GENDER, SEX AND THE LAW

Gender, Sex and the Law

Edited by Susan Edwards

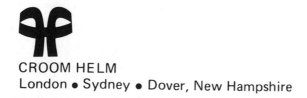

CROOM HELM
London • Sydney • Dover, New Hampshire

© 1985 Susan Edwards
Croom Helm Ltd, Provident House, Burrell Row,
Beckenham, Kent BR3 1AT
Croom Helm Australia Pty Ltd, Suite 4, 6th Floor,
64-76 Kippax Street, Surry Hills, NSW 2010 Australia
New in paperback 1986

British Library Cataloguing in Publication Data

Gender sex and the law.
   1. Sex discrimination against women—Great
Britain—Law and legislation
   I. Edwards, Susan, *1937-*
   344.102'878   KD734

   ISBN 0-7099-0938-1
   ISBN 0-7099-0967-5 Pbk

Croom Helm, 51 Washington Street, Dover,
New Hampshire 03820, USA

Library of Congress Cataloging in Publication Data
Main entry under title:

Gender, sex, and the law.

   Includes index
   1. Sex discrimination against women — Law and
Legislation — Great Britain. I. Edwards, Susan S.M.
KD4103.G46   1985   342.41'0878   84-29309
ISBN 0-7099-0938-1   344.102878
ISBN 0-7099-0967-5 (Pbk)

Printed and bound in Great Britain by
Biddles Ltd, Guildford and King's Lynn

CONTENTS

Contents

PREFACE

The initial impetus for a collection of this kind was
provided following the Woman Law Teachers Group work-
shop on 'Feminism and Law', held in July 1983, when
the issue of biological conundrums as explicated in
various levels of jurisdiction became the focal discussion point. I am grateful to all the participants
and especially to the convenors, Judith Mayhew and
Jennifer Temkin who supported the original idea of
this collection. Only two of the papers presented
appear in a revised form here, but the focus essentially remains the same. The selection of further papers
in the volume was based on the endeavour to examine
dimensions of women's inequality from the lived political experience of women themselves. To this end,
two of the papers have been written by women directly
at the spearhead of political campaign (AIMS), Association for the Improvement in Maternity Services and
(WING), Women Immigration and Nationality Group. Together with the contributors, I would like to thank
Christine Jackson, Equal Opportunities Commission
Manchester, and Alice Leonard, for their ideas and
support.

Sue Edwards

'Over a very large area the law is indifferent to sex.' Yet when property rights are transmitted by marriage the question of legally valid bond becomes a matter of concern. It is no new thing for the law to be drawing the line between biological and social events, choosing the moment when a foetus is enough of a person to require legal protection, deciding when a marriage has been physically consummated, deciding on the definitions of death, rape, cruelty, indecency, a standard of living above starvation. At less public and weighty levels, the same assessment and drawing of boundaries proceeds through the whole social process. Physical nature is masticated and driven through the cognitive meshes to satisfy social demands for clarity which compete with logical demands for consistency.

Mary Douglas, <u>Rules and Meanings</u> (1973) p. 113

INTRODUCTION

This collection of discussion papers examines the many
dimensions and faces of women's inequality as enshrined in law. On a more generic level it explores the
wider questions of the abrogation and denial of equality of access, of decision making of rights between the
sexes. More specifically, it identifies the way in
which these many facets of women's inequality are justified, explained and thereby perpetuated by presenting a picture of women as something different and
special, something different and debilitated. Women's
special status and women's debilitated status stem
from a common ideology, from a belief in an essentialist biological and physiological incapacity which
spans not only assessment of physical capability but also
mental capacity. In law women have been, or so lawmakers proclaim, protected because of these differences, or excluded and exempted.
     The concern is not with positing any implacable
relationship between the multifarious laws discussed
and their various levels of jurisdiction and women's
position, the object rather more involves consideration of the specificity of women's experience as wives,
mothers, childbearers, as women, as plaintiffs, defendants appellants or as victims. Implicitly or explicitly, each interface between gender or sex role and
the legislation codifying one aspect of women's role
is overtly or covertly concerned with the consequence
of 'protective' or exempting legislation in the overall perpetuation of female subordination.
     The history of women before the law is a narra-
tive of total exclusion from certain laws, exemptions
from duties, obligations and responsibilities together
with the accordance with a special status which conferred upon them certain privileges. Yet the rationales promoting each of these were firmly based on a
belief in their incapacity. Such was this special

1

status women were regarded as children! Frances Power
Cobbe (1868), wrote that women were regarded no differently from criminals, idiots and minors and thus
such is that special status that 'The husband being
physically, mentally and morally his wife's superior,
must in justice receive from the law additional
strength by being constituted absolute master of her
property'. (1)

In fact they were non-persons, and through the
work of Ritchie (1975), Sachs and Hoff-Wilson (1978),
we are well acquainted with the manipulative power of
those who negotiate statuses for the sole purpose of
excluding women from public life and participation.
Despite Lord Brougham's Act (1850) and the
Interpretation Act of 1889, women were systematically
excluded from participating in the professions of medicine and of law, and from being admitted as county
councillors; indeed from public life its professions
and its politics, and exclusion was justified since,
'women were inherently incapacitated on grounds of
gender alone'. (2)

Not only were they excluded because of some inherent incapacity, many men feared that their entry into
the professions of law and medicine would desecrate
their hallowed status. The professions of medicine and
law excluded women on the grounds that they were inferior and incompetent and used a statute with which
to support their case. That is the notion that women
were not fully persons. This was undoubtedly a clever
ploy, since indeed women were not regarded as subjects
in their own right and until the 1880's had no right
to their own property nor to their own children, no
constitutional rights; only duties and obligations.
Sophia Jex Blake was one among many women who sought
to challenge such discriminatory practices. In con-
testing her exclusion from the medical profession, she
challenged the precedent that had declared women not
'persons'.

Time and time and time again, women were refused
equal rights alongside men on just this basis. But as
Sachs points out, the exclusion of women on these
grounds was by no means a universal predilection. Law
makers and objectors to women's emancipation held this
trump card high whensoever and wheresoever they chose.
Yet such arguments did not preclude working-class wom-
en from the toil and drudgery of factory life. Indeed
in the 1850's 52% of the labour force were women and
children. Nor did it exclude women from work which
had been seen as an extension of women's domestic
roles, therefore women's work. C.A. Briggs writing on
Poor Law Guardians (1885) observes that such work is,

Introduction

'only domestic economy on a large scale'. Sally
Alexander in a study on women's work in 19th century
London, examines the types of work women were engaged
in, discovering not surprisingly that 'only those
sorts of work that coincided with woman's natural
sphere were to be encouraged'. In consequence, 'Most wom-
en workers in London were domestic servants, washerwom-
en, needlewomen or occupied in some other sort of home
work. These traditional forms of women's work were
quite compatible with the Victorians' definition of
the home and so passed almost unnoticed. (3) As one
writer remarked in excluding women from the public
sphere, they were indeed classed together with prodig-
als, bishops, monks and imbeciles. (4)
        This justificatory rationale was widely shared by
public and legal mentality alike. Fitzgerald B., asserting that 'the law in recognising the distinction
of the sexes assumes a greater worthiness in the male
than in the female, is manifest from the law of descent;
that it has regard to the infirmity of bodily strength
and ability in the female, by rendering her incompetent for some offices and privileges, or incapacitating her from the discharge of the duties thereto belonging, cannot be questioned. Again, that she is
subject to incapacities, from a presumed inferiority
of discretion and judgment, seems also certain: a
woman was not admitted as a witness in case of villein-
age against a man; and the reason assigned is, because
of her "frailty".' (5)   Sir James Fitzjames
Stephens, uncle of Virginia Woolf, considered such
assertive women 'mutinous towards their husbands'. (6)
But then these rationales for exclusion were not unan-
imously held or applied. The pregnancy or maternity
rationale did not exclude certain women from working,
in fact employers habitually turned a blind eye to the
needs of mothers in the post-natal period. Engels observed with horror how from sheer economic necessity,
women were forced to return to 'the mill three or four
days after confinement'. (7)
        If motherhood was extolled and revered and
women had this special status, one wonders how the
lawmakers could maintain this illusion of protecting
women when they were denied rights to the custody of
their own children. In opposition to the Guardianship
of Infants Bill proposing joint guardianship, Earl
Beauchamp declared that such provision 'would open out
sources of the greatest disorders'. (8)
        The protective philosophy under its wing denied
women the most basic of rights whilst enshrining a
husband's right to sex and her duty to submit and a
man's right to chastisement of his wife since he has

3

Introduction

'...by law power and dominion' over her. Justificatory rationales for their exclusion, exemption or differential treatment were founded on two modes of thought, physiological and mental constitution. Such explanations have constrained and entrapped women, providing always an immutable reason why she should be and remain passive, why she should limit her horizons to that which is of her body-child birth and its cultural projection, childcare. This story of course has a beginning long before the rise to power of medical men in the 18th century who like gods, declared that anything other than quiet domiciliary activities were potentially dangerous for women. The contemporary biological representations of women have a heritage rooted in the theories of powerful men in the work of Henry Maudsley, Edward Tilt, Charles Mercier and Lawson Tait. The view that women are weak, inferior, not fully capable, is a characterisation which has been authorised and given credence by the medical model which post facto gave a new scientific credibility to a view which had been for some time held, advancing the theory that women were biologically incapacitated natural invalids, who, totally dictated to by their uterus and ovaries were unable to act rationally. Each generative stage was regarded with a great sense of foreboding as precipitating some mental and behavioural crisis. From the onset of menstruation to the cessation of reproductive life, women were to varying degrees regarded as incompetent; as Maudsley, Ellis and others agreed, 'women were on the borderland of pathology'. The absurdest paradox of all time was generated since as Wynter and Marshall agreed, women in their 'normal' state were indeed 'pathological'. (9) Such powerful arguments and contentions coming from so-called scientific mouthpieces of the era, medical men, were to have impact on the liberties of women. The consequences which followed from these characterisations was to have a profound effect and impact on civil liberties, constitutional and legal rights, and on the treatment of women as criminal defendants, plaintiffs, applicants and victims. At various levels of jurisdiction, this debilitating iconography provided the authorisation for their less than adult treatment in public and private life.

During the 19th century, women were also excluded from education and gross inequalities perpetuated so long as they were viewed from a standpoint of biological essentialism. Where women were to receive an education, the curriculum was limited to traditional teaching of domestic skills, embroidery, painting and such like and aspiration to anything other was met

with the argument that mental activity would have a
positively harmful effect. Allan MacGrigor writing in
1869, located intellectual differences between the
sexes in menstruation, 'In intellectual labour, man
has surpassed, does now, always will surpass women,
for the obvious reason that nature does not periodic-
ally interrupt his thought and application'. (10) But
the most influential treatise which justified the already divisive treatment of men and women was contained in Edward Clarke's Sex in Education (1873), where
he powerfully contended that higher education actually (
destroyed the reproductive functions of American wom-
en. In Britain, Henry Maudsley used Clarke's book for
an attack on educational and professional aspirations
of women. Such views were perpetuated throughout the
19th and 20th centuries. The British Medical Journal
echoing this sentiment reported, 'It is not merely her
mind that is unsexed, but her body loses much of that
special charm that attracts men. In America the college woman when she does marry is often barren'. (11)
In the sphere of civil liberties, enfranchisement of
women in particular, biological characterisations
served to provide a convincing justificatory rationale
for their lack of constitutional status. Women were
deemed incapable, incompetent and irresponsible.
These views were sentiments frequently echoed by politicians in their opposition to attempts to change the
status of women in public life. In opposition to the
Qualification of Women Bill (1907), Earl Halsbury observed of women, 'I think women are not safeguards in
government....' (12) Lord James of Hereford, another
conscientious objector described women in these terms,
'Her mental constitution is supposed to be so ill balanced that it is practically certain that she will
devote her days and nights to breaking up political
meetings and assaulting the police'. (13) The fact
that the suffragettes were forced to adopt militant
tactics only served like a tight knot to reinforce
such beliefs of instability and hysteria.
     This brief historical overview provides an impor-
tant backcloth for a contemporary discussion and analysis of some of the key rights, liberties and freedoms
and the battle for their recognition on, by, and behalf of women today. Despite certain progress women's
exclusion, exemption, differential or special treatment remains predicated on anatomical differences and
the assumption that certain gender roles are incumbent
on this essentialist criterion. It is the endeavour of
this collection to consider some of those interfaces
experienced by women and between women in specific sex
and gender roles and the legislation which shapes and

moulds women's overall status, defined and codified by
social and cultural ascriptions of appropriate rights,
responsibilities and duties.
    In bringing together a variety of discussions of
women in sex, gender and work roles, as plaintiffs,
appellants, applicants, defendants and victims, the
collection examines through a consideration of the various statuses, the rights, duties and obligations which
are conferred or expected in relation to particular
classes, physical and cultural.
    The collection opens with a discussion of the law
as it defines and codifies sexual categories as founded on biological and essentialist criteria. The transsexual is for many intents and purposes a modern medical creation since through the intervention of surgical
advances, a new physical and gender role is facilitat-
ed. The law and certain areas of social policy and
welfare refuse to recognise this new status, preferring instead the rule that sexual status is designated
at birth for the duration of one's life and cannot be
altered by surgical means. Katherine O'Donovan's paper, Transsexual Troubles: The Discrepancy Between
Legal and Social Categories, examines the essentialist
rigidity of the legal ascription of sex predicated on
some clear cut vision of appropriate heterosexual
functions and the institution of marriage. In so doing, she exposes the way in which law organises a particular ordering of society on sex lines and reveals
how rights and duties are ascribed not to persons but
to sexes, often regardless of gender considerations,
based on the error that sex and gender are synonymous.
    In considering the interface between women in
their roles as wives and mothers, essentially dependent on men, Susan Maidment in Women and Childcare:
The Paradox of Divorce, discloses the way in which
custody and maintenance are battles won or remuneration awarded on sexist grounds, that of traditional
gender role fulfilment. The paradox or conundrum
explored is that in order to achieve some kind of par-
ity of treatment, and some kind of 'justice' women who
otherwise might reject such anachronistic ideologies,
are either required to manipulate them, or else find
themselves destitute without any financial support,
and without custody of their children.
    Another important much eclipsed and marginalised
concern from the central debates on women's rights, is
the gradual erosion of women's demands from the child-
bearing and childbirth process. Beverley Beech in
The Politics of Maternity : Childbirth Freedom v
Obstetric Control explores the interface between women
as mothers and medical law which continues to mirror

the interests of a male dominated medical profession
whilst totally excluding any real consideration for
the mother at the centre of the birthing process.
Peggy Kahn, in Unequal Opportunities: Women, Employment and the Law examines the way in which women's access to work mirrors and reflects women's position in
the family and in society where opportunities exist
for women in work roles which are an extension of gender roles and where opportunities are severely restricted in other areas considered 'men's work'. She
presents a practical and political programme for
change spanning social and welfare policy, she calls
for improvements in childcare facilities and greater
flexibility in working hours which would facilitate a
greater participation of women in work.

Judith Mayhew in a paper entitled Pregnancy and
Employment Law focuses on specific interfaces of contemporary legislation, the Employment Act (1980) in
particular and the restrictions placed on the pregnant mother relating to maternity pay and the right
to return to work exposing how employment law reinforces gender ideology by not fully acknowledging the
particular needs of women at this time. The paper
entitled Women, Immigration and Nationality by
Women Immigration and Nationality Group (WING), examines how all women are discriminated against when immigration and nationality is at issue. Addressing the
way in which 'in immigration policy women have not
been seen as people in their own right but as "dependants" of men living here, or as agents of male settlement'.

Susan Edwards, in Gender 'Justice'? Defending
Defendants and Mitigating Sentence turns our attention
to women as wives, mothers, single women and dependants in a consideration of new directions in women and
crime, exploring the way in which gender characterisations have influenced the legal processing of homicide defendants particularly as far as defences to
homicide are concerned. She argues that the development of legal defences in themselves, may contain an
implicit sex bias, which results in women being less
convincingly able to allege provocation and points to
the already growing concern over the role cumulative
provocation should or might play in defences to murder. Additionally turning to mitigation, she examines
the impact appropriate role models particularly of
family centredness, play in mitigating sentences and
allowing appeals arguing that in this, the court may
be favouring a middle-class version of the heterosexual family, whilst single women and working-class
mothers who may not appear in the assessment of the

Introduction

magistracy and judiciary to be 'good mothers', may
lose out. Linda Luckhaus in A Plea for PMT in The
Criminal Law examines the interface between criminal
law and physiology. In a stimulating paper she examines
the re-invocation of the view that women may be debilitated and irresponsible immediately before and during
menstruation. She examines the legal consequences
this notion has had in tracing through the courts the
progress of several recent cases and offers some assessment of the overall consequences this may have for
women generally. Finally, Susan Edwards in a paper
entitled 'Male Violence Against Women: Excusatory and
Explanatory Ideologies in Law and Society' draws together the various dimensions of law and of sex, sexuality, and gender presented in this volume with a
paper which considers the legal processing of domestic
violence, assault, the civil and criminal law, the remedies available and the perpetuating ideologies which
have resulted and continue to ensure that male violence against women will persist so long as every agency
is convinced of the wisdom of 'laissez faire' policies.

REFERENCES

(1)   Frances Power Cobbe (1868), Criminals, Idiots,
        Women and Minors - Frasers Magazine LXXVIII
        777-94, reprinted in C. Bauer and L. Ritt
        (1978) Free and Ennobled, Pergamon at p. 179.
(2)   Sachs, A. and Hoff-Wilson, J. (1978), Sexism
        and the Law, Martin Robertson, Oxford p. 5.
(3)   Alexander, S. (1976) 'Women's Work in Nine-
        teenth Century London: A Study of the Years 1820-
        50' p.59, in J. Mitchell and A. Oakley (eds.), The
        Rights and Wrongs of Women 1976, Penguin
(4)   Anon. (1876), The Legal Position of Women,
        The Westminster Review, Vol. 49: 335.
(5)   Ritchie, M. (1975) Alice Through The Statutes,
        McGill Law Journal,Vol. 21 pp. 685-707 at p. 692.
(6)   Sachs, as above p. 25.
(7)   Engels, F. (1844), The Condition of the Work-
        ing Class in England, 1969 (ed.) Panther
        London pp. 171-172.
(8)   Hansard (1885), Vol. 297 c 298.
(9)   Edwards, S. (1981), Female Sexuality and the
        Law, Martin Robertson, Oxford Ch. 3.
(10)   MacGrigor, Allan (1869), On the Real Differ-
        ences in the Minds of Men and Women Anthropologic-
        al Society of London, Journal 7: 195-219
(11)   British Medical Journal, March 2nd 1907,
(12)   Hansard, 1907 Vol. 175, c 1347.
(13)   Hansard, 1907 Vol. 175, c 1355.

Chapter One

TRANSSEXUAL TROUBLES: THE DISCREPANCY BETWEEN LEGAL
AND SOCIAL CATEGORIES

Katherine O' Donovan

INTRODUCTION

"One is not born, one rather becomes a woman", according to Simone de Beauvoir. (1)   This much-quoted
statement suggests that society rather than biology
determines the meaning attached to the category woman.
Yet for most women their own experiences probably con-
vince them that anatomy is destiny.   Their bodies define them.   Their physical differences from men ground
their place in the world.   So can de Beauvoir's view
that woman is socially constructed be sustained, or
does culture mirror nature?
        English law's approach to issues of sex and gend-
er proceeds on untested assumptions about biological
determinism.   From the entry on the birth certificate
to the drawing up of the death certificate persons are
assigned to category female or category male.   This
affects the regulation of sexuality by the criminal
law, employment law, capacity to marry, social security law, and even sex discrimination law.   Since the
law demands that persons be so classified, have the
tests to determine a person's biological sex been sta-
tutorily or judicially defined?   The answer seems to
be that there is no clear test for sexual classification, but there are a variety of practices that vary
according to the branch of law in question.
        Customary practices are applied in relation to
the birth certificate.   When a child is born one of
the first questions asked is whether the newcomer is
female or male.   The answer given constitutes the
baby's assigned sex.   The test is to look at the external genitalia which are taken as a sign of the appropriate classification.   This casual glance and categorisation affects the future goals, behaviour, identity,
personality, emotions, sexuality and gender role of
the child.   Under the law the birth must be registered

within forty-two days, and the infant's birth certificate records the assigned sex. (2)

In the great majority of cases the sex assignment
made at birth is correct, but cases of error, indeterminacy, and later   dissatisfaction with the assigned
category illustrate the centrality of sex category to
social structure. Error and indeterminacy can arise
for various reasons. Seven variables affecting sex
determination have been identified. These are chromosomal sex; gonadal sex; hormonal sex; the internal
accessory organs - the uterus in the female and the
prostate gland in the male; the external genitals; assigned sex; gender role.(3) Within these criteria
there may be considerable variation. For instance,
the amount of the hormones oestrogen or testosterone
present in the body varies from person to person, and
according to such matters as psychological state and
monthly cycle. Errors are made when an individual's
external organs suggest one category which later turns
out to be incorrect, or where there is no predominance
among the variables indicating one sex or the other.
Dissatisfaction with the assigned category leads to
the phenomenon of transsexualism, in which a person
believes, despite biological evidence to the contrary,
that she or he is inherently of the opposite sex.

It might be thought that in cases or error. and
even of transsexualism, the birth certificate
could be amended. There is such a procedure available in cases of medically certified error; (4) but the
point being made here is that the centrality of sex to
social structure and the reflection of this in law
creates many of the problems which cannot be dealt with
by an amended birth certificate, particularly in relation to transsexuals. This point can be sustained by
reference to substantive law such as criminal and family law.

THE SOCIAL CONSEQUENCES OF SEX CLASSIFICATION

Sex assignment, whether correct or incorrect, has enormous consequences for the individual. It is no exagg-
eration to say that one's whole life is determined by
it. Whilst this might be an argument for careful testing of infants, the more important question is whether
such a division of people should be so important in the
first place. Stoller's research shows that there are
considerable variations amongst persons with one biological male having different hormonal patterns and different degrees of maleness from another. (5) Oakley
argues further that at the simple biological level

women and men are not two separate groups: rather,
each individual takes a place on a continuum with no
single dividing line between male and female. (6)
This is supported by the fact that the embryo human
being is sexually undifferentiated initially. Normal
sex differentiation which commences about forty-two
days after conception is determined by the father's
sperm. Each ovum contains an X chromosome and the in-
faiil's sex depends on whether the fertilising sperm
contains an X or a Y chromosome. The XX pattern will
develop as female, the XY pattern as male. "Since
both the female and the male gonads (primary sex
glands) originate from an identical primitive gonad,
its cortex (outer layer) can develop into an ovary in
the female, or its medulla (centre) can develop into
a testis in the male. During this early stage, at
about the fifth or sixth week, two sets of ducts,
Wolff's and Muller's, also appear in the embryo. The
former can develop into the Fallopian tubes, uterus,
and upper vagina in the female. At about nine weeks
in the development of the normal male embryo, and
slightly later in the female, the appropriate duct continues to develop and the other one retrogresses." (7)
The gonads, and even the external genitalia, are in
their origin more similar than is generally realised.

Despite the similarities in the biological make-
up of the sexes, once an individual is categorised female or male significant social consequences follow.
Studies of maternal behaviour have revealed that even
with newborn infants mothers behave differently according to sex category. (8) This is the beginning of
learning what it means to be classified as female or
male. As the child develops it will gradually become
aware of society's expectations in the way of behaviour, manners, attitudes, activity, and modes of relationship to others. It learns the meaning of being
a girl or a boy, that is, its gender role.

Gender is the term used to denote the social
meaning of sex categorisation. Sex is determined through physical assessment; gender refers to the social
consequences for the individual of that assessment.
Gender stereotypes embody society's view of appropriate
behaviour for women and for men. These take the form
of gender roles, reinforced by law, through which
persons conform to their assigned sex and to society's
conventions. A further aspect is gender identity which
is the individual's psychological experience of being
female or male; it is the sense of belonging to one
gender category. Gender identity, although psychological, relies on the social construction of femininity
or masculinity as its basis.

11

Transsexual Troubles: The Discrepancy between Legal
and Social Categories

   The pervasiveness of the social construction of
gender is revealed by research at Johns Hopkins Hospital
showing that there are people who are sexually concor-
dant at birth - born with the same kind of genitals,
gonads, chromosomes, and hormones - who were differentially labelled female or male. The problems and
successes these patients had in conforming to their
labels, and the difficulties they faced if the label was
changed, have revealed a great deal about what it
means to be a woman or a man in the social world. (9)
   Errors occur in the sexual classification of persons. There may be gonads of both sexes; the initial
indicia of genitals may develop in the opposite direction; internal organs may be missing; genitals may not
develop; there may be too few or too many sex chromosomes; there may be confusion over assigned sex. Money
and Tucker give an example of a child who at birth was
labelled male and raised as a boy, because he had a
rudimentary penis but no testicles. At puberty breasts
developed and an exploratory operation revealed ovaries, uterus and vagina, but no male reproductive organs. Gender identity was so firmly established that
the patient's description was "they'd found some kind
of female apparatus in there by mistake." (10) His
belief in himself as a male was unshaken and male hormones were used to develop external male physical
characteristics such as a beard. He married and had
a satisfactory sexual relationship with his wife. By
contrast another case with very similar external organs at birth was labelled and raised as a girl. At
puberty male hormones gained ascendancy over the ovarian hormones. Drug therapy was used to suppress the
androgenising effect of male hormones and the woman,
who had rejected with horror the idea she might be
male, married and gave birth to children. These case
histories show the centrality of gender identity to
the individual's conception of herself, but they also
show how the social construction of gender different-
iates human beings who are not necessarily biologically differentiated.
   The Australian case C and D (11) provides an example of a person who belongs neither to the female
nor to the male category but who is intersex. The
hermaphrodite in this case had an ovary and a Fallopian tube on the right side with nothing internal on
the left, but had been classified male at birth because of a small penis and a testicle on the left side.
Having grown up psychologically and socially as a male,
in adulthood he sought surgical treatment for correct-
ion of the penile deformity. An article in the
Medical Journal of Australia written soon after the

12

decision to intervene surgically gives an account of the problem faced by the medical and surgical specialists. It was decided "in spite of the bisexual gonadal structure, the female chromosomal arrangement, the female internal genitalia and the equivocal results of the hormonal assays, there was no doubt, in view of the assigned male sex, the male psychological orientation in a person of this age and the possibility of converting his external genitals into an acceptable male pattern, that he should continue in the sex in which he had been reared." (12) Surgery was performed over a period of time to remove the female internal organs and breasts, and to reconstruct the penis into one of normal size and shape. The patient married, but was later held by the courts to be neither male nor female for the purposes of marriage. In a legal system which insists that persons belong to one or other of the sex categories the intersex illustrates the unnecessary rigidity of, and calls into question the necessity for, this classification.

The case of the identical male twins raised differentially as female and male reported by Money shows how sexuality is differentiated in the course of growing up and not at birth. One of the twins lost his penis through medical negligence at the age of seven months. As a result of advice received at Johns Hopkins Hospital the parents decide to reassign the child's gender, permit surgical intervention, and raise the child as a girl. This happened at seventeen months. Money reports that "by the time the children were four years old there was no mistaking which twin was the girl and which the boy. At five the little girl already preferred dresses to pants, enjoyed wearing her hair ribbons, bracelets and frilly blouses, and loved being her daddy's little sweetheart." (13) By the age of nine the two identical (genetically male) twins showed two clearly differentiated personalities, with sharply differentiated behavioural structure based on conventional ideas of what is gender appropriate.

> Regarding domestic activities, such as work in the kitchen and house traditionally seen as part of the female's role, the mother reported that her daughter copies her in trying to help her in tidying and cleaning up the kitchen, while the boy could not care less about it. She encourages her daughter when she helps her in the housework. (14)

Having been placed in separate gender categories these

identical twins of the same sex have learned to perform social rôles considered appropriate to their
gender.

Gender is socially constructed. It is clear in
the examples given above that individuals respond to
their experience of gender in the social world by
creating their own gender identities. Yet for some
people there is confusion when faced with this rigidly
bipartite structure in which they must belong to one
or other of two categories. In the case of transsexuals their response is to insist that their gender
identity is in one category whilst their biological
sex is in the other. It is doubtful whether it is
necessary for society or for law to present such a
bifurcated system. It is likely that the problems
faced by transsexuals by the victims of error, and by
hermaphrodites, are created by the rigidity of the bis-
ection.

LEGAL DEFINITIONS OF GENDER CATEGORIES

Biological and social classification of women and men
as belonging to different and separate categories
leads to similar legal classification. Biology forms
the material base on which an elaborate system of social and legal distinctions is built. Until recently
it was not realised that this base was unsteady. Some
medical psychologists and other researchers, have
questioned the use of biology to support a dichotom-
ised gender system. They suggest that the categories
woman or man are not opposite or closed. Legal reasoning regards these categories as closed. This partly
results from a failure to keep up with medical research but it also arises from the nature of legal reasoning itself. The lawyer is continuously engaged on
a process of classification. "The law must predominantly, but by no means exclusively, refer to <u>classes</u>
of persons, and to <u>classes</u> of acts, things and circumstances." (15) Legal reasoning uses gender as a basis
of classification at a number of stages in the legal
process. At the legislative stage different rules for
men and women may be laid down, or certain acts may
be made sex-specifically criminal. Even where legislation is not gender-specific judges and administrators may interpret and apply it as if it is. For
instance the word 'person' in legislation was interpreted by the judiciary as meaning 'male person' in
nineteenth century cases denying women access to education, the professions, and the vote. (16) Officials
when faced with individuals who do not conform to

Transsexual Troubles: The Discrepancy between Legal
and Social Categories

their expected social role will, even where the law
does not require it, attempt to enforce gender distinctions. (17)
     The apparent opposition of women and men has led,
in legal reasoning, to the approach in which the individual must belong to one of two categories. This
affects aspects of family law, criminal law, welfare
law, employment law, and sex discrimination law.

Capacity to Marry
Although gender classifications permeate family law,
it was a case on capacity to marry which laid down the
fundamental definitions of sex and gender. In Corbett
v Corbett a couple had married with the knowledge of
the fact that, whereas both had been classified male
at birth, one had undergone a sex-change operation in
an attempt to move into the female category. The
marriage was a failure and the male partner brought an
action to have the marriage declared null and void on
the grounds that both parties were members of the male
sex. The court upheld this view. Sex, it said, "is
clearly an essential determinant of the relationship
called marriage because it is and always has been recognised as the union of man and woman. It is the institution on which the family is built, and in which
the capacity for natural hetero-sexual intercourse is
an essential element." (18) Sex, as a concept, seems
to have been used here both in the sense of biological
category and in the sense of sexual intercourse.
     The court went on to distinguish sex as biolog-
ical category from gender. Dealing with the argument
that society recognised the transsexual as a woman for
national insurance purposes and that therefore it was
illogical not to do the same for marriage, the court
said "these submissions, in effect confuse sex with
gender. Marriage is a relationship which depends on
sex and not gender." (19) Social appearance or gender
identity, or other psychological considerations are
irrelevant in determining whether a person is male or
female; the Corbett case makes clear that the legal
test is, for marriage at least, biological.
     The respondent in the Corbett case was born with
male external genitalia. After treatment with female
hormones the respondent had a sex-change operation involving the removal of the male genitalia and the construction of an artificial vagina. The respondent
lived as a woman and was issued with a national insurance card as a member of the female gender category.
A chromosome test showed that the cells examined were
XY, that is the male pattern.

15

Transsexual Troubles: The Discrepancy between Legal
and Social Categories

The biological test laid down by Ormrod J. is
"the chromosomal, gonadal and genital tests, and if
all three are congruent, the law should determine the
sex for the purpose of marriage accordingly, and ignore any operative intervention. The real difficulties, or course, will occur if these three criteria
are not congruent." (20) The respondent, notwithstanding matters of gender identity, social appearance, and post-operative female genitals, was classified as a biological male.
    It is possible to criticise this decision on a
number of grounds. At an individualistic level it may
result in hardship to persons who belong to neither
the female nor the male sex, and who therefore cannot
marry. Transsexuals who have undergone surgery cannot
validly marry in their new category, yet in their
post-operative state they will be incapable of consumm-
ating a marriage as members of their former category.
The male twin raised as a female would face this dilemma in English law. On an abstract level the decision reinforces belief in the categories woman and man
as closed categories, rather than as points along a
continuum.
    The Australian case of C and D in which the
husband, although raised as a male, was a genuine intersex on whom surgery was performed to bring his body
into conformity with his gender identity, illustrates
the rigidity of the gender dichotomy. After some
years the wife sought to nullify the marriage on the
grounds that the husband had been unable to consummate
the marriage. The Australian court held that the
marriage was null because of an absence of consent on
the part of the wife who was the victim of mistaken
identity. The explanation was that "the wife was con-
templating immediately prior to marriage and did in
fact believe that she was marrying a male. She did
not in fact marry a male but a combination of both
male and female and notwithstanding that the husband
exhibited as a male, he was in fact not, and the wife
was mistaken as to the identity of her husband." (21)
    Critics of the Corbett case, who have called its
approach "disturbingly simplistic", (22) argue that
the chromosome pattern which can never be changed
should be ignored. The genital test should consider
the post-operative, rather than pre-operative, state
of the genitals. If the apparent sex, that is, genitals, gender identity and gender role are congruent,
then the individual should be categorised accordingly.(23)
These criticisms are based not only on compassion to
individuals but also on logic. It is said that in
relation to adultery and rape, two areas of the law

16

where penetration of one sexual organ by another is
an essential element, no inquiry as to sexual identity
is necessary, and that this should be the general
approach. The requirement of penetration presupposes
an organ capable of penetration possessed by one person, and an organ capable of being penetrated possessed by the other, and that this establishes a sufficient degree of sexual differentiation. The legal test
for consummation of marriage is penetration.

Fair though this criticism may be it nevertheless accepts that the law should continue to operate
on an assumption that the two sexes are completely
different categories. "As a working hypothesis this
is not unreasonable, but... it does not quite corres-
pond with physiological reality and is therefore liable to break down from time to time." (24) Concern is
expressed because errors may be made, but the premise
that the law should be organised on a basis of gender
dichotomy is not queried. Hitherto criticisms have
been levelled at the lack of logic or of compassion in
legal handling of difficult cases and the suggested
reform is that the courts should consider a variety of
factors including the post-operative state and gender
identity instead of one essential determinant of sex.

There is no doubt that Ormrod J.'s approach can
be described as essentialist. He said that "the biological sexual constitution of an individual is fixed
at birth (at the latest), and cannot be changed either
by natural development of organs of the opposite sex
or by medical or surgical means." (25) Yet the genuine
intersex husband in C and D did not belong essentially to one sex. Neither do many of the patients at
Johns Hopkins Hospital. Furthermore, the objective of
the medical profession has been to bring the physical
appearance of patients into line with gender identity.
"Since it is possible to alter anatomy and hormone
ratio but not gender identity, finding out which way
the child's gender identity inclined was the crucial
concern." (26) In many cases this means confirming
individuals in the gender category in which they were
socialised as children. But to Ormrod J. "a person
with male chromosomes, male gonads and male genitalia
cannot reproduce a person who is naturally capable of
performing the essential role of a woman in marriage."
(27) The judgment does not clarify whether this role
is social, sexual, or reproductive.

The legal view of marriage, as evidenced in
Corbett, is that the essence of the marriage relationship is heterosexual intercourse. Why is this? The
ability to procreate children is not essential to valid marriage, for if this were so, involuntarily

17

childless marriages would be void, and even possibly
voluntary childless marriages. It is true that marriages which have not been sexually consummated are
voidable in English Law, but there have been a number
of decisions holding that the use of contraceptives
does not prevent consummation. (28) If procreation
is not the purpose of marriage, but the law nevertheless requires that the parties belong to different
biological categories, then it seems that marriage is
not a private matter to be negotiated between individuals but a public institution for heterosexual
intercourse.

The essentialist approach presupposes two fixed
and immutable categories. All human beings are assumed to fall neatly into one or other category. "Performing the essential role of a woman in marriage",
suggests certain fixed social, psychological, and
behavioural traits of femininity which depend on biology. My objections to this approach are that it is
based on a false premise, that it is not consonant
with modern medical theory, that it is undesirable on
the grounds of public policy, and that it is largely
unnecessary.

The false premise is the assumption of two closed
categories into which all human beings can be classified on an either/or basis and the attaching to these
of qualities of femininity or masculinity. Whilst it is
true that the great majority of people can be so
classified biologically, there are nevertheless a minority who cannot be. Social and psychological behavioural traits are socially constructed and "the differences within each sex far outweigh the differences
between the sexes." (29) Using the chromosome test
might be seen as a way of sustaining the closed category approach, but even chromosomes can be awkward.
Cases of XO, XXY may cause problems. Furthermore
medical opinion does not support exclusive reliance on
chromosomes.

A better approach is to look at a variety of factors concerning the individual as now presented including psychological identity, and to base the conclusion on the sum of these factors, rather than to look
at one essential feature. Ormrod J.'s objection to
this method was that it is illogical to state that a
person belonged to one category at birth but has
changed to the other category. Yet Ormrod J. suggested that a person may belong to one category for
purposes of contract, employment or social security
and to the other for the purposes of marriage."

In some contractual relationships, e.g. life

assurance and pension schemes, sex is a relevant factor in determining the rate of premium or contributions. It is relevant also to some aspects of the law regulating conditions of employment and to various state-run schemes such as national insurance, or to such fiscal matters as selective employment tax. It is not an essential determinant in these cases because there is nothing to prevent the parties to a contract of insurance or a pension scheme from agreeing that the person concerned should be treated as a man or as a woman, as the case may be. Similarly, the authorities, if they think fit can agree with the individual that he shall be treated as a woman for national insurance purposes, as in this case. (30)

In a system which insists on a dichotomous gender system it seems equally illogical to suggest that a person who is essentially a man for marriage can be a woman for other purposes.
Medical theory according to Money, Stoller and Green, the major modern exponents, favours the adaptation of physical appearance to follow gender identity. This is done in some cases of error, of intersex, and also for transsexuals. Money finds the question whether an individual is really a woman or a man meaningless. "All you can say is that this is a person whose sex organs differentiated as a male and whose gender identity differentiated as a female." (31)
Public policy as expressed in the Sex Discrimination Act 1975 and the Equal Pay Act 1970 is against discrimination between the sexes in certain public areas of life. There is agreement amongst researchers on sex discrimination and by the Equal Opportunities Commission that attitudes which stereotype women or men in particular inflexible ways can lead to sex discrimination. Indeed much of the research suggests that sexual differentiation is socialisation and in education may be inimical to anti-discrimination goals. This is not to suggest that gender identity is unimportant. In a world in which gender is a central principle of social organisation the evidence is that the development of a sense of identity depends on gender identity. It might be otherwise in an androgenous society. However significant gender identity is in a society which is gender organised, the question is whether it is necessary for law to reflect this. If legislative policy goals are aimed at reducing sexual differentiation in the public sphere should the law itself not attempt to eliminate gender distinction

where possible?
     The view that it is unnecessary for the law to classify human beings according to sex or gender can be attacked on various grounds. It can be argued that the great majority of persons do fall into one of two categories biologically. Why should the law not reflect this? Furthermore there are biological functions which can only be performed by one sex, such as menstruation, gestation, lactation. It is necessary for employment laws to recognise this. Another objection can be raised in favour of legal recognition of gender roles, where the state privileges motherhood, for example. Further objections can be based on present realities such as unequal power of women, protection from sexual crime. An androgenous society might be an ideal but empirical evidence suggests that women's special needs must be recognised.
     Establishing the case that sexual classification by law is largely unnecessary requires a deepening of the debate on anti-discrimination. It has long been a major tenet of liberal feminists that differentiation of women leads to discrimination. The counter-argument is that needs, life-style, and life-cycle alternative to the dominant male model must be recognised. I have gone into this debate in some detail elsewhere, (32) but the major point I am making here is that the organisation of society on a gender basis exacerbates gender dysphoria, as exhibited by transsexuals.

Criminal Law
The decision in the Corbett case has influenced criminal law despite Ormrod J.'s statement that the "question then becomes what is meant by the word 'woman' in the context of a marriage, for I am not concerned to determine the 'legal sex' of the respondent at large." (33) In R v Tan and Others (33) the Court of Appeal decided to apply the Corbett decision to an area of criminal law where the sex of the defendant is an essential determinant of guilt. Under S.30 of the Sexual Offences Act 1956 it is an offence for a man to live on the earnings of prostitution. One of the accused, Gloria Greaves, who had been born a male but who had undergone a sex-change operation and who lived as a woman, appealed against conviction under S.30. This defendant submitted that a person who was philosophically, psychologically, or socially a woman should not be convicted of an offence limited to men. The crime of living on the earnings of prostitution is based on the model of the pimp who exploits women for

sexual purposes.   In Greaves' case this rationale
does not seem relevant.
     The Court of Appeal held that for reasons of
common sense, certainty, and consistency, the precedent set by the decision in the Corbett case would be
followed.   Thus the defendant's biological sex remained male despite appearances, gender identity and
surgery.   The decision in Tan can be criticised for
extending Ormrod J.'s definition beyond his specific
limitation to marriage and for ignoring gender identity and medical theory, but the point I am stressing
here is that prostitution law is held to operate on
biological sex and not gender.   The court faced with
female-specific offences such as that of prostitution
in a public place under the Street Offences Act 1956
or male-specific offences under S.30 is obliged to
decide what constitutes a woman or a man.   Legislation
drafted in sex-specific terms creates this problem.
What is not inevitable is the decision to focus on
biological sex rather than gender.
     The outcome is curious.   A male to female trans-
sexual cannot be the victim of rape.   Heterosexual
soliciting by a female prostitute is not a crime for
such a transsexual who can, however, be convicted of
male homosexual soliciting and face more stringent
penalties. (34)   A female to male transsexual cannot
be guilty of the offence of unlawful sexual intercourse with a girl under sixteen. (35)   Consistency,
the goal of the court in Tan, remains elusive.   At the
root of these inconsistencies is sex-specific legislation.   The post-operative male to female transsexual
is incapable of being raped yet in other legal jurisdictions, such as Canada, the law has been reformed to
encompass aggressors and victims of both sexes. (36)

Social Security
April Ashley the male to female transsexual who was
the respondent in the Corbett case was issued with a
national insurance card as a member of the female category.   On her status as a woman would depend such
matters as her age for qualification for the state
pension.   At present this is sixty for a woman and
sixty-five for a man.   Yet, despite the recognition of
the post-operative gender of the transsexual for
purposes of issuing a card, the relevant authorities
have decided that biological sex is the test to be
applied in relation to the age of retirement. (37)
This inconsistency calls into question, again, the
necessity for the differentiation between women and
men.

Transsexual Troubles: The Discrepancy between Legal
and Social Categories

Employment
Legislation regulating the hours that women can work
in factories and excluding them from mining is presented as being for their protection. This is a matter
of debate, but these laws do require a decision as to
what constitutes a woman. In E.A. White v British
Sugar Corporation the female to male transsexual complained of sex discrimination when dismissed on
grounds of deception as to sex. The employer had believed the complainant to be male when the offer of employment was made. Dismissal followed the discovery
that the complainant had previously been classified as
female. The industrial tribunal which heard the case
held that the complainant was a woman. The reasoning
was as follows: "The current edition of The Shorter
Oxford English Dictionary defines males as of or belonging to the sex which begets offspring or performs
the fecundating function. The same dictionary defines
female as belonging to the sex which bears offspring.
On her own evidence the applicant, whatever her physiological make up may be, does not have male reproductive organs and there is no evidence that she could
not bear children." (38) Since the employers required
the employee for the particular job as electrician's
mate to work on Sundays, and since the protective legislation did not permit a woman to do so, the employers did not dismiss the complainant unjustly.

Sex Discrimination
Sex discrimination legislation in Britain has as its
goal the elimination of discrimination between women
and men in the public sphere. It operates on an individualistic level through the comparison of a particular woman with a particular man. A person directly discriminates against a woman when "on the
grounds of her sex he treats her less favourably than
he treats or would treat a man." (39) Individual men
can also complain of less favourable treatment by comparison with an individual woman.
     The complainant in E.A. White v British Sugar
Corporation relied on the Sex Discrimination Act 1975
in making her complaint to the industrial tribunal.
The tribunal held that the test for discrimination led
to the conclusion that the complainant had not been
treated less favourably than a man, because a man who
held himself out to be a woman would also have been
dismissed. The case makes clear that biological sex,
if in question, must be determined for application of
sex discrimination legislation, and that courts and
tribunals are likely to continue with an essentialist

22

approach. It is indeed an irony that in attempting
to abrogate sexual stereotypes the means Parliament
has chosen is to require all individuals to be classified in an essentialist fashion. Whilst the Corbett
test allows for some variation within a category the
White tribunal's use of a dictionary definition is
crude. The tribunal concluded "the laws of this
country and the [1975 Act] in particular envisage only
two sexes, namely male and female." (40)
     One possible solution to the problem of sex dis-
crimination legislation reinforcing the injustice it
attempts to rectify would be for the courts to accept
gender rather than biological sex as the criterion for
the category woman or man. But, as already argued,
there is evidence that gender dysphoria and the transsexual impulse are aggravated, or even created, by
society's insistence on gender dimorphism. Furthermore, such a solution remains individualistic and does
not tackle the general issue of legal dichotomy between the sexes. As Catherine MacKinnon notes "there
is a real question whether it makes sense of the evidence to conceptualise the reality of sex in terms of
differences at all, except in the socially constructed
sense - which social construction is what the law is
attempting to address as the problem." (41)

THE RESPONSE TO TRANSSEXUALISM

Legal writers discussing the problems faced by the
transsexual have argued for a more compassionate
approach and for flexibility in sexual stereotypes.(42)
Examples from other jurisdictions such as Germany,(43)
France, (44) Switzerland (45) and the United States,
(46) where the post-operative transsexual is classified according to chosen rather than ascribed gender
are held up for English law to emulate. Furthermore
the European Commission on Human Rights has held that
it is a violation of private and family life to require the transsexual to carry documents of identity
manifestly incompatible with personal appearance. The
Commission found that the state's refusal to recognise
gender identity treats the transsexual "as an ambiguous being, an 'appearance', disregarding in particular the effects of a lawful medical treatment aimed
at bringing the physical sex and the psychical sex
into accord with each other." (47)
     This response is understandable, for it permits the
maintenance of the gender status quo whilst disposing
of the troubling problems of transsexuals. Quite
another response has come from feminist criticism of
those medical persons, the transsexers, who are osten-

23

sibly dealing with a psychological problem, but who
are accused of engaging in political shaping and
controlling of feminine and masculine behaviour.
Janice Raymond argues that the definition of transsexualism as a medical problem and the development of
sex conversion surgery has given sovereign power to
medical specialists. She sees transsexualism as an
attempt to wrest from women the power inherent in
female biology and in women's creative energies. This
is linked in her thesis to the mutilation of female
flesh in footbinding, clitoridectomy and infibulation.
"Now, patriarchy is moulding and mutilating _male_ flesh,
but for the purpose of _constructing women_." (48)
   Janice Raymond's case is that transsexualism
offers a unique perspective on gender role stereotyping in a patriarchal society. By giving examples of
statements by male to female transsexuals she supports
her case. A central figure in this is Jan Morris of
whom Money admits, "most transsexuals embrace the
stereotype of their identity, even a person as sophisticated as Jan Morris." (49) As James Morris, a
correspondent for the _Times_, he accompanied the
Mt. Everest climbing expedition and scooped the
story. The experience is described as "this feeling
of unfluctuating control, I think, that women cannot
share, and it springs of course not from the intellect
or the personality, nor even so much from upbringing,
but specifically from the body. ' ...I never mind the
swagger of young men. It is their right to swank and
I know the sensation." (50)
   Later Morris, after a sex-change operation in
Casablanca, had a first experience of "being liked"
by a taxi driver in London who "boldly" kissed her
"roughly and not at all disagreeably on the lips",
after which he said, "There's a good girl" and "patted
her bottom." (51) "I like being a woman but I mean
a _woman_. I like having my suit case carried. ...I
like gossiping with the lady upstairs. ...And yes,
I like to be liked by men." (52) As Janice Raymond
points out, Morris switches from one stereotype to the
other without understanding the significance of either.
   April Ashley, the respondent in the _Corbett_ case
was described by Ormrod J. as follows: "Her outward
appearance at first sight was convincingly feminine
but on closer and longer examination in the witness
box it was much less so. The voice, manner, gestures
and attitudes became increasingly reminiscent of the
accomplished female impersonator." One of the medical
experts put his opinion in the words: "the pastiche of
femininity was convincing". (53) Neither transsexuals, nor experts, question the gender stereotypes

24

against which behaviour is judged. The stereotypes
themselves are not confronted but merely frowned upon
when acted out by persons of the 'wrong' sex. Faced
with this transsexuals cling even harder to their notions of femininity and are resentful of 'Gennies',
that is, biological females. "Genetic women are becoming quite obsolete, which is obvious, and the future
belongs to transsexual women. We know this, and perhaps some of you suspect it. All you have left is
your 'ability' to bear children, and in a world which
will groan to feed 6 billion by the year 2000, that's
a negative asset." (54)
     The argument that transsexualism is a result of
socially produced gender role stereotyping is powerful. It is society's definitions of femininity and
masculinity and the connection of these to particular
physical appearances that create the desire in the
transsexual for different sex organs. "The sexual
organs and the body of the opposite sex come to incar-
nate the essence of the desired gender identity and
role, and thus it is not primarily the body that is
desired, but what a female or male body means in this
society." (55) If one accepts Janice Raymond's thesis, then it follows that a society concerned about
transsexual troubles would concentrate not on surgery
to bring about physical and psychological conformity,
but on eliminating the rigidities of beliefs about
appropriate gender behaviour.

CONCLUSION

Gender is socially constructed and the law, insofar as
it builds on gender dichotomies, is part of that process. An important step in the dismantling of harmful
stereotypes is for the law to cease its insistence on
classifying people according to sex. To finish, as I
started, with Simone de Beauvoir: "Woman is determined not by her hormones or by mysterious instincts, but
by the manner in which her body and her relation to
the world are modified through the action of others
than herself." (56)

Transsexual Troubles: The Discrepancy between Legal
and Social Categories

NOTES

(1)   de Beauvoir S., The Second Sex, p.295 (1972).
(2)   Births and Deaths Registration Act, 1953, S.2.
        S.1. 1968, No. 2049, reg. 16.
(3)   Smith, D.K., "Transsexualism, Sex Reassignment
        Surgery and the Law", 56 Cornell L. Rev. 969
        (1971).
(4)   Supra, note 2, S.29 (3).
(5)   Stoller, R., Sex and Gender, Science House,
        (1968).
(6)   Oakley, A., Sex, Gender and Society, Temple
        Smith (1975).
(7)   Bowman, K. and Engle, B., "Sex Offences: The
        Medical and Legal Implications of Sex Variat-
        ions", 25 Law and Comtemp. Pbs. 292, at p. 293
        (1960).
(8)   Archer J. and Lloyd B., Sex and Gender, Pen-
        guin, Ch. 9 (1982).
(9)   Money J. and Tucker P., Sexual Signatures,
        Abacus (1977).
(10)   Ibid., p.50.
(11)   (1979) F.L.C. 90-636; Finlay H.A., "Sexual
        Identity and the Law of Nullity" 54 A.J.L.
        115 (1980).
(12)   Fraser, Sir K., O Reilly, M.J.J. and Ritoul,
        J.R., "Hermaphroditus Versus, with Report of a
        Case" I Med. J. of Aus., 1003 at 1006 (1966).
(13)   Supra, note 9, at p.75.
(14)   Money J., "Ablato Penis: Normal Male Infant
        Sex-Reassigned as a Girl", 4 Archives of Sexual
        Behaviour, 65 at p.69 (1975).
(15)   Hart, H.L.A, The Concept of Law, Clarendon
        p.121 (1961).
(16)   Sachs, A. and Wilson, J.H., Sexism and the Law,
        Martin Robertson, Ch. 1 (1978).
(17)   O'Donovan, K., "The Male Appendage - Legal Def-
        initions of Women" in S. Burman (ed.), Fit Work
        for Women, Croom Helm, pp. 134-152 (1979).
(18)   [1971] p. 83 at 105.
(19)   Ibid., at 107.
(20)   Ibid., at 106.
(21)   Op. cit., note 11, at 78, 327.
(22)   Op. cit., note 3, at 1005.
(23)   Bartholomew, G.W., "Hermaphrodites and the Law",
        2 Mal. L. J. 83 (1960).
(24)   Ibid., at p.84.
(25)   Op. cit., note 18 at p.104.
(26)   Op. cit., note 9 at 81.
(27)   Op. cit., note 18 at p. 106.
(28)   Baxter v Baxter [1948] A.C. 274.

Transsexual Troubles;   The Discrepancy between Legal
and Social Categories

(29)   White Paper, Equality for Women, Cmnd. 5724, para. 16 (1974).
(30)   Op. cit., note 18 at p. 105.
(31)   Op. cit., note 9 at p. 69.
(32)   O'Donovan K., "Protection and Paternalism", in M. Freeman (ed.), The State, The Law and the Family, Tavistock (1984).
(33)   The Times, 15 Feb. 1983.
(34)   Sexual Offences Act 1959, S.1; Sexual Offences Act 1956, S.32.
(35)   Sexual Offences Act 1956, S.6.
(36)   Annotated Criminal Code of Canada (Snow), SS. 244, 246.
(37)   Dec. CP 6/76 (Nat. Ins. Comm.).
(38)   [1977] I.R.L.R. 121 at p. 123.
(39)   Sex Discrimination Act 1975, S.1.
(40)   Op. cit., note 38.
(41)   MacKinnon C., Sexual Harassment of Working Women, Yale U.P., p.155 (1979).
(42)   Pannick D., "Homosexual, Transsexuals and the Sex Discrimination Act", [1983] Public Law 279; Bailey R., note on C and D, 53 Aus. L. J. 659 (1979).
(43)   Horton K.C., "The Law and Transsexualism in West Germany" (1978) Fam. Law. 191.
(44)   Pace P.J., "Sexual Identity and the Criminal Law" [1983] Crim. L. Rev. 317.
(45)   In Re Leber. Neuchatel Cantonal Court, July 2, 1945.
(46)   Walz, M.B., "Transsexuals and the Law", 5 J. of Contemp. L. 181 (1979).
(47)   Van Oosterwijck v Belgium 3 E.H.H.R. 557 at p.584 (1980).
(48)   Raymond, J.G., The Transsexual Empire Women's Press, 1980, p. xvi.
(49)   Ibid., at p. 83.
(50)   Morris J., Conundrum, Signet, pp. 89-91 (1974).
(51)   Ibid.,
(52)   New York Times Magazine, March 17, 1974, p.94.
(53)   Op. cit., note 18, at p. 104. See also Fallowell, D. and Ashley. A., April Ashley's Odyssey, Arena, Ch. 10 (1983).
(54)   Cited by Raymond op. cit., note 48, at p. xvii.
(55)   Op. cit., note 48, at p. 70.
(56)   Op. cit., note 1, at p.734.

27

Chapter Two

WOMEN AND CHILDCARE: THE PARADOX OF DIVORCE

Susan Maidment

This chapter explores the paradox of divorce for
women with children. The areas of custody and maintenance are investigated to expose the contradictions
which face women who as an ideal believe in equality
between men and women but in reality find themselves
making claims in law which depend on asserting the
traditional role of women as childcarers and economic
dependants of men.
    In the past fifteen years two major developments
have highlighted and exposed some contradictions and
ironies in the position of women. The first is the
dramatic increase in the number of divorces, from 4.1
per 1000 married population in 1970 to 12.1 (estimated)
in 1982 (OPCS Monitor Ref. FM2 83/4). These divorces
are overwhelmingly instigated by women; according to
the Judicial Statistics about 75% of divorce petition-
ers are wives, for which there are social and psychological as well as economic explanations, such as the
availability of legal aid and advice, and of supplementary benefit to mothers heading one-parent families.
    The second development has been the growth of the
women's movement, of women's employment and in a more
general sense a greater awareness by women of all ages
and classes of their lack of equality and advantages.
The claim for equality of treatment has manifested
itself in areas such as employment and education. It
has also been forcefully made in the context of the
family. The sharing of household chores and of childcare responsibilities for example has been one aspect
of the claim for equal partnership in marriage on a
social level. There have however also been legal ram-
ifications. The writing down of the practicalities of
equal partnership in marriage in the form of legally
binding marriage contracts has been particularly evident in the Unites States (Weitzman, 1981). These contracts are intended as alternatives to the traditional

legal consequences of marriage, whereby, it is alleged, the law upholds male domination and sex discrimination in the division of labour within the family. In this country mothers were finally given equal parental rights with fathers over their children in the Guardianship Act 1973, more than a century after such claims had first been made by militant Victorian women. Proposals for equal rights over family property within the marriage have also been made, and were taken up in the 1970s by the Law Commission, although to date governments have resisted such changes. And divorce laws, covering the grounds of divorce and consequential issues of children, property and money, were rewritten in 1969-1971 to be gender-neutral, so that at least in theory, differential treatment of men and women on divorce was not legally justified.

The coincidence of the rise in divorce and the claims of women to equality has however in practice only served to expose the enormous gap between the ideal and the reality. While espousing an ideal of equal partnership within marriage, on divorce women are forced by reality into making claims based on their traditional role as dependants and childcarers. Despite the social changes that have undoubtedly taken place in the employment of women and the greater participation of fathers in childcare (Lewis, Newson and Newson, 1982), the reality of family life is that women are still largely economically dependent on their husbands for their support and accommodation, and that mothers still bear the responsibilities if not all the chores of childcare (Oakley, 1982). Divorce therefore not only affects women on a personal or psychological level, for example by causing a loss of self-esteem, but also serves to expose the hidden poverty of women within marriage. The reality and contradiction of divorce for women is therefore that they find it necessary to make claims which on principle of equality with men they would not countenance.

Some of these contradictions of divorce for women which arise out of the gap between the ideal and the reality of family life can be seen in two particular areas: these are the claims made by women after marriage breakdown to the custody of children, and to financial support.

WOMEN AND CUSTODY

The custody of children after divorce is popularly associated with their mothers. It is certainly the case that in practice in about 90% of divorces with

dependent children the courts do grant custody, or
care and control of the children to the mother. One
major explanation for this is that only about 6% of
custody applications are contested (Eekelaar and
Clive, 1977; Maidment, 1976, 1984), so that the general practice of making custody orders in favour of the
mother is a result of private ordering between the
parents, which the court merely confirms in a formal
order. The court can and in effect does only respond
to the proposals put before it by the parties; it is
not interested in the social context which dictates
such proposals. In those cases that are contested
there is little evidence of any widespread maternal
preference (Eekelaar and Clive, 1977), although in
custody disputes which go on appeal a maternal preference is more likely to be articulated (Maidment,
1981). The empirical evidence suggests that far more
significant in practice than any maternal preference
both in uncontested as well as contested cases is a
judicial desire to maintain the residential status quo
of the child, to avoid unnecessary or undue physical
or psychological disruption of the child's life.
Where children remain in the care of their mothers
after the marriage breakdown therefore, as they usually
do, the most likely outcome even of a custody contest
is that custody will be awarded to the mother. In
other words, the reason why fathers do get custody in
some cases is usually to be explained by the fact that
they have physically cared for the child since the
breakdown of the marriage (Maidment, 1981).
    Contested custody cases are particularly signif-
icant, firstly, in terms of the mother's and father's
motives and self-perceptions. There is evidence that
a much higher percentage of children are resident with
their father at the time of the divorce petition in
contested than in uncontested cases, which suggests
that residence with the wife is more likely to go unchallenged than is residence with the husband (Eekelaar
and Clive, 1977; Luepnitz, 1982). Wives, it seems,
are "more tenacious than husbands in their attempts to
obtain possession of the children" (Eekelaar and
Clive, 1977: para 3.6). It would seem likely that
social values concerning the role of women and motherhood underpin and explain such differential behaviour,
although this has not been explicitly studied. The
father's position has been given more attention, in
itself an interesting fact since it suggests that
fathers who contest custody are in some way and to
some extent considered deviant. Reasons for fathers
seeking custody include genuinely wanting it, or believing that the mother does not, feeling wronged or

sufficiently vindictive to use custody to intimidate or harass ex-wives, or "as a means of economic gain if they believe their ex-wives would be willing to take less property or support in the divorce settlement"(Santrock and Warshak, 1979:113). Claims for custody cannot also be entirely separated from claims to the matrimonial home. Gersick (1979) noted that nearly all fathers with custody remained in the marital residence. Gersick did not find any greater interest by fathers in sons, nor had the fathers who sought custody participated more in childcare prior to the divorce, although they were all described as "active". Gersick (1979) suggests four variables which in his study identified fathers with custody: relationships in their family of origin ("men with custody showed more closeness towards their mothers and less towards their fathers; they were more likely to be later-born children with both male and female siblings...men from traditional families are more likely to make the extremely non-traditional decision to seek custody"); feelings about the departing wife ("the more wronged, betrayed or victimised that a man felt, the more likely he was to have sought custody...Anger and revenge seemed to be components of many decisions to seek custody"); the wife's intentions about custody; and the attitudes of lawyers.

The second aspect of the contested custody cases is the judicial response to the parental claims. In the majority of contested cases, the custody outcome appears to be broadly dictated by the residential status quo of the child, rather than by any maternal preference, although the actual outcome will often be to confirm the mother's existing care of her child. This can be illustrated by considering those cases where the mother does not have the status quo on her side.

> The very low success rate of wives where they did challenge their husbands' possession of the children shows that the courts do not necessarily share that assumption (that the wife is seen as prima facie the proper person to have care of the children) or, if they do, they have regard to other factors in making their decisions. This point is of extreme importance.
> (Eekelaar and Clive, 1977: para 3.6).

There nevertheless remains a minority of cases where the status quo is not confirmed by the court. In Eekelaar and Clive's study (1977) although any change of status quo by the court was exceedingly rare,

where it did occur it was never in the father's favour but only to the mother. They therefore conclude
that there is "evidence of a certain judicial caution
about allowing husbands to look after children"
(para 6.5). They are at pains to emphasise however
that this is not to be thought of as typical: "Occas-
ional instances of 'favouritism' for the wife may
still, therefore, be found, but they are quite unchar-
acteristic of the general practice" (para 13.14).

Where decisions in contested cases are appealed
against to a higher court, a different picture emerges. In a study of reported appeal cases (Maidment,
1981) it appeared that some 37% (14 out of 38) did
not maintain the status quo, and children were moved
by court order from their father to their mother,
after a status quo of between one and five years, on
such articulated grounds as a simple maternal preference, reuniting siblings, assessment of a parent's
personality, and punishment for refusing or obstruct-
ing access. In terms of outcome, therefore, a bias
at this level towards mothers is evident, since it is
these appeal cases which on paper present the best
chance of success for fathers, by having on their side
the single most significant indicator of custody outcome, the status quo.

Both uncontested as well as contested custody
cases therefore confirm a general pattern of mothers
as childcarers. In uncontested cases, over three
quarters of children who are living with one or other
parent, live with their mother, and the court confirm
this arrangement in over 99% of cases (Maidment, 1984:
62-3). In contested cases, mothers seek custody more
often than fathers when the child is not living with
them; the judges' response is normally to uphold the
residential status quo of the child, but when they do
not it is to return the child to its mother. Fathers
who believe that custody decisions are stacked against
them are not totally incorrect, although judges have
almost total discretion in these matters (which is why
it is difficult to impugn their subjective discretion
even by a formal appeal). It may be that the solution
to these contests cannot lie in favouring one parent,
whichever it is to be, over the other; it may have to
be found in some more radical approach to the whole
issue of parental responsibilities, both legal and
actual, in the post-divorce arrangements for children.

This discussion of child custody has served to
illustrate that, whatever the reasons, and these have
never been explicitly investigated, women usually seek
the legal rights to the care of the children on the
breakup of their marriages, and that by and large, and

again for various reasons, not all of which
are directly based on a maternal preference, the judges
respond on the basis of the traditional childcaring
role. Indeed in one sense the prevalence of the judicial confirmation of the status quo in uncontested
cases may be contingent on the fact that the judges
do indeed approve of the division of labour evident
in the parties' private arrangements.

It might be said that, despite the general rais-
ing of the level of consciousness which few women in
this country have not by now been exposed to, nevertheless many if not most women still accept and desire
a traditional childcaring role, and that this role
within marriage is merely being reflected in the public formalities of divorce. There are reasons to
believe however that the claim to the childcaring role
is of a deeper dimension for women, even for those
of a feminist persuasion. This may be illustrated by
considering two specific groups, lesbian mothers and
unmarried mothers.

Judges have evidenced a certain unwillingness to
uphold claims to children by homosexual parents of
both sexes (for example in the adoption case of Re D
[1977] 1 All ER 145 and in the access case of G v G
(1981) 11 Family Law 149). Lesbian mothers however
allege that there is a particular judicial hostility
to granting them custody, and groups such as Action
for Lesbian Parents have been set up to provide support for members in custody and access disputes (Sunday Times, 15 January 1978). It is not true that a
lesbian mother will never get custody. Cases have
been reported in which the Court of Appeal has over-
turned an initial refusal of custody to a lesbian
mother, although this outcome may have been based more
on the father's inability to provide immediate housing
for the two children, and the resulting choice of
allowing the girls to remain with their mother rather
than going into local authority care.

It may be that a more typical judicial response
is the decision in S v S (1980). A mother who had a
lesbian relationship lost custody of her daughter aged
7½ and her son aged 6 because of "the risk of children, at critical ages, being exposed or introduced to
ways of life which, as this case illustrates, may lead
to severance from normal society, to psychological
stresses and unhappiness and possibly even to physical
experiences which may scar them for life." The welfare report had recommended custody to the mother on
the grounds that the sexual identity of both children
was well established, both children expressed wishes
to be with their mother, and the mother could provide

better material care for the children than the father.
Both sides had called expert witnesses: for the mother
it was said that "there was no danger in this case of
the children being led into deviant sexual ways"; for
the father the consultant psychiatrist agreed as regards sexual deviation, but considered that the "social
embarrassment and hurt" resulting from local knowledge
of their mother's lesbianism would be very harmful to
the children. In other words the fears for the children were more concerned with social stigma than with
sexual deviation.
    There is in fact little evidence to suggest that
living with a homosexual parent is psychologically
damaging to a child. In the United States research on
the effects of being reared in lesbian-mother families
is more advanced because the issue has arisen more
often than here in child custody litigation. Early
reports comparing children in divorced or separated
lesbian mother and heterosexual mother families find
no significant differences in children's sex-role
behaviour as measured by toy preference tests (Hoeffer,
1981), no difference "in the type or frequency of
pathology as evaluated by blind psychological testing
and a playroom evaluation", nor any differences in
gender development "by evaluation of the sex of first-
drawn figure, the history of play preferences and
sexual interest, and behaviour exhibited in the playroom" (Kirkpatrick et al, 1981). Nor can the absence
of a father or other male in the lesbian household be
said to damage the child, or to make him or her grow
up as a homosexual (Rutter, 1978).
    To the divorced lesbian mother, then, the central
issue is why should her lesbianism be of any significance in the custody decision. Yet behind this issue
lies her claim as a mother to custody of her child.
The lesbian mother is asking, given that she claims
that her homosexuality is a legal irrelevance, for the
same treatment by the divorce courts as all mothers,
that is an expectation that she will get custody, especially where the children have so far been living
with her.
    Unmarried mothers also have recently been making
a case of uninterrupted childcare. In 1979 a Law
Commission Working Paper explored the extent to which
English law discriminated against illegitimate children. For example, the child's mother is his sole legal parent and guardian and he is not treated as having
a legal father although the father may apply to court
for custody or access to his child. Nor is the child
treated as having any legal relations; the child's
legal right to maintenance is limited, is technically

known by a different name of "affiliation" and may only be applied for by his mother and only in a magistrates' court. The Law Commission's view was that if one took the welfare of the child as the first and paramount consideration such legal discrimination was unjustifiable. They therefore recommended abolition of the status of illegitimacy so that all children would be treated equally in law regardless of the marital status of their parents. The main effect of this proposal however from the parent's point of view was to equate the legal position of parents of a legitimate child to that of an illegitimate child. Thus, according to the Law Commission, fathers would have equal parental rights with mothers over all children. Recognising that in some instances to give the father automatic parental rights would give rise to difficulties, for example in rape or incest cases, they proposed that the mother should be able to take the father to court if she wished to have his parental rights removed.

The response to these proposals was exceedingly hostile. Rights of Women (ROW) thought it was "a means of extending male control over women rather than enhancing the rights of children" (Sunday Times, 12 February 1980). The National Council for One Parent Families (NCOPF) submitted: "Evidence from mothers, social workers and lawyers shows the extent to which both married and unmarried fathers use their rights of custody, access and the payment of maintenance as a lever to harass women when their relationship is breaking down" (Sunday Times, 12 February 1980). In An Accident of Birth (1980) (NCOPF) argued against giving fathers automatic parental rights.

> In our experience, the majority of illegitimate children during early childhood are living with and being cared for by their mothers alone, and have either no contact, or very erratic contact with their natural fathers. We believe that giving fathers automatic rights will remove the existing protection and security an unmarried mother has in bringing up her child alone, and will lead to increased pressure and distress, caused not only in the event of intervention by an estranged father, but also by the uncertainty of never knowing whether or not the father will exercise his rights, unless the issue is decided in court.
> If an unmarried father is to be given automatic parental rights, the question of establishing paternity takes on increased significance.

> We believe that many mothers will be deterred
> from entering the father's details on the birth
> certificate or will deny the identity of the
> father if automatic parental rights flow from
> paternity being established. This will act
> against the child's rights to know the facts
> about his or her origins and will undermine the
> Law Commission's recommendation on this subject.

In practice nowadays over 50% of illegitimate births
are jointly registered and therefore publicly recognised by both parents, and it is estimated that over
a third of illegitimate children are born into relatively stable unions (Lambert and Streather, 1980).
(ROW) and (NCOPF) did therefore accept that in these
situations there ought to be the possibility of a
"mutual declaration of parentage" but only with the
mother's consent, and not otherwise.
     The Law Commission in its final Paper (1982)
recapitulated. They now propose that a legal distinction between "marital" and "non-marital" children
should remain, although most of the legal disadvant-
ages which flow from that distinction should be removed. The basic difference remains therefore whether the
child's parents were married or not, and the effect of
that on the rights of the parents. The father,
according to the Law Commission will not therefore
have automatic parental rights, but it is proposed
that he will be able to apply to court for a full parental rights and duties order. This will not depend
on the mother's consent as such, although that will
obviously be a serious issue for the court, but purely
on the welfare of the child as the first paramount
consideration.
     The reasons behind the opposition to the Law
Commission's original proposal are various (they are
set out at Law Commission No. 118 para 4.26.).
     Behind them however may be detected, at least in
part, a certain female exclusivity. At its most crude
and simplistic, the militant unmarried mother is saying that if she chooses to bear her child outside
marriage, then that child is hers and she does not
want any interference from whoever happened to be the
biological father. Such a stance unfortunately smacks
not only of a claim to the natural role of childcare,
but also of an assertion of property rights over
children, for which many generations of mothers rightly attacked their husbands at a time when in law the
"sacred rights of fathers" over their children were
paramount.
     Although the circumstances differ therefore, both

Women and Childcare: The Paradox of Divorce

lesbian and unmarried mothers have made claims to the
care of their children, which are essentially based
on social and cultural perceptions and expectations
of motherhood. The irony for many of these women is
not simply that they make such claims, but that being
unconventional and possibly more politically conscious,
they may perhaps be aware of the contradictions which
underlie such claims. It may be that giving birth to
and caring for their children has given these particular women a certain social and psychological security
which they are not willing to give up or even share
with the father of the child. The social realities
of their lives therefore demand for them exclusive
claims to their children. As has already been suggested, this position creates some difficulties for a
feminist theory which at the same time is seeking a
non-gender-exclusive approach to childcare. It also
poses a challenge to feminist theory to confront the
competing principle of the best interests of the
child, a matter which will be returned to.

WOMEN AND MAINTENANCE

. Until 1971 the right of women to maintenance after
separation or divorce was severely limited by the principle of the matrimonial offence. A wife who was
guilty of adultery or desertion had in principle lost
her right to maintenance in law, and on being divorced
by her husband would receive no maintenance at all
although in some cases she might be allowed " a compassionate allowance to save her from utter destitution" (Dailey v Dailey [1947] 1 All E.R. 547). Indeed
prior to 1971 many contested divorce petitions must
have been fought more with an eye to the issue of
maintenance.
     Under the present Matrimonial Causes Act 1973,
the matrimonial office is no longer the theoretical
basis for divorce. Divorces are granted on the sole
grounds of irretrievable breakdown (although issues of
fault do appear in three of the five facts needed to
prove irretrievable breakdown); maintenance is an entitlement arising out of the status of having been
married (this derives from the overriding guideline to
the court in awarding maintenance, that is "so as to
place the parties in the financial position in which
they would have been had the marriage not broken
down": Matrimonial Causes Act 1973, section 25); and
this entitlement to maintenance is gender-neutral and
in theory equally applicable to both husband and wife.
The same is essentially true of maintenance on break-

down of marriage in the magistrates' courts (Domestic
Proceedings and Magistrates' Court Act 1978).

Men may, and some men do, claim maintenance from
their wives, and in principle the courts treat them
in the same way as applications from women. There are
certainly some reported cases of this kind, although
statistical information is not available indicating
the extent of such applications. In practice of
course it is mainly women who claim maintenance or
financial support from men, and the reason for this is
pre-eminently because they <u>need</u> it. The financial dependency of women after breakdown of marriage arises
from two particular sources: firstly the economic
inequality of men and women in employment, and secondly from the traditionally different roles played by
men and women within marriage. Both of these explanations are accepted by the courts in the present practice of maintenance law. Faced with women's financial
claims to resources which are insufficient in most
cases to keep both parties at the standard of living
they enjoyed as an intact family, the courts tend to
be guided in practice, whatever the theory contained
in the Matrimonial Causes Act 1973, section 25, by
the principle of trying to satisfy the "needs" of the
parties (Eekelaar, 1979), but also (though this is
rarely articulated) within a context of trying to
achieve a comparable, even if lower than previously,
standard of living for both parties.

In recent years, the debate about maintenance
after divorce has turned on two issues. The first
concerns whether the law should recognise the financial dependence of women, and the second is whether,
if that dependence is accepted, it should be the ex-
husband or the state who should bear the cost.

The two main arguments against legal recognition
of the financial dependence of women are quite different and result in uncomfortable bed-fellows. Groups
such as Campaign for Justice in Divorce, whose members
are mainly well-educated, middle-class ex-husbands
together with some bitter second wives, have argued
that the ex-wives receive maintenance even where they
do not need it, to the extent that the man's second
family suffers and is provided for less than the ex-
wife. This is the so-called "meal ticket for life"
or "alimony drone" syndrome. CJD particularly wants
to have matrimonial conduct reintroduced into maintenance law in far more cases than at present (according
to <u>Wachtel v Wachtel</u> [1973] 1 All E.R. 829 these
should only be the exceptional cases where the conduct
is "so obvious and gross" that it would be repugnant
to a sense of justice not to take it into account),

so that wives who are deemed in actual fact to have
broken up the marriage (though not in law) are penalised financially.

A more thoughtful argument against maintenance
for ex-wives have been expressed by Ruth Deech (1977).
Essentially she argues that divorce law should recognise a partnership of equals, and eliminate any recognition of female dependency or sexual stereotyping,
so as to encourage women to be independent. She
argues for legal equality both within and after marriage, for individual responsibility to meet one's own
needs. She concedes that there may be special cases
where a woman can prove her "needs" for maintenance
such as where she is caring for children or is unable
to work, but argues that such maintenance should only
be temporary and rehabilitative, with exceptions for
example in the case of older or incapacitated women.

Deech starts from a position of independence but
concedes that there will be cases of dependence.
Katherine O'Donovan (1978) represents a view of inevitable female dependence within the existing social
structure. She argues that marriage requires a woman
to sacrifice a cash income for her husband and children, which in justice has to be recognised on divorce
by making the wage-earner responsible for the support
of the non-wage-earner. Maintenance for ex-wives also
recognises the inequality of earning power between
husbands and wives, the value of the work done by the
wife in the home, and the lack in English law of a
community of property system (i.e. equal shares in
family property) during the marriage. She concludes
that Deech's equality principle is inappropriate: it
only operates as between husband and wife, and can
hardly be served by making the wife dependent on the
state, for in reality this is the only way her dependence will be met.

The Law Commission (1981) having reviewed the
current maintenance debate tried to steer a middle
path; it sought to promote the desirability of self-
sufficiency for both parties, but in two major ways
recognised that in practice it was likely to be extremely difficult for women to become financially independent. Thus the report encourages limited term financial orders or a clean break, but at the same time
insists that the law recognises the financial needs
of women who are childcarers, or of older women with
low employment prospects. Indeed the current Matrimonial and Family Proceedings Bill which will give
effect to the Law Commission's proposals by the end
of 1984 is intended to embody this compromise and is
expected to continue to recognise women's needs to

maintenance despite fears to the contrary (see the evidence of Sir John Arnold, President of the Family Division, to the House of Commons Special Standing Committee on the Bill).

Recognition of women's financial dependence on divorce leads to the second issue: whether it should be the ex-husband or the state who bears the cost. Kevin Gray (1977) has argued that on divorce an equal division of property between husband and wife would give recognition to their (possibly) separate but equal contributions to the marriage, but that future needs should become a state responsibility through the social security system. He suggests that this scheme would present an incentive to the wife to retain financial independence during marriage. On O'Donovan's arguments this remains an unrealistic ideal; and indeed she is not impressed by a scheme which merely transfers the wife's dependence from her husband to the state.

In one sense this part of the debate is absurdly academic. At the present time the <u>private</u> law of maintenance is expected to reallocate finances on divorce and provide for the support of the economically weaker party. In practice the state through the supplementary benefit system is already providing the main economic support for ex-wives with dependent children, by virtue of the rule that these women are entitled to supplementary benefit without the requirement that they register for work. The Law Commission (1981) itself in its report recognised that the private law of maintenance could not solve the poverty of mother-headed one-parent families created by divorce, but the question of public support was beyond its terms of reference.

The issue therefore is not whether the financial responsibility for ex-wives and children should be transferred from ex-husbands to the state, for the fact is that it already is. The little empirical evidence that there is (and based on very small samples) suggests firstly that ex-wives who are employed are more likely to be receiving some maintenance, whereas those who are unemployed are more likely to be receiving no maintenance and living on supplementare benefit (Davis, McLeod, Murch, 1983); secondly that although a large percentage of ex-wives do receive some maintenance (68% of single mothers and 47% of remarried mothers according to Maclean and Eekelaar, 1982, and 72.5% of ex-wives with children according to Davis, McLeod, Murch, 1983), nevertheless maintenance is the <u>sole</u> source of income for only 12% of them (Davis, McLeod, Murch, 1983) (and according to the

National Council for One Parent Families it is the
. main source of income for only about 6% of them).
According to Maclean and Eekelaar (1982) the only way
out of poverty for ex-wives is remarriage, since
employment even if full-time does not usually lift her
family out of poverty, nor does maintenance, and most
women who remarry move into accommodation provided by
the second husband.

Indeed the most acute criticism of the new Matrimonial and Family Proceedings Bill, which has been
made by the National Council for One-Parent Families,
is that it is ultimately a red-herring, since reform
of the private law of maintenance can never solve the
poverty of one-parent families. If over 75% of women
receiving maintenance are also in receipt of supplementary benefit (Davis, McLeod, Murch, 1983), this is
because the amounts of maintenance are too low, even
by state subsistence levels. According to Maclean
and Eekelaar, in 1981 50% of women who received maintenance for themselves and their children received
less than £10 a week, and only 25% received over £20.
The Finer Report (1974) had commented, and it appears
to be still true, that even if court maintenance orders made in favour of supplementary benefit claimants
were paid regularly and in full (and only about a
half of them are so paid), the claimant and her children would, almost without exception, still be better
off as a recipient of benefit that as a recipient of
maintenance. Better enforcement of maintenance orders
then is ultimately irrelevant.

Carol Smart (1982) has highlighted the source of
the problem of maintenance for women. She supports
the arguments for the legal recognition of the financial dependence of ex-wives because, she claims, divorce on a large scale is now merely exposing the hidd-
en poverty of most women within marriage. Even apart
form the issue of childcare, it is the problems of
women's lower wages, unemployment or inability to re-
enter the labour market which make them the economically weaker party on divorce. The argument is therefore that society cannot expect women to be independent on divorce when it has already made them dependent within the family and employment.

The contradictions for women are obvious. Most
women, if asked, would presumably be only too eager
to be financially independent on divorce. The clean
break idea is enormously attractive to women as well
as men. Women have reported the great feeling of
relief which accompanies the receipt of supplementary
benefit, from being in control of their own finances
for the first time since they were married (Davis,

Women and Childcare: The Paradox of Divorce

McLeod, Murch, 1983). Most women, one may presume,
would therefore dearly love to be financially independent on divorce - if only it were possible. The
reality is that they cannot be anything but dependent,
whether that dependency falls on their ex-husbands or
on the state. They may have their own preferences as
to on whom they wish to be dependent; but the number
of maintenance applications is no guide to this since
there has been a certain amount of pressure put on
claimant wives by the Department of Health and Social
Security to bring maintenance proceedings so that the
DHSS can recoup some of the money paid out to claimants.

THE WELFARE OF THE CHILD

It is inappropriate to discuss the law of custody
without noting that in English law "the welfare of the
child is the first and paramount consideration" in
all legal questions concerning the custody or upbringing of a child. (Guardianship of Minors Act 1971,
section 1). It will also be impossible to ignore the
welfare of the child in maintenance cases because the
new Matrimonial and Family Proceedings Bill is introducing a "revolutionary" change into the law by making
the welfare of the child "the first consideration" in
these cases (this will become a revised Matrimonial
Causes Act 1973, section 25 (1)).
    The problem of the interests of children is a
particularly difficult one for feminists to confront.
Mica Nava (1983) has touched on this:

    The interests of children, their dependency and
    vulnerability, have never really been explored
    within feminist theory. Various related explan-
    ations for this are possible: there are the
    political fears that too much concern about the
    needs of children could feed into the anti-fem-
    inist backlash; at a personal level, the issue
    might be too contradictory to face; finally, a
    satisfactory feminist theory of children's needs
    may simply not be possible. Where the question
    has been addressed, the tendency has been to
    designate the work non-feminist, in that women's
    interests are not given priority.
    (Nava, 1983 : 88-89).

    This is an issue which will need systematic anal-
ysis (although here is not the place), since the problem of divorce is becoming the problem of children.

42

In other words childless divorces do not pose problems
of the same kind or same degree as divorces where
there are now, or even have been, dependent children
(Maclean and Eekelaar, 1984). It is clearly the presence of children which creates the custody issue, and
which largely results in the wife's economic dependence. This however affects most divorces, since nearly 60% have dependent children under 16, and over 70%
have children under 18 (OPCS Monitor Ref FM2 83/84).
(Indeed in some ways the question of marriage is also
one of children, since the trend may be to cohabit and
delay marriage until children are planned or produced.
So also may it be the real problem of sex discrimination, for much discrimination against women arises
because the woman has dependent children, particularly
in employment).
     The child-centredness of English law is not it-
self entirely unproblematic. Firstly, it is doubtful
whether the motives of the proponents of such law were
as child-centred as they appear. In the case of custody law, the introduction of the welfare of the child
as the first and paramount consideration in the first
Guardianship of Infants Act 1925 (now Guardianship of
Minors Act 1971) can be attributed to a blatant political compromise by the government of the day to stem
the growing pressure by militant women's groups to
reform the patriarchy of the common law under which
the father had absolute rights over his children
(Brophy, 1982; Maidment, 1984). Originally the father's rights were enforced both during and after marriage; from the 1830s onwards however inroads had been
allowed by mothers into the father's absolute control
over both access to and custody of the children on the
breakdown of marriage. The welfare principle was at
this same time beginning to be developed by the judges,
as a justification for derogating from the father's
common law rights (both in favour of the mother, or
of others who had been caring for the child). From
the 1850s onwards however women's groups had also been
campaigning for equal parental rights <u>within marriage</u>.
The chance of legislative success by the 1920s was
then met by a government proposal which, far from addressing the question of parental rights within marriage, elevated into a statutory criterion the existing
judicial principle of the child's welfare, but only
when questions of custody came before the courts. It
was not until 1973 that equal parental rights within
marriage were written into English law. The historical
origins of the welfare principle are therefore not as
illustrious as they might appear.
     The same may be said of the new maintenance law.

There can be no doubt that the Matrimonial and Family
Proceedings Bill has its origins in political pressure
from groups of ex-husbands to reduce their maintenance
liabilities. It is also quite apparent that the government is realistic about the financial needs of divorced women (and may be concerned at the prospect of
even more of their financial support falling on the
state). Political recognition of these competing
claims of both husbands and wives has been quite apparent in the debates surrounding the passing of the
Bill, and in the suggested judicial interpretation of
its provisions. The appearance of the welfare of the
child as the first consideration in maintenance cases
(originally proposed by the Law Commission (1981)) can
therefore be seen as an attempt to deflect the political debate away from "spousal support" by seeming to
promote the welfare of the child. The lack of guidelines as to how in fact the welfare of the child principle is to operate in maintenance cases appears to
confirm the analysis. For example, it has been asked,
should maintenance for the child be considered first
in time before maintenance for the wife? If so, and
the Lord Chancellor has indicated that this is intended, then what began as a political ploy may in fact
turn out to be a revolutionary change of practice. It
has also been said that courts have no guidelines as
to the real cost of maintaining a child; the Lord
Chancellor has responded by circulating courts on the
fostering rates recommended by the National Foster
Care Association. The welfare principle may therefore
become a meaningful reform, but it is unlikely that
the promoters of the new Bill had thought out its
implications in this way.
      The second difficulty with the child-centredness
of English law is that even if the law becomes in
interpretation totally child-centred there are grave
problems about giving effect to such a principle,
given the lack of a scientific base for knowledge and
understanding of the needs of children, and the lack
of professional agreement about how best to promote
their interests (Maidment, 1984). And thirdly there
is a very real question as to how a child-centred law
can take account of the interests of the parents. In
one sense divorce laws may need to take account of the
interests of the welfare of the family as a whole, of
the competing and interdependent claims of all of its
members who have participated in the past and should
participate in the future. There is a very real sense
in which the law, despite espousing a welfare of the
child principle, in fact allows the parents to determine what arrangements are made for the children.

44

This is most evident in the widespread practice of
judicial confirmation of the parents' private ordering
and the rather cursory judicial investigation into
whether the arrangements for the child's welfare are
satisfactory as a condition of the parents' divorce
(under the Matrimonial Causes Act 1973, s.41) (Davis,
McLeod, Murch, 1983; Dodds, 1983). It is even more
fundamentally evident in the fact that parents choose
to divorce, and are allowed to by the legal system,
when it is the child's overwhelming wish that his
parents stay together in the intact family(Wallerstein
and Kelly, 1980). In this respect the main interests
of children and parents at the time of divorce are
usually in direct conflict, and the parental right is
given precedence. The welfare of the child in English
law does not therefore incorporate a right to self-
determination, nor are his wishes necessarily relevant
(Maidment, 1984).
      The welfare of the child could become a more
meaningful principle. In custody cases there is a
strong argument for the law requiring both divorced
parents to participate legally and actually in the
life of the child, so that equal parental rights continue to operate, and childcare is shared, to the benefit of the child (Wallerstein and Kelly, 1980; Maidment, 1984). If sole custody orders were not the
norm, then contests which push mothers into making
claims to childcare would be elimated. The law would
on the contrary reinforce an ideal of shared or equal
parenting; not for reasons of equality between men and
women, but because this is now considered to be the
optimum circumstance for children to cope with their
parents' divorce (Wallerstein and Kelly, 1980). In
the context of maintenance the welfare of the child
requires not only financial support for the child, but
also for his carer. Maclean and Eekelaar (1984) have
rightly argued that a child can only take his standard
of living from that of the parent with whom he lives.
Anything that reduces the parent's income, only serves
to reduce the resources available for the child. This
is therefore the best argument against allowing the
wife's conduct to be reintroduced as a factor in reducing her maintenance entitlement and exposes a serious contradiction in the new Maintenance Bill.
Maclean and Eekelaar (1984) argue that the only realistic way to give effect to the welfare of the child
is to consider the resources of the household in which
the child lives. The court's task is therefore to
seek to equalise the standard of living of the two
households created by the divorce, on the one hand the
parent (usually the mother) with the child or children,

and on the other hand the father and any new wife or children who become his dependants.

The welfare of the child as a criterion for decision-making is not as uni-dimensional as it appears. There are ways in which it could be developed in a genuine attempt to treat the parents' claims as subsidiary to those of the child. The welfare principle however can also be an easy "liberal" stance behind which to hide when difficult or political choices have to be made between claims by mothers and fathers. The feminists' dilemma over how to accommodate the interests of children is no less real for that, but feminists who ignore this problem are in some ways being honest. In truth the present custody and maintenance debates are being held between adults, they are arguments about justice between the husband and wife or the father and mother.

In the case of custody, it was suggested that social or psychological needs compelled women into making claims for legal recognition of childcare responsibilities. In the case of maintenance it is financial need which leads to claims based on the economic dependence of women. In both cases women find themselves putting forward claims which in an ideal world they might not wish to make.

BIBLIOGRAPHY

Brophy,J. (1982) 'Parental Right and Children's Wel-
    fare: Some Problems of Feminists' Strategy in
    the 1920s'. International Journal of the Sociol-
    ogy of Law 10: 149-168.
Davis,G., McLeod, A. and Murch, M. (1983) 'Undefended
    Divorces: Should s.41 of the Matrimonial Causes
    Act 1973 be Repealed?' Modern Law Review 46:
    121-146.
Deech, R. (1977) 'The Principles of Maintenance'.
    Family Law 7: 229.
Dodds, M. (1983) 'Children and Divorce'. Journal of
    Social Welfare Law: 228-237.
Eekelaar, J. (1979) 'Some Principles of Financial and
    Property Adjustment on Divorce'. Law Quarterly
    Review 95: 253-269.
Eekelaar, J., Clive,E. with Clarke,K. and Raikes,S.
    (1977) Custody after Divorce. Oxford: Centre for
    Socio-Legal Studies.
Finer Report (1974). Report of the Committee on One-
    Parent Families. Cmnd. 5629. London: HMSO.
Gersick, K. (1979) 'Fathers by Choice: Divorced Men
    who Receive Custody of their Children'. In G.
    Levinger and O. Moles (eds) Divorce and Separ-
    ation. New York: Basic Books.
Gray, K. (1977) The Reallocation of Property on Divorce.
    London: Professional Books.
Hoeffer, B. (1981) 'Children's Acquisition of Sex-Role
    Behaviour in Lesbian-Mother Families'. American
    Journal of Orthopsychiatry 51: 536-544.
Kirkpatrick, M., Smith, C. and Roy,R. (1981) 'Lesbian
    Mothers and their Children: A Comparative Study'.
    American Journal of Orthopsychiatry 51: 545-551.
Lambert,L. and Streather, J. (1980) Children in Chang-
    ing Families: A Study of Adoption and Illegitimacy.
    London:Macmillan.
Law Commission Working Paper (1979). Illegitimacy.

Working Paper No. 74 London:HMSO.

Law Commission (1981). The Financial Consequences of Divorce. Law Com. No. 112. H.C. 68 1981-1982. London: HMSO.

Law Commission (1982). Illegitimacy. Law Com. No. 118. H.C. 98 1982-1983. London: HMSO.

Lewis, C., Newson, E. and Newson,J. (1982) 'Father Participation through Childhood and its Relationship with Career Aspirations and Delinquency'. In N. Beail and J. McGuire (eds) Fathers. Psychological Perspectives. London: Junction Books.

Luepnitz, D. (1982) Child Custody: A Study of Families after Divorce. Lexington, Massachusetts: D. C. Heath.

Maclean, M. and Eekelaar, J. (1982) Children and Divorce: Economic Factors. Oxford: SSRC Centre for Socio-Legal Studies.

Maclean, M. and Eekelaar, J. (1984) 'Financial Provision on Divorce: A Re-appraisal'. In M. Freeman (ed) The State, the Law and the Family. London: Tavistock. .

Maidment, S. (1976) 'A Study in Child Custody'. Family Law 6: 195-200, 236-241.

Maidment, S. (1981) Child Custody: What Chance for Fathers. London: National Council for One-Parent Families.

Maidment, S. (1984) Child Custody and Divorce: The Law in Social Context. London: Croom Helm.

National Council for One-Parent Families (1980). An Accident of Birth - A Response to the Law Commission's Working Paper on Illegitimacy. London: NCOPF.

Nava, M. (1983) 'From Utopian to Scientific Feminism? Early Feminist Critiques of the Family'. In L. Segal (ed) What Is to be Done About the Family? Harmondsworth: Penguin.

Oakley, A. (1982) 'Conventional Families.' In R.N. Rapoport, M.P. Fogarty and R. Rapoport (eds) Families in Britain. London: Routledge and Kegan Paul.

O'Donovan, K. (1978) 'The Principle of Maintenance: An Alternative View'. Family Law 8: 180-184.

OPCS Monitor Ref. FM2 83/4. London: Office of Population Census and Surveys.

Rutter, M. (1978) Quoted in The Sunday Times, 15 January.

Santrock, J.W. and Warshak, R.A. (1979) 'Father Custody and Social Development in Boys and Girls', Journal of Social Issues 35: 112-125.

Smart, C. (1982) 'Justice and Divorce: The Way Forward'. Family Law 12: 135.

Bibliography

Wallerstein, J. and Kelly, J.B. (1980) Surviving the
    Break Up: How Children and Parents Cope with
    Divorce. London: Grant McIntyre.
Weitzman, L. (1981) The Marriage Contract. New York:
    Free Press.

Chapter Three

THE POLITICS OF MATERNITY: CHILDBIRTH FREEDOM v
OBSTETRIC CONTROL

Beverley Beech

The law, in various ways, has been used to protect the interests of some while controlling the activities of others. Where medical expertise is concerned it is only during the last three hundred years
that childbirth has been considered to be an appropriate domain of medical interest, and during that time
the medical profession has sought to protect and extend its interests with the support and protection of
the law. The mother is perceived to be "sick and
incapable" and childbirth is viewed as a pathological
process which cannot be judged to be safe until after
the event. It is clear that women have, bit by bit,
lost all control of the normal natural process while
the medical profession have, inch by inch, sought to
control and dictate.
    In this chapter a number of contemporary cases
demonstrate the struggle for basic rights and freedoms in the childbirth process. The medical profession justifies its activities on the grounds that after
all it is only in the mothers' best interests. Unfortunately, the profession has yet to produce evidence
to substantiate that claim; and in the meantime British women are daily humiliated, defiled and assaulted
in ways that any civilised society should consider
intolerable and unacceptable.
    Since time immemorial the business of delivering
babies was the sole domain of women. Midwives are
mentioned in the Bible (Genesis Ch. 35, 17, and Exodus
Ch. 1). In ancient Greece obstetrics and gynaecology
was the province of the midwife, many of whom were
skilled surgeons and physicians. Unfortunately, the
history of medicine, written by medical men, marginalised the role women played. Throughout the ages
childbirth, contraception, abortion and healing were
all integral aspects of women's lives and those women
who undertook midwifery would already have had a great

50

deal of experience observing and assisting with births
that took place in their localities. Midwifery skills
were handed down from mother to daughter and many
entered apprenticeships -. in the 1690s a three year
apprenticeship cost £5. (1) In this country changes
began to take place around the 13th century when men
began to organise themselves into guilds, resulting
in the development of the barber surgeon guild and
restrictions on the right to practise. As the male
interest in the science of medicine developed so
became more interested in restricting and controlling
midwifery practice.

The first formal control of midwives was provided
by the Act of 1512 which on the one hand established
a system of licensing skilled and approved practitioners, and on the other restricted the practices of
those without a licence. The Church authorities were
responsible for its implementation and a midwife who
offended against the Act, ran the risk of appearing
before the churchwardens of her parish at the Bishop's
Court where she might be prohibited from practice,
made to do penance, or excommunicated. (2) The Act
was only concerned about her social and religious
behaviour, making no provision for any kind of training, and as women midwives were excluded from admission to the universities any midwife wishing to improve her
knowledge and expertise found the battle for admission
for training almost impossible. By the end of the
17th century midwifery was still a woman's profession,
with the majority of women being attended by midwives,
whilst male surgeons were called in for the difficult
cases requiring surgical intervention. Gradually men
began to take over midwifery in the more upper class
homes where it was considered fashionable to be attended by the more expensive doctor. It was during this
time that the Chamberlen family invented the forceps.
They were extremely careful to ensure that their
secret instruments were not copied by anyone else, so
they kept them covered in a large wooden box and when
they came to use them the woman was blindfolded and
the door was locked. The secret was passed down the
family from father to son for generations, and forceps
did not come into general use by the medical men until
the 18th century.

Jean Donnison, in her book <u>Midwives and Medical
Men</u>, a definitive history of midwifery, shows how in
1761 Elizabeth Nihill, a midwife, who had worked for
the prestigious.Hotel Dieu in Paris, where midwives
worked without male supervision or intervention, observed that instruments were seldom, if ever, necessary and argued that the man-midwife was for "dispatch".

51

She considered that he used instruments unnecessarily
to hasten the birth and save his own time, as well as
to impress the family with his dexterity and justify
charging a higher fee. Consequently more infants were
lost than formerly, and if the mother did not die of
the injuries she might have sustained or of resulting
childbed fever, she was frequently left with fearful
and lasting disabilities. Worse still, complained
Mrs. Nihill, "the male practitioner, adding insult to
injury, was so adept at concealing his errors with a
'cloud of hard words and scientific jargon', that the
injured patient herself was convinced that she could
not thank him enough for the mischief he had done."
(3) It is interesting that those sentiments are just
as applicable today! During the 18th century the
male involvement in midwifery continued with the more
affluent members of society employing the services of
a doctor, and because of the social attitudes to such
"delicate" subjects the art of midwifery was no longer
considered a "respectable" profession for the more
educated women in Society. The image of Sairey Gamp,
a dirty, disreputable and drunken midwife, described in
Charles Dickens The Life and Adventures of Martin
Chuzzlewit was pounced upon and promoted by the medical men. Midwives were held to blame for any calam-
ity, although the standards and knowledge of medical
men, with their theories of "complexions", "miasmas"
and "temperaments" were often far worse. The midwives'
traditional role of healer was constantly denigrated
and the medical men's view that childbirth was a dangerous time began to be promulgated. In addition,
because there were no midwifery societies, no midwifery journals and as women were barred from the medical
schools and universities there was no means by which
an intelligent professional midwife could improve her
practice and share her expertise with other midwives.
There were attempts, however, to legislate for control
of midwifery practice but the medical profession were
very opposed to any legislation. It was, after all,
a threat to their own practice and income, and they
were worried that good midwives would undermine their
interests.
    By 1890 the first Midwives Bill was introduced
to the House of Commons - it failed. The Bill's opp-
onents effectively arguing that it was designed to
provide an occupation for the increasing numbers of
working women in the population, if not to oust men
from midwifery practice. Midwives they considered,
were quite unnecessary, since the services of a doctor
could be provided through provident clubs and dispen-
saries, lying-in charities, and the Poor Law Medical

Service.   In 1902 the first Midwives Act was made law,
50 to 100 years after similar steps had been taken by
most continental countries.   Although the Act represented a massive defeat for the medical profession it
did give them an enormous say in midwives' affairs and
the local regulation of midwives passed into the hands
of Medical Officers of Health and the Central Midwives
Board, which, unlike other professional bodies, had
representatives of a competing profession (the doctors)
as members.   Furthermore, the Board was not actually
required to include even one midwife.   It was only
because of the Privy Council's right to nominate a
woman,   and the fortuitous representation on the
Board of two nursing organisations, that any midwives
were in fact appointed.   It was not until 1920 that
midwives were appointed to the Board, although they
were still debarred from becoming a majority; and it
was not until 1973 that a midwife became Chairman. (4)
By 1983 the Central Midwives Board was disbanded, midwives joining with nurses and health visitors in a
joint board of control - The United Kingdom Central
Council for Nurses, Midwives and Health Visitors.
England, Northern Ireland, Scotland and Wales has a
National Board consisting of a majority of elected and
some appointed members, each National Board sending five
members to the UKCC.   Complaints about midwives' conduct are submitted to the Investigating Committee of
the National Board.   If they decide that there is a
case to answer then the complaint is referred to the
Professional Conduct Committee of the UKCC.   When the
Investigating Committee of the English National Board
met they decided that it was only proper that members
of their Committee should hold qualifications in nursing, midwifery and health visiting.   As obstetricians
did not hold these qualifications it was, therefore,
not proper for them to be invited to sit on the Committee.   For the first time in England the medical
profession have been excluded from involvement in
controlling midwifery practice at its highest level.

THE HOSPITALISATION OF CHILDBIRTH

The move to hospitalise women for childbirth began
during the 18th century with the emergence of lying-in
hospitals which gave medical men the opportunity of
studying and examining large numbers of healthy women
and babies.   These hospitals were not interested in
admitting women who had problem pregnancies, indeed
their criterion was that the women should be fit and
healthy and free from any illness or disease.   The

main requirement for admissiion was proven poverty, a
letter of recommendation from a hospital subscriber,
proof of settlement in the parish in which the hospital was situated, together with an affidavit of marital
status. Only two of the lying-in institutions, the
General Lying-In and Queen Charlotte's, admitted unmarried mothers, and then only if the first pregnancy,
so as not "to encourage vice". (5) Although, it was
argued, at the time, that maternity cases had no place
in a hospital at all, hospitals offered a very much
less safe environment for childbirth than a home
birth, with high rates of infection and maternal death.
Puerperal fever was associated with hospitalised doctor controlled childbirth, and what figures there are
show just how dangerous hospitals were. Calculations
of maternal mortality in Westminster and London, during the late 18th century juxtaposed a rate of 1 in
277 for the Westminster district as a whole with a
rate of 1 in 3 for the Westminster Lying-In Hospital.
(6) Notwithstanding this very damning evidence, the
proportion of institutional confinements steadily increased.

The 1970 Peel Report (7) recommended that there
should, at a time when there was a shortage of beds,
for high risk women, be sufficient beds available for
those mothers who wished to have their babies in
hospital. A goal of 100% hospital confinements was
recommended, without any empirical data to support
it. (8) By 1980, when the Short Report (9) was published, the recommendation had changed to one that
ensured that all women would be delivered in hospital : "an increasing number of mothers should be delivered in large units; selection of patients should
be improved for smaller consultant units and isolated GP units; home delivery should be phased out."
The Committee quoted OPCS data on perinatal mortality
and noted that by 1977 perinatal mortality in home
deliveries was actually higher than in consultant units. Following the publication of the Short Report,
a letter from them was published in the Lancet sharply
criticising the Committee's misuse of their material.
(10) In a letter to the Minister AIMS also criticised
the figures.

> Closer investigation of the figures shows that
> from a statistical or epidemiological point of
> view this has not been proven (that perinatal
> mortality in home deliveries was actually high-
> er than in consultant units).

AIMS went on to state that:

The Politics of Maternity: Childbirth Freedom v
Obstetric Control

Removing the option of a home birth, and closing
down small maternity units, will remove the freedom of choice for parents and will not necessarily improve the perinatal and neonatal mortality
rates...We feel that it is imperative that parents are able to have freedom of choice in the
place of confinement and we will oppose vigor-
ously any attempt to reduce further this option
(11)

Despite the complaints of consumer groups the
move to hospitalise childbirth is now almost complete. By 1927 15% of all births were delivered in
hospital, in 1946 it was 54%. (12) In 1964 69.7% of
all births took place in hospital, in 1972 it was
91.4% and by 1980 it was 98.7%. (13) Yet there are
no authoritative figures available which show hospital births to be safer than home births and the figures
demonstrating the reverse to be true have been consis-
tantly and continuously ignored.

HOME BIRTH: A WOMAN'S FIGHT

It is the right of every woman in Britain to give
birth to her baby at home if she so wishes, yet the
exercising of that right is severely restricted, and
in some localities a right that is irrevocably denied.
One of the worst areas in the country in which to
arrange a home birth is Wolverhampton as revealed in
the following case. In 1981 Michelle Williams became
pregnant and decided that she would have a home birth.
She delivered her first baby in New Cross Hospital,
Wolverhampton, an experience which left her deeply
upset and determined that any subsequent birth[s]
would be at home.

In the written statement Michelle Williams made
for the court she described an incident that
occurred during the labour. "My main complaint
about what happened subsequently was that I was
given drugs against my wishes. Large purple
capsules were given to me to take. I asked
what they were and was told relaxants. I said
that I did not want relaxants and the nurse concerned went away to speak to the sister saying
'she is being a naughty girl and won't take her
tablets.' The sister therefore came over and
without further ado stabbed me in the leg to give
me an injection of pethidine without even asking
me to turn over or saying what she was going to
do. I vomited instantly...The whole process was

> like a production line. I was disgusted and
> determined not to let it happen again. ...The
> NHS has got to realise that women aren't just
> pieces of meat."

Having made the decision to have a home birth she and
her partner, Brian Radley, set about booking a midwife
by writing to the Divisional Nursing Officer. Follow-
the receipt of the letter, they were told that they
were irresponsible and were putting the mother and the
baby at unnecessary risk. A process of intimidation,
co-ercion, argument, and mainly subterfuge then commen-
ced.

First, they were incorrectly and deliberately informed that they would have to find a GP willing to
give medical cover. Few women are aware that there
is no necessity for GPs to be involved in home births.
Health Authorities insisting upon GP involvement do so
as a means of applying further pressure upon parents
to give up and have their babies in hospital. Midwives, in this country undertake three years midwifery training and therefore, it is they who are the experts in
normal childbirth, whilst the few GPs involved with
home births do not have adequate midwifery qualifications. If a midwife finds that a labour is not
progressing normally she can call for an expert in
abnormality to attend - the obstetrician and the fly-
ing squad. Some GPs do have obstetric training and
in such an emergency the midwife can call out any GP
on the obstetric list. He has to attend, and is required, by law, to do so. The Radleys, were unaware
that they were perfectly within their rights to inform
the Health Authority that they were not able to spend
time searching for a suitably experienced GP. The
midwives also contributed to the browbeating. A midwife was sent to assess the home conditions and determine the wisdom of arranging a home birth, and she concluded that Michelle Williams was a "High Risk" case
and ought to have her baby in hospital. "High Risk"
was assessed, not on a medical basis but on a moral
one because she was unmarried, the flat was considered
dirty and cold and the requests the Radleys were making
were considered unacceptable.

The reality was somewhat different, the Radley's lived in a perfectly clean, tidy, but sparsely furnished flat
and Brian Radley had taken the precaution of obtaining a
small heater to ensure that the flat was warm for the birth.

> In her written statement to the court Michelle
> Williams stated "...they showed themselves to be
> very hostile to me right from the start...I got

the feeling they regarded me as a silly little
girl." The midwives also made it clear that they
had conditions to me met. The bed would have to
be raised off the floor to "the required minimum
height."

Michelle Williams protested "I am not going
to lie down to give birth but would like to ass-
ume another position such as standing up or
crouching." The midwives responded "No. We cannot
do it like that."

The Radleys requested that Michelle would stand, or
crouch for the labour and delivery, that neither cath-
eters nor drugs be used nor was the cord to be cut
immediately. The midwife informed them that they
would have to sign a form (which was not produced)
which would mean that all the decisions about the birth
would be made by the midwives. The Radleys refused.
The midwife left stating "we can't help you if you
won't sign the form." The Radleys then decided that
perhaps the baby could be delivered by a private midwife. There are no private midwives in Wolverhampton
and they were not in a position to pay for one. Up
until two weeks prior to the birth Brian Radley was
still trying to find someone to deliver his girlfriend's baby, and it was not until the last moment
that it became apparent to them that if they were going to get the kind of birth they wanted then they
would have to deliver the baby themselves. In her
written evidence to the court, Michelle Williams
stated "It never entered my head that Brian would deliver the baby himself although the thought was coming
into my mind that he might have to if all else failed".
The Radleys were not aware that they could have in-
structed the DNO to assign another midwife to them as
they were not prepared to accept a midwife who had
little sympathy with their views.

The Health Authority has a legal obligation to
provide a qualified midwife to attend in childbirth,
whether the birth takes place at home or in hospital.
A pregnant woman has the right to dismiss her attend-
ants, at any time, should she feel that they are not
supporting her, and can demand that another midwife
be assigned. Instead, the Radleys prepared to deliver
their baby themselves, and Sunny Radley was born at
home without any support from the midwives. Michelle
Williams had an easy labour, the baby was born with
Michelle in squatting position, she needed no drugs
nor did she tear. The baby was perfectly fit and
healthy.

Such an affront to the integrity of the Health

The Politics of Maternity: Childbirth Freedom v
Obstetric Control

Authority could not be allowed to go unchallenged.
The West Midlands Regional Health Authority decided to
prosecute Brian Radley, under Section 9 of the Midwives Act (1951) which stated:

> If a person, being either a male person or a wom-
> an who is not a certified midwife attends a wom-
> an in childbirth otherwise than under the direct-
> ion and personal supervision of a duly qualified
> medical practitioner, that person shall - unless
> he or she satisfies the court that the attention
> was given in a case of sudden or urgent necessity,
> be liable on summary conviction to a fine not ex-
> ceeding ten pounds.

This particular Act had its origins in Section 1(2) of
the Midwives Act of 1902 which was designed to regul-
ate the midwifery profession and prevent the practice
of lay midwifery. In other words the 1902 Act was
designed to ensure that only qualified midwives were
practising and those who were doing it in order to
make a bit of extra cash would be penalised. The Lancet (1902) made the following comment:

> Legislation is absolutely necessary to prevent
> ignorant and incompetent women from practising
> for gain to the danger of those women who employ
> them. A drunken old hag could not obtain a sit-
> uation as a nurse to a hospital or workhouse, but
> there is nothing to prevent her putting a brass
> plate with "Midwife" under her name on the door.

On August 4th 1926 the Midwives and Maternity Homes
Act received the Royal Assent. Section 1 of the Act
makes substantial amendment to the "Public Health"
penal clause in S1 (2) of the 1902 Act. It was consolidation of the 1926 Act (viz the 1951 Midwives Act)
under which Brian Radley was prosecuted and convicted.
Although the exceptional saving in the case of "anyone
rendering assistance in the case of emergency" (1902
Act) was elaborated in the 1926 (and 1951) Act to
"unless he or she satisfies the court that the attention was given in a case of sudden or urgent necessity", it was immediately noticeable that the condition
"habitually and for gain" was absent.
   From the 1926 Act onward it became a criminal
offence to give unqualified attendance to a woman in
childbirth on a single occasion, and for free. The
offence became one of absolute liability, which meant
that Brian Radley was accused of committing the prohibited offense and his reasons for so doing were irrelev-

ant. That he had asked for midwifery care and that
this care had been grudgingly hedged with unacceptable
conditions was also irrelevant. There was only one
excuse that he could have used and that was that his
actions were as a result of "urgent necessity". In
other words the baby arrived suddenly and unexpectedly
and he dealt with the emergency. Brian Radley, however, could not plead this as he had acknowledged that
he and his girlfriend had agreed that, in view of the
actions of the Health Authority and the midwives, they
would deliver the baby themselves. He was duly convicted on the 6th August 1982 at the Stipendiary Magistrates Court, Wolverhampton and fined £100. (The
Act allows for a fine of up to £500, but the magistrate decided on a lower fine having taken into account
Brian Radley's financial state). A few weeks later another father, Rupert Baines, was convicted of a similar
offence in Bristol Magistrates Court. The couple had
stated that they had booked a midwife for the delivery
but when his wife went into labour it was late at
night and Mr. Baines was not prepared to abandon her
and search for a public telephone, in an area where he
ran a considerable risk of being assaulted. He too,
was judged to have acted "irresponsibly" and was fined
£40. It appears that fear of muggers resulted in a
reduction of £60 for such a heinous offence!

The Nurses, Midwives and Health Visitors Act
1979 which came into force on the 1st July 1983 has
given even greater power to midwives whilst reducing
parental choice still further, making it an offence
for anyone other than a midwife or a doctor to "attend
a woman in childbirth" except in situations of emergency or training. Any father, who wishes, under the
guidance of a sympathetic and caring midwife, to
"catch" his own baby will not be allowed to do so because he would not be acting "in a situation of emergency or training". The scope for authoritarian and
dictatorial midwifery has been further extended, those
parents who wish to make their own arrangements for
the delivery of their babies may find that if a
midwife refuses to co-operate, then the parents insis-
tance may become a criminal offence. The offence
will be one of absolute liability and the midwives
will have to prosecute. This section of the Act has
taken a significant step towards a professional midwifery police force. The medicalisation and policing
of childbirth will have been completed, and the threat
to individual self-determination and liberty will have
taken a significant step backwards. Following the
prosecutions of Brian Radley and Rupert Baines childbirth pressure groups have been approached by numerous

women determined to have a home birth and adamant that
the birth will be conducted according to their wishes.
These women have lost confidence in midwives, each
one of them has already had a number of previous births, most of which were conducted in hospital, where
they found their wishes overruled.

It is an appalling indictment of our midwifery service that some women feel that they have to run the risk of
unattended delivery in order that they and their babies
have the kind of birth they wish; and that fathers are to
be prevented from being at the birth of their own
children, as a direct result of the loss of trust in
the midwifery profession.

The "Patient" Mother

It is generally recognised that hospitals are places
for sick people and because of the attitude and management of patients in these institutions it is not surprising that the admission of a normal, healthy young
woman should also be treated in much the same way.
Treatment of the sick has been standardised and routine procedures are adopted to ensure their welfare and
care. Similarly, routine procedures have been introduced for the care of normal healthy women who are
expecting to deliver normal, healthy babies. Yet,
many of the procedures have never been properly evaluated whilst those that have, have been shown to have
little or no value. (14) Until recently it was accepted that when a woman entered hospital for maternity
care she assented to whatever treatment the medical
profession considered necessary. For other patients
it is generally accepted practice that treatment cannot be given without the patient's consent and that
to do so without such an undertaking would amount to
assault. Clearly, women admitted to hospital for maternity care have fewer rights than any other same patient entering a British hospital, and one of the reasons for this denial lies with the Medical Defence
Union. Its booklet Consent to Treatment (1974) contains the following entry on maternity patients:

> The Union does not consider that a maternity
> patient need give her written consent to any
> operative of manipulative procedures that are
> normally associated with childbirth. When she
> enters hospital for her confinement it can be
> assumed that she assents to any necessary proced-
> ure, including the administration of a local,
> general or other anaesthetic.

The Politics of Maternity: Childbirth Freedom v
Obstetric Control

In February 1983 AIMS challenged this presumption.(15)
Significantly, the Medical Defence Union has withdrawn
this presumption from the most recent edition of the
booklet. Yet beliefs, ideologies and practices die
hard, women and babies are still subjected to 'treatment' to which they do not consent.
      Consider the total and irrevocable abrogation of
the mother's rights in the three cases that follow:

Case No. 1. This case involves a woman who was transferred during labour to Bangor Hospital, North Wales.
The consultant insisted that the husband leave the
labour ward; when he refused to do so the consultant
called the police who removed him on the grounds that
he was trespassing. An episode indelibly marked on
the mind of the wife:

> They took my husband away from me despite my
> begging for him to stay. He did not come back
> for two hours. The consultant obstetrician gyn-
> aecologist had wanted the police to prosecute my
> husband but thankfully they didn't, this incid-
> ent marred this happy occasion for us.(16)

Those who wish to have a second companion, or their
children present at the birth are on even shakier
ground. Whilst the Short Report and the Maternity
Services Advisory Committee Report (17) recommended
that fathers should be welcomed and encouraged, hospitals can and do ignore the recommendations if they
feel so inclined. AIMS recommends that any mothers
faced with such an ultimatum should reply "If he goes
- I go", and refuse to be attended by the staff until
it is established that her companion can stay. This,
of course, is very difficult indeed for any woman to
ensure during her labour.

Case No. 2. The second case concerned a woman who,
in 1980, became pregnant and asked her GP to arrange
for the delivery to take place in the local GP unit,
which was one floor up from the consultant unit at
Preston Royal Infirmary. It soon became apparent that
she was expecting twins and she was told that she
should be admitted to the consultant unit. She had
already had a previous set of twins in another consultant unit, Marsdon Green, and the experience was so
dreadful that she refused to be admitted.
      During the pregnancy she had written to the Area Nurs-
ing Officer explaining that if she agreed to a consultant

The Politics of Maternity: Childbirth Freedom v
Obstetric Control

unit delivery she would like to be accompanied by the community midwife, who providing the twins were presenting
normally, would at least deliver the first twin. She
also listed her needs:

That the babies would be delivered on her stomach.
That after the delivery the babies would be left with
her and her husband.
That the babies remain with her so that she could
breast feed as necessary and that the babies would
not be given a bottle.

She refused consent to:

Shaving her pubic hair.
An enema unless she was constipated.
A routine episiotomy.
Any drugs without adequate discussion beforehand.
Any mechanical foetal monitoring.
Any routine drips without discussion.
Any uninvited audience, and the presence of any male
doctor or consultant without adequate discussion bef-
orehand.

The consultant refused to agree to any of her requirements, refused to explain why she could not have her
babies in the GP unit and was offensive to both her
and her husband. "He was very overbearing. He never
gave me a chance to explain my position and feelings
about the last experience." (18) He told her that
she could have her babies at the bottom of a field if
she wished but in his opinion she should have her
babies in a consultant unit. There then developed a
stalemate - lasting seven months, during which time
the mother was browbeaten, coerced and bullied. Her
questions and repeated requests were never answered
and the psychological pressure to comply with the consultant's ruling continued. Eventually after months
of searching for a suitable alternative, she much
relieved found another consultant unit that agreed to
her requirements.
     In November 1981 she was admitted, in labour, to
Blackburn consultant unit and after a perfectly normal labour she gave birth to the twins, whom the midwife delivered. She had no drugs, no episiotomy and
she had all her requests acceded to. Following the
birth the mother made a formal complaint to the first
hospital about her treatment. The hospital administ-
rator justified the consultant's actions:

     Until the fundamental question of admission to

> a specified hospital unit was determined the
> possibility of detailed discussion on the other
> points you wished to make could not take place...
> the decision by the consultant obstetrician to
> insist upon your confinement in a consultant unit
> was taken in your own best interests and those of
> your babies...

As the mother herself put it "it is rather like agreeing to the hanging ahead of the trial!"
    AIMS prepared an extensive dossier on the case,
describing what had happened over those months and
enclosing copies of all the correspondence, sent to
all the prestigious bodies asking for action - the
Royal College of Obstetricians and Gynaecologists,
the Royal College of Midwives, the Royal College of
General Practitioners, the Royal College of Physicians,
the Royal College of Psychiatrists. None of them took
any action. AIMS did not ask the General Medical
Council to act because it was well aware of their conditions of investigation:-

> By law, the Council can act on a complaint about
> a doctor's actions or behaviour only if the matt-
> er raised appears to be so serious that it might
> justify holding a formal enquiry to decide whether
> the doctor should retain his registration. (19)

Were such conditions applied to the police force it
would result in them being unable to investigate anything other than murder or rape! When Professor Peter
Huntingford (an eminent obstetrician and gynaecologist)
saw the details of this case he was moved to write to
the Minister and the Royal College of Obstetricians
and Gynaecologists:

> I would like you to know that I am ashamed to
> belong to a profession that can humiliate a wom-
> an in these ways and that allows such behaviour
> to continue. (20)

The case has since been referred to the Ombudsman (who
has yet to rule) but none of the prestigious bodies,
or the Minister of Health, took any action whatsoever.

Case No. 3. The third case concerns a woman who, in
January 1981, gave birth, four weeks prematurely, to
a son at the Royal Free Hospital, London. The mother
had already discussed with her obstetrician the kind
of birth she wanted and was confident that the staff

63

would be supportive. Once she had been admitted however the staff were unco-operative and unwilling,
informing her that she was not a private patient and
could not squat for the delivery but would have to lie
down. Shortly after she was admitted she was put on
a syntocinon drip which was steadily increased in in-
tensity. In her official complaint she stated that
the pain was so intense she was suffering periods of
unconsciousness, though she repeatedly asked for the
level to be rectified. She had wanted to stand during
the labour, in order to be better able to withstand
the pain of the artificially induced contractions, but
she was not allowed to do so. She had wanted to squat
for delivery but the nursing staff insisted that
she lie flat on her back, and eventually the baby was
delivered with the mother in that position. She had
already made it clear that she did not want an episiotomy but the staff stated that for a baby that was
one month premature an episiotomy was always carried
out. The birth was not a difficult one, the baby was
not distressed and the mother believed that the episiotomy was carried out as a routine in spite of her
objections. Although she had agreed with the consultant that the baby would be delivered in accordance
with a "Leboyer Style birth" she found that as soon as
the baby was born he was whisked away, and despite her
repeated requests to hold her baby he was not returned
to her for two and a quarter hours; and only then
after she had threatened to get out of the bed and go
and get him. It was very important to her to be able
to hold her baby immediately after the birth and she
was particularly distressed about being separated from
her baby for such a time. The Senior House Officer
meanwhile insisted that the baby be taken to the special care baby unit. The mother protested, pointing
out that there was nothing the matter with her baby,
but eventually very reluctantly agreed on the understanding that no treatments were to be given to her
baby without her permission being sought first. The
SHO agreed and told her that it was necessary for the
baby to go into the unit for observation.

When the mother visited the SCBU later in the day
she discovered, that her baby had a tube inserted in his
nose, had been given a stomach pump and had been given
dextrose solution. In explanation the SHO told her
that she had "forgotten" to pass her instructions on
to the unit staff. Later the baby developed a "sleepy"
eye. The SHO told her that antibiotics would be administered as a prophylactic measure. The mother informed her that she did not wish her baby to be given
antibiotics and argued with her for over an hour. The

64

mother was so outraged and upset by the treatment, she
and her baby, received at this hospital, she put in a
formal complaint to the ombudsman.

OMBUDSMAN - OBJECTIVITY OR PARTIALITY?

The office of Ombudsman was set up 12 years ago in
response to the need to provide for an objective investigation of serious complaints about the Health
Service. Whilst he can investigate complaints about
administration, he cannot investigate those concerning
clinical judgments. The present Ombudsman Sir Cecil
Clothier was approached by the mother described in
case history 3.
    The mother first of all complained that she had re-
quested that the level of the syntocinon drip be reduced,
finding her request ignored. The Ombudsman found that:

> "there were occasions when, in response to her
> request, the level was reduced " and "...the
> decision as to how much syntocinon should be giv-
> en is one which, in my view, the midwives took
> solely in the exercise of their professional
> judgment. As such I am not permitted to question
> it."

It is interesting that he considered that a clinical
judgment takes precedence over the expressed wishes of
the patient. In the evidence in this section of the
complaint he quotes one of the midwives who stated "midwives are not trained in supervising deliveries in the
squatting position." Yet, in 1982 the Chairman of
AIMS wrote to the Secretary of the Royal College of
Midwives precisely over this claim. The reply received read:

> Midwives have the necessary knowledge, under-
> standing and skills to manage a labour in the
> squatting position. Sadly, and for a multitude
> of reasons many midwives are either lacking in
> confidence or are too rigid to draw upon these
> when faced with an alternative way of assisting
> a delivery. Midwives do not need information
> about the management of any type of labour or
> delivery. They have all the knowledge and under-
> standing they require. (21)

Unfortunately, this was not known by the Ombudsman.
And again regarding delivery position his 'independent' evaluation was partisan:

65

it was for them (the staff) to decide whether to
agree to her requests about the conduct of her
labour and delivery. Their decision not to do
so, was, in my opinion, taken solely in the exercise of their professional judgment and I may
not question it.

The mother's objection to "routine episiotomy" and
subsequent complaint was similarly handled:

I do not doubt Mrs X statement that she told
the medical and nursing staff at various times that
she did not want an episiotomy...It is clear that
the consensus of opinion amongst the staff was
that, in the case of a premature birth, it was
the hospital's practice to perform an episiotomy
in order to avoid the risk of injury to the
baby's head. I am satisfied that that practice
was based on a decision taken solely in the exercise of clinical judgment and that it took into account the duty of the medical and nursing
staff to ensure the safety of both the mother
and child. For these reasons I cannot question
the decision to perform an episiotomy.

Yet the Ombudsman upheld not clinical judgments but
hospital policy. In his own report he states "it was
the past hospital's <u>practice</u> to perform an episiotomy
in order to avoid the risk of injury to the baby's
head."
When his investigation turned to the issues surrounding the treatment of the baby in the SCBU his
reasoning can only be described as manifestly absurd.

According to the medical records...the SHO prescribed the application of neomycin ointment to
each of A's eyes.   ...The SHO explained that,
as far as she could recall, Mrs X was worried
about antibiotics which were given by mouth or
by injection - whereas neomycin had a local effect only and was not absorbed into the system.
For this reason the SHO tended not to regard
neomycin as an antibiotic even though it was.

The Ombudsman found that "I do not doubt Mrs X
statement that she made it clear to the SHO that she
did not want A to be given antibiotics...she (the SHO)
suggested that there may have been confusion as to
the type of antibiotic to which she thought Mrs X was
objecting. I am not satisfied that the SHO's decision
to prescribe an antibiotic ointment for A was taken

in deliberate disregard of Mrs X's wishes. It follows
that I cannot find this complaint made out."
   The investigative impartiality of the Ombudsman
has been called into question before. (22) The Association for Improvements in the Maternity Services is
so disgusted with the Ombudsman's rulings that they
no longer advise women to take their complaints to
him. They point out to anyone seeking their advice,
that the only advantage in complaining to him is to
draw his attention to yet another complaint about maternity care and to demonstrate to the Health Authority
and the medical and midwifery profession that the care
that is on offer is less than satisfactory. Of the
complaints that go to the Ombudsman that no complainants do not receive a sympathetic investigation, particularly those who complain about being badly treated. If, however, the complaint is of an administrative shortcoming then he has no difficulty at all in
criticising the Health Authorities.
   In Administrative Law a "reasonable suspicion of
bias" debars people from sitting on tribunals. A relationship between the adjudicator and one side in the
dispute has been held to be sufficient to arouse such
reasonable suspicion. Sir Cecil Clothier's previous
employment was as Legal Advisor to the General Medical and Dental Councils, strong grounds for reasonable
suspicion of bias in a man whose job is to investigate
complaints about his former employers. (23) Those
not satisfied with the Ombudsman's rulings have a further and more restrictive channel of complaint in taking legal action against him. In the last case the
mother investigated the possibility of legal action,
finding that she could have obtained a writ of Mand-
amus, forcing him to rule on the item of complaint
about which he had made no comment i.e. the nurse who
continued the treatment in spite of the mother forbidding her to do so. She could also have appealed to the
High Court to quash the Ombudsman's ruling about the
SHO on the grounds that it was "manifestly absurd".
Any such action has to be taken within three months of
the Ombudman's ruling, and unfortunately very few
people are aware of this. The wheels of the complaints procedure grind slowly. Many litigants find the
procedures so complicated and lengthy that they drop
the case against the Ombudsman evading legal action.

WOMEN CARING FOR WOMEN

There is too yet another dimension: many women are
concerned about being treated by men and are adamant

that they will not consult a male doctor.   Up until
1983 the majority of pregnant women would be treated
by male doctors, while they could be confident that
at least the midwives looking after them would be female.

MALE MIDWIVES

In 1982, the European Court of Justice ruled that
Britain was acting illegally in preventing men from
training as midwives and in March 1983 the Secretary
of State announced that restrictions on the training
and employment of men as midwives were to be lifted.
This followed a report "Male Midwives: A Report of Two
Studies" (24) which concluded that the majority of
women were not opposed to male midwives and in general
accepted them.   The report was criticised by AIMS,
which pointed out that the form of questioning used in
the study was unsatisfactory.   The women were asked
whether they objected to being attended by a male midwife.   AIMS felt that the question was subtly loaded,
it should have asked whether the women would wish to
be attended by a male or female midwife, and leave
them to make the choice. as it was the women were under subtle pressure to agree.   Indeed the study quoted
the example of one woman who had refused to be attended by a man, but because of a mix-up with the notes
a man did attend her.   The report noted that she did
not complain because she felt too shy to do so.
    As a result of this legislation every training
school in the country is bound to offer midwifery
training to men who apply and the onus is still on
the mothers to make it quite clear that they do not
wish to be attended by a man.   Bearing in mind how
particularly vulnerable pregnant women are and especially when in labour, very few are likely to refuse
the attendance of a man.
    The appointment of male midwives can only be a
retrograde step, and it is interesting that the Sex
Discrimination Act was very quickly used to the disadvantage of the majority of women.
    ' Following the lifting of the restrictions on the
training and employment of men as midwives the Department of Health issued a Health Circular (25) stating:

    Health Authorities MUST make appropriate arrange-
    ments locally to ensure that a. women have the
    freedom of choice to be attended by a
    female midwife.   b.   where male midwives are
    employed, provision is made for them to

be chaperoned as necessary.

Again, another right conveniently masked, few women
realise that they have the right to refuse the attendance of a male midwife (or any individual midwife
for that matter).

HOSPITALS FOR WOMEN

For women who wish to be attended by women their
choice is exceedingly limited. Certainly they have
every right to refuse to be attended by a man, but many
of them will find considerable difficulty in locating
a woman who can treat them. The result is that women
often do not come forward for treatment. The Elizabeth Garrett Anderson Hospital in London was established to provide treatment by women for women and together with the South London Hospital for Women they are
the only two hospitals in the country where women can
be assured of being treated by a woman. The EGA hospital was the focus of an enormous campaign to prevent
its closure; and assurances were received from the
Government that it would be retained (though greatly
reduced in the services it offers).
     As a result of the pressure applied by the Royal
College of Obstetricians and Gynaecologists, the EGA
is now facing the proposition of the appointment of a
male registrar. The RCOG has refused to allow the EGA
training status unless it agrees to a link with UCH, and
the UCH staff have pointed out that it would be against
the Sex Discrimination Act to advertise for a female
registrar; therefore. it is very likely that one of
the three registrars appointed will be male. Both the
RCOG and the medical staff and administrators at UCH
have shown themselves to be very much against any progress in the care of women by women and no doubt by the
time this volume is published the campaign against
these proposals will be well under way.
     In May 1984 AIMS received the following letter:

     I am expecting my second baby in October/November
     this year, but I am having a problem with any
     "rights" I thought I had. I am having shared care
     with my GP and the local hospital. The trouble
     is, I thought I had the right to be examined/att-
     ended by a female doctor, which is very important
     to me. I have been told that if there is no fem-
     ale available at the time, I would have to have
     a man.
          I have discussed this with the hospital, my

> health visitor, and the Rape Crisis Centre. I
> contacted the Rape Crisis Centre because I was
> sexually assaulted by a male doctor during a vis-
> it to the Casualty Department of my local hospit-
> al, when no nurse was present, although I didn't
> report it because I was too upset.
>
> I thought of writing to the hospital but my
> health visitor tells me that this is a bad idea
> as they could use it against me and give me a
> rough time.
>
> My immediate worry is that I next go to the
> hospital for a 32 week check, which includes a
> blood test. I have enquired in advance, and there
> will be no female doctor there on that day. I
> tried to make another appointment, but they said
> that I had to go then because of the blood test,
> which must be done at 32 weeks. I have to have
> the examination that goes with it and they said
> "Don't worry - there won't be an internal." Why
> are you always told to take your knickers off,
> in that case?
>
> I'm sorry to go on, but I'm upset. Please
> help me.

In March 1984 Frank Dobson MP raised the question of
the EGA's role of providing a service by women for
women and in April 1984 he received a reply from the
Prime Minister, Mrs. Margaret Thatcher, which stated
the reasons for having a male registrar appointed and
ended her letter with the following comment:

> it does seem unfortunate that the re-opening of
> the rebuilt EGA, to which the Government has dem-
> onstrated its commitment by substantial capital
> investment, should be greeted with such dissent
> over a minor problem.

These "minor" problems are being faced every day by
women in this country. One wonders why it is that the
woman who is expecting her baby in October/November is
unable to consider her dilemma to be a minor problem.
For the consumer groups her dilemma also poses a problem. The obstetric department at the EGA was closed
many years ago, and the South London Hospital has been
threatened with closure this summer. If these plans
go ahead by the autumn of this year it will not be
possible for any pregnant woman to be confident that
she will receive care only from women. Where are they
to go? According to Mrs. Thatcher we have nothing to
worry about because being attended by a man is only a
"minor" problem. During the campaign to save the EGA

letters were received from women aged 11 to 96. Every
one of them objected to being attended by a man and
many of them expressed their anxieties about having to
share wards with male patients. Mrs. Thatcher is wrong,
it is <u>not</u> a "minor" problem, but it does appear that
the consumers are going to have to voice their objections loud and strong before politicians, and the medical profession, consider the problem anything more
than one of "minor" proportions.

ASSAULT IN CHILDBIRTH

The Association for Improvements in the Maternity
Services was founded in 1960 and one of its first cam-
paigns was to fight for fathers to be present in the
labour wards. AIMS did not launch this campaign out
of a far-sighted desire to improve family relationships or to encourage the fathers' involvement in the
birth process, they did it because they were worried
by the numbers of women who were complaining of being
assaulted in labour and they felt that if the fathers
were there these assaults would be less likely to occur.
When one talks about assault the usual assumption is
that someone has been punched on the nose or suffered
a similar kind of violence. In a medical context, an
assault occurs when treatment is administered against
the expressed wishes of the individual. In other
words, if Mrs. Smith states that she does not want an
injection and the midwife or doctor, administers the
injection, they are committing an assault, or to be
strictly accurate: a battery. John Finch in his article "Litigation: A Simple Step Forward" stated that
"A 'routine' (unnecessary or objected to) episiotomy
is a serious assault (and battery) against a patient.
It is no different <u>in law</u> from a knife wound delivered
in a fight. Likewise the giving of drugs, say pethidine, against a person's will is an assault. Just like
a security guard being chloroformed in a bank raid."(26)
     It is not just the mother who requires protect-
ion from medical procedures, her baby is also subjected to "routine" procedures, many of which are carried
out without the consent or knowledge of the parents.
The Maternity Services Advisory Committee in its report on intra-partum care (27) states "It is also common practice to give all new born babies Vitamin K to
prevent haemorrhage which is an uncommon but serious
complication. The reasons for this should have been
explained to the mother during the antenatal period."
You will note that the committee states that the reasons should have been "explained" to the mother, not that

the parent's permission should have been obtained.   This
committee then had accepted that it is not necessary for
permission to be obtained for a routine procedure that had
yet to be shown to be of benefit to low-risk babies!   The
next paragraph of the report goes on to say "In the rare
event of a mother objecting to either of these measures,
this should be recorded in the notes."   Not a single comment to the effect that should the mother object the procedure should not be carried out - merely recorded!
Mothers don't object to these procedures because very
few of them even know that they are being carried out,
and when they do find out it is questionable that the
law would support them in any legal action they may
wish to take.   In 1974 parents took the Exeter and
Mid-Devon Hospital Management Committee to court. (28)
Their baby had been admitted to a Special Care Baby Unit
and the nurse had forgotten to take a hot-water bottle out
of the baby's cot; as a result the baby was badly burned.
The parents sued.   The Judge, Mr Justice Cantley, did not
support their case.   He found that while the baby was
in hospital she remained "in the custody of" her parents.   Where children are cared for by the hospital
and doctors they are being so "by the authority and
on behalf of the parents who remain in a position to
exercise powers of control (my emphasis) should they
wish to do so."   These parents had no idea that a hot-
water bottle had been put in their baby's cot, and it
is interesting that the law had been used against
them in this instance.   One wonders what the legal
ruling would be for parents who sued a hospital for
having given their child a routine injection of Vitamin K without their knowledge or consent.

THE MATERNITY DEFENCE FUND

In response to growing evidence of the extent of malpractice and assault in 1982 seven women, members of
the most prominent childbirth groups, and one midwife,
gathered together in a South London terraced house to
discuss the problems of assault in childbirth.   Concerned about the issue for many years, they had recognised that the campaign to ensure a father's entry into labour wards, in order to protect their partners,
had failed, because although the fathers are
now generally welcomed into the labour wards, they
were ineffective in preventing assaults to their partners.   Mothers were still being assaulted, and complaints and appeals through the complaints procedures
have had little influence on current medical and midwifery practice.   Indeed it is clear that at every

level; Health Authorities; Family Practitioner Committees; Central Midwives Board; the General Medical
Council; the Royal Colleges; the Minister of Health;
and the Ombudsman cherish as their primary consideration the protection of the profession whilst justifiable complaints of individual patients take second
place.

It is clear that the only time the medical profession takes any notice of patients' complaints is when
the patient threatens, or takes legal action. Every
other channel of complaint had been tried, and none has
yet provided any evidence that doctors, or midwives,
were willing to confront these issues.

At the 1982 Consumer Groups' meeting, it was decided that a fund would be launched in order to advise
parents, and prospective parents of their rights during pregnancy, childbirth and the post-natal period;
and particularly to take legal action in the cases of
assault. It was hoped that not only would legal action for assault actually define parents' rights in
law, but it would also give midwives the confidence
to stand up for the wishes of the woman. It had become
accepted that women had to accept "routine" treatment,
and those midwives who were responsive to individual
women's wishes often had to face the wrath of the con-
sultants (and sometimes their colleagues) because they
had not carried out the "routine" procedure. Also, it
was hoped that women who were fearful of entering
hospital to have their babies would have their fears
allayed because they would know that their views would
be respected.

The decision to launch the fund was not taken
lightly; the members of the childbirth organisations
hesitated for some time before deciding that taking
legal action was the only effective channel left open
to them.

When it was announced that a fund was being raised to sue the profession, the doctors were quick to
point out that such an action could only lead to more
litigation, defensive medicine, and a situation similar to that happening in America where the patient
rushes to the lawyers at the first opportunity. They
omit to mention that a possible cause of large numbers
of medical litigation cases in America could possibly
be high levels of medical malpractice.

The current medical attitude to patient litigation, in this country, is illogical and not supported by
the facts. The numbers of patients taking legal action is very small indeed. It is recognised, within the
consumer groups, that although there are many individuals who have grounds for legal action, very few are

willing to do so, indeed there is considerable reluctance amongst parents even to complain about maternity
care, let alone sue, often on the grounds that if
they said anything it would be "taken out on them" if
they became pregnant again. Unfortunately, there is
evidence available to show that their fears are justified.

Since the launching of the Maternity Defence Fund
over £4,000 has been raised. There are two cases of
assault currently going through the legal process, and
a number of negligence cases are being advised and
supported. Contrary to the widely held view, of the
medical profession, that patients want to rush into
litigation, the largest single block of complaints are
those who have come to the Maternity Defence Fund for
advice and assistance and then decide not to go ahead
with litigation. The anxieties about appearances in
court, potential costs and also, most important of
all, the clear indications that very little medical
litigation succeeds prevents many from taking such
action. (Many of those who are anxious about the implications of legal action are, however, taking their
cases through the complaints procedures and are also
approaching the professional bodies with formal complaints about their members).

In civil actions the majority of cases are found
in favour of the litigant. In medical cases exactly
the opposite applies. The legal profession deals very
leniently indeed with the medical profession. John
Finch in his article "Law Can Be a Doctor's Friend"
states:

> medical practitioners are undoubtedly the most
> protected by the application of legal rules and
> principles of liability. During the past three
> decades, the Court of Appeal has time and again
> reiterated principles which shield doctors from
> the worst effects of the normal rules of liabil-
> ity in negligence. (29)

THE FUTURE

At one time the practice of medicine was an elite and
closed world, where the profession considered its business in the confident knowledge that the information
would be restricted to its own ranks and medical myst-
ique would be preserved. No longer is that so, already
the consumers are reading and analysing medical papers; attending medical conferences; sharing information and resources; and helping those who have just-

ifiable complaints.

Over the last ten years there has been an enormous change in attitudes and practice within the medical and midwifery professions. Unfortunately these changes do not occur overnight, but as a result of consistent and continuous consumer pressure. There was a time when the views of Leboyer were derided and considered outrageous. Today, his views are accepted and practised by many British hospitals. No longer are they considered the views of a crank and therefore unacceptable.

On the plus side maternity care is changing, and the good hospitals are responding to consumer pressure. No longer are women required to deliver babies flat on their backs; no longer do women have to suffer the indignities of routine shaves and enemas; no longer are babies fed by the clock; no longer are husbands left to pace the corridors alone, and there are more changes yet to come.

Parents are now questioning routine medical procedures, and are finding and sharing the research papers to support their views. They are no longer prepared to accept routine medical treatment and are asking questions about routine use of syntometrine during the third stage of labour, routine episiotomy, induction and acceleration of labour; the safety of ultrasound and the routine injecting of perfectly healthy babies with Vitamin K. The value of all these treatments is being questioned and the professions are being required to justify their continued use. Slowly, the public are beginning to realise that the rush to hospitalise all women for the birth of their babies has been achieved at a cost.

In April 1982 over 5,000 parents demonstrated outside the Royal Free Hospital, Hampstead about their practice of insisting that women give birth flat on their backs. For the first time in British history parents took to the banners and the streets to demonstrate that they were not prepared to accept the hegemonic dictates of the medical and midwifery professions. Parents have begun to reclaim control over childbirth, and the professionals are beginning to realise that they fight against that lobby at their peril.

The birth of a baby is far too important an event to be left to the hegemony of medical practitioners. For the last thirty years technological interventions have been used, not to support and encourage normal childbirth, but to replace it; and countless thousands of women have been persuaded into believing that the routine technological births would have been far worse

The Politics of Maternity: Childbirth Freedom v
Obstetric Control

without all the interventiions which often became a
necessity because nature was forced to deliver in time
to the obstetric tune. One day there will be a proper
evaluation of the costs, both physical and emotional,
that have been paid by the ordinary, average British
mother and baby. No-one doubts that high technology
has saved the lives of some very high-risk mothers and
babies. Unfortunately the costs have had to be paid
by the ordinary and 'normal' low-risk mothers and babies, whose labours have been required to fit into the
perceived medical model, whilst the casualties of the
system have often found that they have been left to
fend for themselves. Those mothers who have decided
to complain have often been asked "What are you complaining about? You have a beautiful, fit and healthy
baby, haven't you?" In other words the goal of a fit
and healthy baby has been achieved and let's forget
about the damage the mothers may have suffered. Those,
therefore, who have had justifiable complaints about
their care have found that on the whole they have had
to battle through the complaints procedures alone and
unaided. The medical profession however, has been
confident in the knowledge that their decisions and
deliberations will not receive the publicity they
deserve. No longer is that so, the consumer organisations now have a system of help and assistance for
those who are taking formal complaints and they are
also helping and advising those who wish to take legal
action. Certainly, the first few cases of legal action will most probably fail, but the courts will soon
realise that they cannot continue to accord the medical profession a superordinate status. They will also
realise that not only must justice be done, but it
must be seen to be done.

REFERENCES

(1)   Oakley, A., 'Wisewoman and Medical Man: Chang-
        es in the Management of Childbirth' in The
        Rights and Wrongs of Women, Mitchell, J. and
        Oakley, A. (eds.) Penguin 1976
(2)   Donnison, J. Midwives and Medical Men, Heine-
        mann 1977
(3)   Ibid.
(4)   Ibid.
(5)   Versluysen, M.C., 'Midwives, Medical Men and
        "Poor Women Labouring of Child: Lying-In
        Hospital in 18th Century London"' in Women
        Health and Reproduction, Roberts, H. (ed.)
        Routledge & Kegan Paul 1981
(6)   Oakley, A., 'Wisewoman and Medical Man:

Changes in the Management of Childbirth' in
The Rights and Wrongs of Women, Mitchell, J.
and Oakley, A. (ed.) Penguin 1976

(7)   Standing Maternity and Midwifery Advisory
Committee (1970) Report on Domiciliary Midwifery and Maternity Bed Needs (The Peel Report) HMSO London

(8)   Tew, M., 'The Case Against Hospital Deliveries; The Statistical Evidence' in The Place
of Birth (ed.) Kitzinger, S. and Davis, A.
(eds.) Oxford University Press

(9)   Social Services Committee 'Perinatal and Neo-
natal Mortality'. Second Report from the
Social Services Committee (The Short Report)
House of Commons Paper 1979-80: 663/1 HMSO
London 1980

(10)   McIlwaine et al. Letter to the British Medical Journal vol 281 p. 1067 18.10.80

(11)   AIMS letter to the Secretary of State (Rt
Hon Patrick Jenkins) dated 22 Sept 1980

(12)   Oakley, A., 'Wisewoman and Medical Man:
Changes in the Management of Childbirth' in
The Rights and Wrongs of Women, Mitchell, J.
and Oakley, A. (eds.) Penguin 1976

(13)   Macfarlane, A. and Mugford, M., Birth Counts.
Statistics of Pregnancy and Childbirth, HMSO
London 1984

(14)   House, M., 'Episiotomy - Indications, Tech-
nique and Results', Midwives Health Visitor
and Community Nurse, Jan 1981 vol 17. no 1

(15)   Beech, B.A., 'Denial of Parents' Rights' in
Maternity Care, AIMS 1983

(16)   Ibid.

(17)   Maternity Services Advisory Committee Maternity Care in Action-Part II Intra-Partum
Care, HMSO London 1984

(18)   Angela Phillips Birthplace: 'A Mother's
Fight to Choose', Sunday Times 15 Nov 1981

(19)   Correspondence from the GMC to AIMS dated
30 Dec 1983

(20)   Prof. Peter Huntingford's letter to the
Minister of Health, the President of the
Royal College of Obstetricians and Gynaecol-
ogists and others dated 11 Sept 1980

(21)   Correspondence from the Royal College of Midwives to AIMS dated 27 May 1982

(22)   Beech, B.A. and Claxton R. (1983) The Health
Rights Handbook for Maternity Care, Community
Rights Project

(23)   Ibid.

(24)   Male Midwives: A Report of Two Studies

The Politics of Maternity: Childcare Freedom v
Obstetric Control

DHSS 1982
(25)   Health Services Management - 'Male Midwives'
         Health Circular, HC(83)15
(26)   Finch, J., 'Litigation: A Simple Step For-
         ward', in Nursing Mirror, 8 Sept 1982
(27)   Roger v Exeter and Mid-Devon Hospital Manage-
         ment Committee (1974)
(28)   Maternity Services Advisory Committee. Mat-
         ernity Care in Action - Part II Intra-Partum
         Care, HMSO London 1984
(29)   Finch, J., 'Law Can Be a Doctor's Friend',
         General Practitioner, 23 Mar 1981
         see also:
         Eekelaar, J.M. and Dingwall R.W.J. (1984)
         'Some Legal Issues in Obstetric Practice',
         Journal of Social Welfare Law,(forthcoming)

Chapter Four

UNEQUAL OPPORTUNITIES: WOMEN, EMPLOYMENT AND THE LAW

Peggy Kahn

In general, employment law is apparently about
relations, between employers and workers without regard
to gender. Employment law regulates the public realm
of work, which it appears to treat as separate from
the private sphere. Yet much employment law and many
collective agreements are predicated upon the male
worker, a worker with few domestic responsibilities in
full-time employment at a unionised workplace. There
is little effective legal regulation of the sort of
work women manage to undertake, work that is often
part-time and low paid and reflects women's family
roles. Where women are excluded from employment, the
law does little to encourage integration of the workforce.
        Changes in employment law and other policies
since the return of a Conservative Government in 1979
have further weakened already inadequate regulation of
women's work. While Government economic policy has
encouraged the growth of categories of disadvantaged
workers such as the low paid, the Government has repealed or weakened regulatory measures, arguing that
employment protection creates "labour market rigidities" and prices even the lowest paid out of jobs.
What law remains is more difficult for both individual
women and trade unions to use, as unemployment makes
workers fearful of claiming their legal rights. In a
period of economic crisis, trade unions, still mainly
orientated towards the interests of male members, are
both generally weakened and not likely to see women's
issues as a high priority.
        Even if employment law were stronger with respect
to women's work, it would by itself be inadequate to
involve women equally in paid employment. Other policies and practices, most notably the division of labour in the family and public provision for those in
need of care, structure women's entry to and exit from

79

employment. Formal equality in employment law is bound to be an inadequate remedy for work inequalities which are intertwined with other structures of interests and attitudes. In fact the weakness of the law in regulating women's work and in altering gender divisions in employment reflects and reinforces a society in which men continue to dominate public life while women bear the majority of domestic responsibility, though what legislation exists has to a very limited extent improved women's legal rights and actual employment position.

WOMEN'S EMPLOYMENT

Despite family commitments, women work in large numbers. In 1981, 47.2% of all women, 49.5% of married women and 43.6% of non-married women, worked. In 1981 the female workforce was estimated at 10.4 million, or 39.6% of the labour force. Since 1979, the number of employees in employment has officially fallen by about 2 million, and the number of women in employment has fallen from a pre-1979 level of 5.5 million to 5.1 million in September 1982. There has also been a substantial increase in unemployment among women, and men. Between 1976 and 1982 the number of women registered unemployed increased by 600,000 and men by 1.2 million.(1) But the regular statistics of registered unemployment do not fully describe unemployment, especially among women; and this shortcoming was accentuated in November 1982 when the basis of the statistics changed to a count of people claiming benefit at Unemployment Benefit Offices. The immediate effect of this change was, according to the Equal Opportunities Commission (EOC), to remove about 130,000 or 14% of women from the statistics because those women, though out of work, are not entitled to benefit.(2)
        The terms and conditions of women's work are largely structured by the division of responsibility in the family. Women work part-time in order to combine care of children with paid employment, and they work when their domestic life-cycle of childbearing and childrearing allows them to do so. The age of the youngest dependent child in the household tends to influence both the decision to work and the number of hours worked. Around 30% of women with a dependent child up to four years are in employment, of whom 75% work part-time. 70% of all women with a youngest dependent aged ten or over are in employment, and 59% of these women work part-time. Of women without dependent children, 61% work and only 26% of those are part-

time. (3)   The increase in women's employment in the
1970s was, in fact, largely due to the increase in
female part-time employment, from 2.8 million in 1971
to 3.7 million in 1979. (4)
    Women are concentrated in industries and occupat-
ions which are largely female and reflect women's
traditional role in the family.   The ten industries
containing the largest number of female employees are
all in the service sector.   These industries account
for nearly 60% of all female employees but nearer a
quarter of male employment.   The concentration of
part-time female employees is even more marked, with
nearly two thirds of employees in ten industries. (5)
In almost all manufacturing, women as a percentage of
the workforce have declined, while in services the
trend is the opposite. (6)
    Women's earnings remain well below those of men,
reflecting assumptions about women as "secondary"
wage earners.   Women are concentrated in low-paid occ-
upations where trade unionism is weak and remuneration often determined by wages councils.   Women experience vertical as well as horizontal job segregation:
they receive little training and so occupy less skilled jobs, and they have few promotion opportunities.
The 1983 New Earnings Survey (NES) figures show wom-
en's full-time hourly earnings at 72% of men's.   But
the effect of overtime is to widen further the gap
between male and female earnings since men work substantially more overtime than women.   Women's full-
time gross earnings, including overtime, average 65%
of men's.   The 1983 NES, which excludes significant
numbers of low-paid part-time women, shows part-time
women's gross hourly earnings at 57% of male hourly
earnings excluding overtime.   Nationally, one half of
all full-time women were low paid in 1982 according
to accepted definitions. (8)

WOMEN, PART-TIME WORK AND THE LAW

Officially there are about 4.3 million part-time workers in Great Britain, about 20% of the total workforce.
Of these 83% are women.   In recent decades, while
full-time work has declined, part-time work has steadily increased.   Between 1961 and 1981 the number of
part-time workers doubled from 2 to 4 million. (9)
High levels of part-time work are due to large numbers
of women working, while still bearing primary responsibility for childcare, and to a shift from primary
and manufacturing sectors towards services.   Part-time
workers are officially those who work less than 30

hours a week, but can also be understood as any workers who work less than the number of hours worked by
a majority in the workplace.

Despite large numbers of part-time workers, regulation of their employment is poor: part-time workers
receive neither the pay nor terms and conditions of
full-timers on a pro rata basis by law. In addition,
unless part-timers work more than 16 hours, they enjoy
few legal employment rights. This "firmly rooted
double standard of occupational morality" which discriminates against part-timers is partly due to the
large number of women part-timers who are assumed to
be secondary wage earners whose real place is in the
home, not the labour market.

The rights of part-time workers are established
by both statute and negotiated agreements. However,
because of the need to establish "continuity" of employment for statutory rights and the fact that employment usually only starts to be "continuous" when a
worker has been working 16 hours a week without a
break in employment, many part-timers who work under
16 hours a week are excluded from statutory rights.
However, there have been some useful decisions on
"continuity" of employment. In 1979 the Employment
Appeal Tribunal decided that women employed alternate
weeks at Lloyds Bank by arrangement with the employer
were in continuous employment and therefore entitled
to maternity leave as long as they had the proper
qualifying period. (10) A further important case,
Ford v Warwickshire County Council, was heard in the
Lords in October 1983. The Lords ruled that workers,
such as part-time college lecturers on fixed term contracts which generally expire at the beginning of the
summer holidays and are then renewed when the next
academic year begins, should be regarded as continuously employed if the interval between two fixed-term
contracts could be characterised as short relative to
the combined duration of the two fixed term contracts.
(11)

Part-time workers who can establish continuity
of employment at 16 or more hours, who comprise approximately 53% of part-time workers, generally receive
statutory employment protection, such as the right
to a statement of employment terms, redundancy pay,
unfair dismissal, maternity pay and time off for trade
union activities, after the appropriate qualifying
period. Part-timers working between 8 and 16 hours
receive many rights only after 5 years of continuous
employment. However, over 800,000 workers who work
under 8 hours enjoy no employment rights. Part-timers
are also less likely to be covered by occupational pen-

sions and sick pay schemes or entitled to unsocial
hours or overtime payments. One third of part-time
workers are excluded from national insurance benefits
because their earnings fall below the contribution
limit. (12)

While part-timers are covered by equal opportunities legislation, case law has not always been particularly favourable to them. The decision in Meeks
v National Union of Agricultural and Allied Workers
that lower pay per hour for part-time workers was not
covered under the indirect discrimination provision
of the Sex Discrimination Act because it pertained to
a contractual matter or under the Equal Pay Act because the Act did not cover indirect discrimination
(13) has been superseded by rulings that the Acts are
to be treated as one integrated code. Yet the findings of the European Court of Justice in Jenkins v
Kingsgate were that a difference in pay between full-time
and part-time workers does not amount to discrimination
unless it is in reality merely a way of securing cheap
female labour. An example of a factor justifying the
difference, the Court held, was where an employer was
endeavouring economic grounds to encourage full-time
work. (14) In other words, case law has opened the
way for employers to use economic arguments to justify
wage discrimination against predominantly female part-
time workers.

As redundancies have continued to increase, the
issue of part-timers and selection for redundancy has
become more prominent. Where there have been redundancies in concerns which employ both full-time and
part-time labour both employers and trade unions have
often assumed or formally agreed that part-timers
should go first. The justification is that they are
just "temporary workers", that they are "secondary
wage earners" and that "the majority of the workforce
want it that way".

Two important legal cases have established that
"part-timers first" may constitute indirect sex discrimination. In Powell and Clarke v Eley (IMI) Kynoch
the Employment Appeal Tribunal found that an agreement
between the local Transport and General Workers Union
and the employers that redundancies were on a last-in
first-out basis except that part-timers were selected
first, was indirectly discriminatory. The proportion
of women who could comply with the condition of full-
time work was smaller than the proportion of men. (15)
Similarly an Industrial Tribunal found in the case of
Dick v University of Dundee that the decision to review all part-time and temporary employees with a view
to making selections for dismissal from among them

83

affected a greater proportion of women and was therefore discriminatory. (16)

The case of Powell and Clarke illustrates that
collective agreements have an important bearing upon
the terms and conditions of part-timers. Yet, while
there is little systematic information on collective
agreements as they pertain to part-time work, it is
likely that many part-timers are not covered by agreements and that where they are it is likely that they
are not well protected because they are a relatively
weak and under-represented section of trade union members. Part-time women may have particular difficulty
attending meetings and getting released for trade union training and activities, and union membership fees
are often a disproportionately large slice of a part-
time wage. The TUC and certain individual unions
have, however, begun to pay more attention to part-
timers' rights and opportunities.

One of the potentially more significant measures
to strengthen the position of part-time workers is the
European Commission's draft Directive on voluntary
part-time work, which seeks to improve the status and
practice of part-time work by guaranteeing part-time
workers the same rights as full-time workers "with due
regard to the special nature of part-time employment".
It seeks to extend to part-time workers on a proport-
ional basis rates of remuneration and other financial
benefits enjoyed by full-time workers. The draft
Directive would establish a general principle of non-
discrimination, which would extend to part-time workers the same provisions in respect of working conditions, social facilities, access to training and promotion and rules governing dismissal as full-time employees. The Directive has a twofold purpose: to encourage part-time work as a way of tempering the unemployment problem and to establish equality of conditions and increased employment protection for part-
timers. British employers and the Government have
opposed the Directive on grounds that it will increase
labour costs and thus decrease growth, competitiveness
and innovation and that it is an encroachment on man-
agerial prerogative to agree terms and conditions with
prospective employees at a time when cost pressures
on companies are great. Small businesses see the Directive as yet another legal intervention which has
high administrative costs and detracts from the "family atmosphere" of the firm.(17) Trade unions on the
other hand generally support the Directive, though
some trade union leaders regard part-time working arrangements as solving the economic crisis at the ex-
pense of the workers.

WOMEN, LOW PAY AND THE LAW

Women are low paid not only in the sense that their
average earnings are less than those of men. They are
also low paid in the sense that their earnings conform
to general definitions of low pay: those earnings at
or below two thirds the median earnings of full-time
adult male workers, or £92.70 a week in 1982/83, according to the Low Pay Unit, or those earning less than
£104.31 per week to support a two child family, according to the DHSS. (18) Nationally one half of all
full-time women are low paid. (19) Since 1979 there
has been a deterioration in the earnings of the low
paid, and low paid women's earnings have declined from
69 to 67% of average earnings. (20) Low pay is concentrated in the personal service sector, in small-
scale manufacturing and certain public sector jobs,
where women work in large numbers.
    Much of the personal service sector is comprised
of industries regulated by wages councils, and three
quarters of the wage council workforce is women.
Those industries are highly competitive and labour
intensive, with a high proportion of small firms. In
such a fragmented industrial structure there is little
effective collective bargaining. Low wages, allied
with other poor conditions, mean high labour turnover,
which makes unionisation even more difficult. The
wages council system has been intended to substitute
for collective bargaining at least in setting a minimum wage. But wages councils have not remedied the
problem of low pay for women or others within their
jurisdiction.
    The statutory mimimum remunerations set by the
wages councils are themselves extremely low. For
example, in 1982 the average adult minimum rate was
£55-£60 per week. (21) The average earnings of women
in those industries are closer to the minimum than
those of men, who have more access to other payments,
such as overtime. In addition the enforcement machin-
ery is inadequate. The legalistic language in which
directives are couched and the low visibility of wage-
setting make enforcement of minima by employees or
trade unions less likely, and there are not enough
Inspectors to police the system effectively. A general statutory minimum wage, on the other hand, would
be clear and well known and might have considerable
redistributive potential.
    The Government is clearly hostile to wage coun-
cils, and statutory minimum wages in general, and is
seeking to abolish some of the remaining wages councils. It has already weakened the insufficient Wages

Inspectorate by reducing the number of "outdoor" inspectors from 177 in May 1979 to 119 in March 1983.
(22) In some areas "indoor" support staff have also
been reduced. Yet in a period of high unemployment
and economic pressure on companies, there is every
reason to expect the incidence of underpayment to
increase. The Low Pay Unit reports that the incidence
of recorded underpayment increased from 31.5% in 1979
to 41.3% in 1981 and that 40% of firms were underpay-
ing in 1982. (23) The Government has also exerted
pressure on particular councils to keep minima low.
For example, as Secretary of State for Employment,
Norman Tebbit objected to the Retail Trades (Non-Food)
Wages Council proposal for an 8% increase, which would
have entitled adult shop assistants to £67.50 per
week, on grounds that it was "inflationary" and would
"have damaging effects on employment in the retail
industry." The council reduced the increase. (24)
     In addition to the wages council orders both the
Fair Wages Resolution and Schedule 11 of the Employment Protection Act 1975 have been relevant to the
problem of low pay among workers in general and women
in particular. The Fair Wages Resolution provided
that a government contractor or subcontractor must
observe terms and conditions of employment not less
favourable than those established for the particular
trade or industry in the district concerned or than
the general level of terms and conditions. Until 1974
Fair Wage Resolution comparisons could only be made
with national wage agreements, and the growth of plant
and company-level bargaining reduced its usefulness;
but it remained a useful moral pressure. When a decision in 1974 allowed an extension of fair wage comparisons to plant and company level agreements, use of
the FWR temporarily accelerated. The present Government policy of contracting-out services would have
again made it important. Yet the Government has res-
cinded the FWR, arguing that it was an unnecessary interference in free collective bargaining, inflationary, and unhelpful to the low paid. (25) Similarly,
Schedule 11, which applied broadly similar principles
to all industry, was repealed by the Employment Act
1980. Yet the Government's own statements suggest
that the FWR was of assistance to those earning £75-
£85 or about half of current average male earnings,
and an analysis of Schedule 11 awards between 1977
and 1979 by Warwick University's Industrial Relations
Research Unit showed that 93% of successful claims
by manual workers were made on behalf of those with
earnings below average, as was the case with 87% of
non-manual claims. (26)

EQUAL OPPORTUNITIES LEGISLATION AND EMPLOYMENT

The two equal opportunities Acts, the Equal Pay Act
and the Sex Discrimination Act, might have been expected to make contributions to women's low pay and
segregation into certain, often part-time, jobs. Yet
neither the EPA, which covers contractual matters relating to employment, nor the SDA, which covers such
non-contractual matters as recruitment, promotion, and
redundancy, has had a significant impact. The collective provisions of the legislation have proved very
weak and the Acts have become an uncertain recourse
for the declining number of individuals disposed to
take Tribunal cases.
     Both the EPA and SDA do include collective and
general provisions. The Equal Pay Act required a specifically female rate in either a collective agreement negotiated with a union or in an employer's pay
structure to be raised to at least the lowest male
rate. If there were separate female rates for certain
categories of work, then the women's rate had to be
raised to the men's; but if there were separate female
rates for certain categories of work and no male rates, the women's rate had only to be raised to the lowest male rate. If the employer failed to make these
changes, the union could refer the case to the Central
Arbitration Committee. In the five years between
the passage of the EPA in 1970 and its implementation in 1975 many employers made changes which min-
imised the impact of the Act, such as simply altering
the names of grades and retaining de facto women's
rates and the tightening of women's piece-rates. Many
employers commissioned general job evaluations in order to adjust discriminatory wage rates in compliance
with the Act, and the London School of Economics Equal Pay and Opportunity Project found that the implementation of equal pay through equal value measures
resulted in "considerable and sometimes dramatic"
narrowing of differentials between the basic rates of
main groups of women and men. Evasion of the Act
seemed to occur where there was a high level of job
segregation, a high degree of management confident-
iality and an absence of women's involvement in bargaining on pay. In addition, many women outside of
collective agreements or formal pay structures were
not affected by the collective provisions of the Equal
Pay Act. (27)
     One section of the Equal Pay Act allowed for con-
tinuing referral to the Central Arbitration Committee
(CAC), by a party to a collective agreement or by the
Secretary of State, of any collective agreement which

contained a provision applying specifically to men or
women only. The CAC was empowered to advise how the
discrimination should be removed. In fact, between
1975 and 1980, 51 cases were dealt with by the CAC.
The practice of the CAC was not only to remove "women
only" grades, but also to look beyond the superficial
wording of collective agreements to the distribution
of male and female workers and pay differentials. It
often used job evaluation to assess whether discrimination was occurring, applying an "equal value" test
to grading and pay structures. However this approach
was stopped in 1979 when Hymac Limited took the CAC to the
High Court. The Court upheld the employer's argument
that the CAC had no power to rewrite pay structures to
give women equal pay for work of equal value. If male
and female rates had notionally disappeared, the CAC
could do nothing about continuing pay discrimination.
The Court said that the only exception was where women-only rates were untouched except in name. Trade
union referrals to the CAC rapidly fell to nil after
this judgment. (28)

The Sex Discrimination Act created an Equal Opportunities Commission both to enforce the law and
engage in wide public education. Experience with race
discrimination legislation had exposed the weakness
of relying upon complaints of allegedly unlawful acts
from individuals: such a model assumed that those most
in need of legal protection were aware of their rights
and sufficiently confident to avail themselves of
legal remedies. The EOC was therefore given responsibility for the strategic role of seeking out patterns of discrimination and bringing the law to bear
upon them. In order to identify patterns of discrimination the EOC throughout its history has commissioned research projects, and it has granted financial
assistance in individual tribunal or Court cases which
seem to advance particularly equal opportunities or
expose the weakness of the law. The EOC was also to
have formidable powers of "formal investigation" to
indentify discriminatory practices and order their
removal. Yet these powers have proved legally cum-
bersome and ineffective. The EOC has recently begun
to use power under another section of the Act which
allows the Commission itself to take tribunal cases,
yet whether such cases will make a major impact is
unclear. The general consensus is that the EOC, constituted as a "quango" with representatives from trade
unions, business and other interests recognised by
the Government, its membership balanced between major
political parties, lacking ties with the women's movement, orientated towards encouraging "voluntary"

efforts by employers and unions, and under-resourced,
is not an effective enforcement mechanism. Its efforts have been ad hoc and weak and it has lacked political will. (29)
    Voluntary programmes of positive action in train-
ing and general desegregation of work, which the EOC
was to oversee, have also made little difference to
the overall pattern of women's work. Numerous trade
unions have reserved seats on official bodies for wom-
en, or established equal opportunities committees,
though the impact of such organisational changes has
remained limited. Most use of Acts, therefore, has
been by aggrieved individuals through the Tribunal system. There is no provision in the legislation for
class action, that is, for an individual to seek redress on behalf of an affected class or group of people.
There has, in fact, been a steady decrease in individual Equal Pay and Sex Discrimination cases since the
earliest years. In 1976, 1,742 Equal Pay cases went
to Industrial Tribunals, and 213 complaints were upheld. 243 Sex Discrimination cases were lodged and
24 upheld. In 1982, 38 Equal Pay cases were heard,
and 2 upheld. 156 Sex Discrimination cases were lodged and 24 upheld. (30) Much of the decline in use
of the law has to do with the limits of the statutes
and the Tribunal procedure. In Equal Pay cases in
particular it is easy to reach a compromise outside
of the Tribunal by agreeing on a payment of some sort.
Studies have pointed out that the Advisory, Conciliat-
ion and Arbitration Service (ACAS), to which all cases
are referred, are eager to conciliate rather than
press the principle of equal opportunities before Tribunals. (31) But it is also clear that the high and
rising level of unemployment acts as a deterrent for
individuals with complaints. The EOC's 1982 Annual
Report noted that "significantly more than in any
previous year complainants are voicing their unwillingness to exercise their rights at law for fear of
losing their jobs or, simply, of causing trouble".
(32) It is also likely that for many trade unions
redundancy has dominated other issues, including that
of sex discrimination.
    Nevertheless Tribunal judgments and case law
have provided remedies for individuals and sometimes
for groups of workers. In addition they provide a
set of principles upon which women workers and trade
unions can draw in collective bargaining and grievance
procedures. Finally, insofar as judgments are widely
disseminated, they may generally affect views of women
and work. However, the less use is made of the law,
the less individual women are aware of its potential

for rectifying discrimination and the less society as
a whole is re-educated through the legal process.
   The individual provisions of the Equal Pay Act
require employers to give equal treatment in pay and
conditions to men and women employed on like work or
work which has been given equal value under a job evaluation scheme. A woman is regarded as doing like
work if her work is of the same or broadly similar
nature to a man's work and if the differences between
the things she does and the things he does are not of
practical importance in relation to terms and conditions of employment. A defence against equal pay is
that there is a "material difference" other than sex
between the personal equations of the man and woman.
   Therefore the initial stages of the applicant's
argument must be to establish that a woman and man
working for the same employer are doing like work. The
necessity for a male comparator limits the usefulness
of the EPA due to the fact that women may work in
small workplaces, which are often all or predominantly
female, or predominantly female work. In the early
months of the Act's existence, a great many Tribunals
seized upon trivial differences to justify lower pay
for women. But decisions in the Employment Appeal
Tribunal and Court of Appeal, which unlike Industrial
Tribunal decisions set precedents in law, stated that
trivial differences should be disregarded and that
arguments about work suitable to women were inappropriate. So, for example, arguments by employers that
women cleaning offices worked in comfortable environ-
ments similar to their own homes and therefore should
be paid less than men cleaning warehouses were not
accepted. Further cases made the point that relevant
differences and similarities were in work actually
performed, not simply contractual obligations; that
the regularity and frequency of different tasks had to
be considered and that the time at which work was performed was irrelevant to the basic rate.
   While in general "material difference" has been
taken to apply to the personal equation or qualifications of the man and woman, "market forces" have increasingly appeared as a successful defence. Whether
market factors were material differences for purposes
of equal pay was judged by the Court of Appeal in
Fletcher v Clay Cross. The Court held that an employer
cannot avoid equal pay because the male comparison
could not be recruited for less. But in more recent
cases it has been held that certain market factors,
specifically "the needs of a business, particularly
its profitability" are legitimate reasons for employers to withhold equal pay. In Albion Shipping Agency

90

v Arnold the Employment Appeal Tribunal held that in
the light of Jenkins v Kingsgate, in which the European Court accepted that objective economic circumstances could validly be taken into account when considering a claim of equal pay, reduced profits and volume of work did constitute a "material difference" for
the purpose of the Act. Such an interpretation broad-
ens the escape route for employers, and is likely to
be used, particularly in a situation when businesses
are under economic pressure, to depress the wages of
those with least ability to maintain them. Because
of this expansion of the category of "material difference" to the detriment of women, groups such as the
NCCL have suggested that a schedule of material differences, excluding market factors, be appended to the
legislation. (33) The individual provisions of the
Equal Pay Act require an employer to give equal treatment in pay, terms and conditions not only when men
and women are employed on like work but also when they
are employed on work which, though different, has been
given an equal value under a job evaluation scheme.
Because continuing job segregation means that male
comparators doing similar work are often difficult to
locate, job evaluation remains a necessary legal route
to equal pay for individuals.
      Yet the original "equal value" provisions of the
Equal Pay Act were extremely weak in some respects.
Where an employer refused to undertake job evaluation,
the Act left women not on like work no grounds to
claim equal pay. This was a serious legal weakness
because many women work in unorganised workplaces
where there is no strong union to enforce a demand for
job evaluation. It was also not possible to challenge
an existing job evaluation on grounds that it contained hidden or indirect discrimination. Also, because
job evaluation is carried out on a firm-by-firm basis,
the applicability of any exercise is limited; nor will
equal value provisions necessarily have an impact upon
low-paying, women-only workplaces.
      It was because of shortcomings in the equal value
provisions of the Act that the European Commission
brought infringement proceedings against the United
Kingdom Government. The Commission alleged that the UK
was in breach of its obligations under the Treaty of
Rome by failing to provide adequately in its national
legislation for individuals to pursue claims for equal
pay where they were engaged in work of equal value.
The Commission maintained that the deficiencies in the
Equal Pay Act constituted an infringement of the UK's
Treaty obligations to give full effect to the provisions of Article 119 of the Treaty of Rome and in par-

ticular to the provisions of the Equal Pay Directive. In its judgment of July 1982 the Court ordered the UK Government to endow an appropriate authority to hear and adjudicate for equal pay for work of equal value even if no job evaluation scheme was in existence.

Under pressure of the European Court judgment the Government introduced limited amendments to the Equal Pay Act, which became law in December 1983. The weakness in the amendment may well account for its method of introduction not by amending the Act, which would have required full parliamentary debate, but by an order under Section 2(2) of the European Communities Act of 1972, which limits parliamentary debate to 90 minutes. What amendments were finally made were a compromise between the Government's original weak proposals and outspoken criticism of them from the Equal Opportunities Commission, the National Council for Civil Liberties and the Trades Union Congress.

The amendments did designate Industrial Tribunals to hear claims for equal pay for work of equal value where no job evaluation scheme was in existence. Tribunals were empowered to appoint "independent experts", which would be ACAS officers, to prepare a job evaluation. The new rules stipulate that the expert must prepare a written, reasoned report taking account of representations made by the parties. However, the Tribunal can only reject the report if the expert has failed to comply with the limited stipulations and cannot do so on the grounds that it disagrees with the report's reasoning or conclusions. Whereas the first draft of the amendment prevented equal value applicants from pressing a claim if their job was already covered by job evaluation, the final amendment allows a claim if it can be shown that there are "reasonable grounds for determining" that the system used discrimination on grounds of sex. The thrust of these changes is to have the question of equal value determined more by experts than by judicial process. The amendments contain no provision for amendment of collective agreements to ensure that they conform to the principle of equal pay for equal value. They therefore do not provide a remedy for large-scale discrimination in the valuation of women's work.

However, the nature of the burden of proof will make it possible for employers to evade equal pay claims. The burden of proof that the difference in pay between the man and woman is due to a difference other than sex remains with the employer, but it is a different standard of proof than is required by the other provisions of the EPA. An employer facing an equal value claim will not be obliged to show that the genuine material difference that explains the difference in pay is a difference that relates to the man and woman's case. The existence of a material factor as opposed to a material difference will be sufficient to provide a legitimate justification for a pay difference. In other words the employer may have recourse to extrinsic factors rather than to differences between individuals. The Under-Secretary of State attempted to defend the different burden of proof by saying that it was necessary so as to allow account to be taken of "Skill shortages or other market forces". The admissibility of "market force" factors is a serious weakness: the market awards higher pay to a man than a woman because of the undervaluation of women's work. Their admissibility articulates in statute an argument similar to that which has already made its appearance in case law on the like work provision. (34)

But, in addition to the weaknesses of the amendment itself, job evaluation as a means of redress against sex discrimination in pay remains flawed. In general, job evaluators reflect general assessments of what is skilled work and what is not, and the EOC has previously called attention to the possibilities of hidden or implicit sex discrimination in job evaluation. The underlying difficulty remains the widespread view that what women do is "unskilled". There is, however, considerable evidence that definitions of skill have as much or more to do with social conceptions and the bargaining power of groups of workers as with objective job content. There is considerable historical evidence in the textile industry, for example, that like work has been designated as semiskilled where men did it but as unskilled where women have carried it out. In jobs that women do, aptitudes, such as dexterity, are often regarded not as skills but as "natural" or are ignored altogether. The widespread introduction of job evaluation, therefore, is not sufficient to reduce discrimination. Sexism in job evaluation would need to be eradicated by training job evaluators or involving women themselves in job evaluation. The NCCL has proposed, for example, that Equality Officers be appointed and that they be trained and employed by the EOC to assist and report in equal value cases. (35)

The individual provisions for the Sex Discrimination Act prohibit discrimination in employment, as well as in other fields. A person is regarded as discriminating against a woman for the purposes of the Act if on the grounds of sex he treats her less favourably than he treats or would treat a man, or he

applies to her a requirement or condition which he
applies or would apply to a man but which is such that
the proportion of women who can comply with it is con-
siderably smaller than the proportion of men who can
comply with it, when that requirement is not a necessary one. A person is regarded as discriminating
against a married person if similar conditions apply.
The SDA provides that it is unlawful to discriminate
against a woman he or she employs in the arrangements
made for recruitment, terms of employment, access to
opportunities for promotion, training, transfer, or
dismissal. It specifies that being a man is a genuine
occupational qualification for a job only in very restricted circumstances. The burden of proof in sex discrimination lies wholly with the applicant.

One important but limited development in case law
has been the use of the concept of indirect discrimination. In Price v Civil Service Commission (1977)
Price complained that the Civil Service age limit of
28 for entry as an Executive Officer was indirectly
discriminatory against women as fewer women than men
could comply with such a requirement; many women in
their 20s were engaged in bearing or bringing up
children. An Industrial Tribunal ruled against her on
the grounds that women need not have children. But
the Employment Appeal Tribunal held that it was necessary to ascertain whether women could comply as easily as men in practice with this rule and noted that
knowledge and experience suggested that they could
not. The Industrial Tribunal to which the case was
remitted subsequently found in Ms Price's favour.
Early efforts to use the concept of indirect discrimination to argue for pro rata equal pay for part-time
workers failed. In Meeks v NUAAW the ruling was that
lower pay per hour for part-time workers was not covered under the indirect discrimination provision of the
SDA because it pertained to a contractual matter; nor
did the Equal Pay Act cover such a case, because it
did not cover indirect discrimination. The ruling in
Jenkins v Kingsgate, however, stated that the two Acts
were to be treated as a harmonious code, while opening
new defences against pro-rata equal pay. Selection
for redundancy cases, however, have relied upon arguments about indirect discrimination. However, it is
becoming more difficult for an applicant to show indirect discrimination and easier for an employer to
defend against it. Previously the requirement which
was detrimental to women had to be shown to be "necessary", not simply convenient to the employer. But
the Court of Appeal in Ojutiku v Manpower Services
Commission rejected the test of necessity and said

that a requirement was justified if a person produces reasons which would be acceptable to right-thinking persons as sound and tolerable reasons. (36)

The Sex Discrimination Act has also provided a valuable case enjoining employers that women could not be regarded as unsuitable employees merely because they have children. And a series of cases has also established that the marriage of a woman was insufficient grounds for dismissal or other discriminatory action. However, in the case of a woman apparently dismissed because she was pregnant, the Tribunal ruled that there was no sex discrimination. In Turley v Allders (1979) a majority of the Employment Appeal Tribunal held that sex discrimination involves treating men and women unequally simply because they are men and women. When a woman is pregnant, she is no longer just a woman, she is a woman with child, and there is no masculine equivalent. (37)

WOMEN AND EMPLOYMENT LAW

Existing law, therefore, neither adequately protects women where they manage to work nor does it create significant new opportunities for women to enter employment. Law relating to employment is not particularly useful to women in view of current social practices, such as the organisation of childrearing and domestic work. (38) It allows women to continue to work in low-paid and low-status jobs, with little employment protection. Employment protection in general is directed towards continuously employed full-time workers, which women often are not. Nor does equal opportunities legislation actually break down the forms of employment segregation which result from women's domestic responsibilities and social attitudes towards women. The content of the law itself, the lack of legal rights and opportunities, does not adequately address women's employment concerns. Changes in the law relevant to employment, a lowering of the hours threshold for "continuity of employment", a statutory minimum wage, and a schedule of specific, restricted "material differences" in the Equal Pay Act, for example, would be in the interests of women at work.

Even where employment rights exist however, women do not necessarily enjoy those rights because of the weakness or unsuitability of enforcement procedures or bodies. In Britain, many statutory employment rights are floors of entitlement which trade unions enforce or build upon. Yet trade unions have been unwilling or unable to understand and act upon women's

particular, socially structured employment needs.
Women's "double shift" - at work and at home - makes
it difficult for women to become active and press
their interests within unions. Working women's posit-
ions as "migrants" from the domestic domain, the domain of consumption, into that of production, also affects their commitment to collective action at work.
In addition, women work in a segment of the labour
market which is especially difficult to organise.
Many unions, and the TUC are, however, beginning to
respond to the voices of organised women workers and
campaigning groups, such as the Low Pay Unit. (39)
        The structure of equal opportunities legislation
and the weakness of the EOC mean that much of the legislation is dependent upon individual women taking
cases to Tribunals. Yet partly because social practices locate women firmly in the private sphere, working women, even more than working men, are no doubt
reluctant litigants. This is especially so because
other agencies, such as ACAS, and bodies such as
trade unions are not always particularly eager to
support principles of equal opportunities; because legal aid is not available for representation before Tribunals; and because the employment consequences for
women of even taking cases may be difficulties at work.
British equal opportunities legislation does not allow
for class actions, actions by an individual or small
group on behalf of a larger category of persons, and
so fragments and individualises legal action. Nor is
the structure of legislation such that there is either
an automatic or legally triggered obligation on employers themselves to take substantial initiatives to
desegregate with the obligation backed by legal sanctions. (40)
        The current Conservative Government is weakening
the ability of both organisations and individuals to
secure women's employment rights by pursuing a strategy which elevates "free market" principles into the
greatest social good. Market ideologies and practices
regard the market as autonomous and beneficent. Social practices are not seen as structuring the market
in negative or unfair ways. And so the weak position
of women and other groups is not seen as an appropriate object of state or trade union intervention.
Such interventions are regarded as detracting from the
proper functioning of the market, and the development
of a leaner, fitter economy. Many legal protections
which might have benefited women workers - wage councils, Schedule 11, the Fair Wages Resoluton, the proposed European Directive on part-time work - are being
weakened, withdrawn or opposed. And it is not sur-

prising that market ideology is appearing not only in amendments to the Equal Pay Act but also in case law. The deep economic recession which has resulted from Government policy makes it in some respects less likely that trade unions will make women's particular interests a high priority. Maintenance of existing jobs, rather than alterations in recruitment practices or improvements in women's pay, has become the central issue for most trade unionists. However, as the economy has been re-structured away from traditional manufacturing toward lighter industry and services, trade unions have recognised the importance of effectively unionising women workers, partly in the interest of organisational survival. Yet a Government which creates high levels of unemployment and weakens trade unions makes it very difficult for willing trade unions to act effectively on behalf of women, or other members. And it is certainly not in the interest of capital, especially when profits are under pressure, to itself improve the pay and conditions of a weak and "flexible" group of workers. The state of the economy also makes it more difficult for individual women to use the law, as the threat of unemployment is ever present.

Women are dependent, however, on more than employment law and a reasonably strong economy to improve their position in the labour market. Women's employment is structured by a variety of social practices and policies. Women are tied into a complicated inter-related set of structures and roles: they are mothers, carers for the elderly, and unpaid workers in the home, as well as paid workers. Women's position in employment is related to their other roles and policies which influence them.

Employment-related law does not alter those social practices which create or reinforce inequality in employment; other policies are necessary, alongside improved employment-related law. For example, attitudes and policy which encourage the sharing of labour in the family and provide public facilities for care of the young, ill and elderly are essential to the creation of employment opportunities for women. The present Government's reassertion of the traditional role of women combined with its attack on the public services undermines women's availability for employment and job opportunities. Shorter working hours would, for example, allow working parents to spend more time with children and domestic tasks. But there is also little point in arguing for women's participation in the labour force or men's giving up full-time employment when women have no, or poor, employment opportunities. And if women are to have a full range of employment options they require educational and training opportunities, not only as young people but also as adults. Gender equality in employment, therefore, requires political will mobilised behind a comprehensive programme of change - in employment-related law and elsewhere.

NOTES

(1) Equal Opportunities Commission (EOC), Seventh Annual Report 1982. HMSO (1983), pp. 74-75
(2) Ibid., p. 76
(3) Ibid., p. 76
(4) Ibid., p. 75
(5) Department of Employment Gazette, 91, (September 1983) Table 1.4 "Employees in Employment, June 1983" pp. S12-13
(6) EOC, Annual Report 1982 p. 77
(7) Department of Employment, New Earnings Survey 1983, Part B: Report, Summary Analysis, and Analysis by Agreement; Table 32: "Average Earnings in April 1983 and Increases Since April 1982", p. B12; and Part F: Hours, Earnings of Part-Time Women Workers, Adult Rates Analyses, Table 180: "Median, Quartiles, Deciles and Average of Gross Hourly Earnings and Average of Gross Weekly Earnings and Weekly Hours, By Region", p. F88
(8) Steve Winyard, "Poverty in the West Midlands" Low Pay Review, 15 (September 1983), p.3
(9) Select Committee on the European Communities, House of Lords, Voluntary Part-Time Work London: HMSO (1982), p. viii
(10) Lloyds Bank Limited v Secretary of State for Employment (1979) ICR 258. However in Corton House Limited v Skipper (1981) ICR 307 the contract of employment provided for 4 hours' work every other evening, ie 12 hours in one week and 16 hours in the next. The Employment Appeal Tribunal held that the employee could not count the 12 hour weeks and that her continuity of employment was therefore broken.
(11) Ford v Warwickshire County Council (1983) reported in The Times, 19 February 1983
(12) On employment protection and terms and conditions for part-timers see House of Lords, Voluntary Part-Time Work; Ann Sedley, Part-Time Workers Need Full-Time Rights (NCCL Rights for Women Unit, 1983); Women's Advisory Committee, Trades Union Congress, Report

to the 1980 Women's Conference, Supplementary Report: Part-Time Workers (TUC, 1 981) pp. 30-47; and Jennifer Hurstfield, "Part-Time Pittance", Low Pay Review 1 (June 1980) pp. 1-15

(13) Meeks v National Union of Agricultural and Allied Workers (1976) IRLR 198. This case and other major cases under the equal opportunities legislation are reported in EOC, Towards Equality: A Casebook of Decisions on Sex Discrimination and Equal Pay 1976-1981 (EOC, n.d.)

(14) Jenkins v Kingsgate (Clothing Productions) Ltd. (1981) ICR 592

(15) Clarke v Eley (IMI) Kynoch Ltd and Eley (IMI Kynoch Ltd v Powell (1982) IRLR 131 and IRLR 483; The Guardian, 5 March 1982

(16) Dick v University of Dundee (1982)

(17) House of Lords, Voluntary Part-Time Work

(18) Winyard, "Poverty Wages" p. 1

(19) Dominic Byrne, Chris Pond and Gill Sullivan, "Low Wages in Britain" Low Pay Review 12 (February 1983), pp. 6-7.

(20) Winyard, "Poverty Wages", p. 2

(21) Ibid., pp. 5-6

(22) Ibid., pp. 5-6

(23) "Parliamentary Report: Wages Councils" Low Pay Review 9 (November 1982) pp. 13-14

(24) "Shop Workers' Wages" Low Pay Review 13 (March 1983) p. 18; Financial Times 14 March 1983

(25) On the FWR and its repeal see "Parliamentary Report" Low Pay Review 12; Chris Pond "Abandoning Fair Wages" Low Pay Review 11 (November 1982) pp. 1-7; Emma MacLennan "Contracting Poverty" Low Pay Review 11 (November 1982) pp. 8-17; Penny Wood "Employment Protection Act 1975 and the Fair Wages Resolution 1946" Industrial Law Journal 7 (June 1978) pp. 65-83

(26) "Parliamentary Report" Low Pay Review 12, pp. 15-16, Pond, "Abandoning Fair Wages" Low Pay Review 11, pp. 1-7. On Schedule 11 also see Michael Jones, "CAC and Schedule 11: The Experience of Two Years" Industrial Law Journal 9 (March 1980), pp. 28-44

(27) See Mandy Snell, "The Equal Pay and Sex Discrimination Acts: Their Impact in the Workplace" Feminist Review 1 (1979) pp. 37-58

(28) See John Harris and Helen Snider, "Has Discrimination Been Eliminated in Collective Agreements? The Central Arbitration Committee and Equal Pay" Polytechnic of Central London, Research Working Paper No 16 (April 1982)

(29)   On the EOC, see Elizabeth Meehan, 'Equal
        Opportunities Policies: Some Implications for
        Women of Contrasts Between Enforcement Bodies
        in Britain and the USA' in Jane Lewis, (ed.)
        Women's Welfare, Women's Rights London: Croom
        Helm (1983) pp. 170-182; P. Byrne and J.
        Lovenduski, 'Sex Equality and the Law in Brit-
        ain' British Journal of Law and Society 5
        (1978), pp. 147-165: George Appleby and Evelyn
        Ellis, 'Toothless Watchdogs? The Commission
        for Racial Equality and the Equal Opportunities
        Commission as Law Enforcement Agencies' Univ-
        ersity of Birmingham, Faculty of Law (mimeo);
        and Anna Coote and Beatrix Campbell, Sweet
        Freedom: The Struggle for Women's Liberation
        (London: Pan, 1982)
(30)   EOC, Annual Report 1982, p. 39
(31)   Jeanne Gregory, 'Some Cases that Never Reached
        the Tribunal' Feminist Review 10 (1982), pp.
        75-89
(32)   EOC, Annual Report 1982, p. 1
(33)   Fletcher v Clay Cross (1978) IRLR 361, (1979)
        ICR1; Albion Shipping Agency v Arnold (1981)
        IRLR 525, (1982) ICR 22; Jenkins v Kingsgate
        (Clothing Productions) Ltd (1981) ICR 592;
        Catherine Scorer and Ann Sedley, Amending the
        Equality Laws (National Council for Civil Lib-
        erties, Rights for Women Unit, 1983)
(34)   On the original equal value provisions and
        amendments see the speech by Anthony Lester QC
        to the Institute of Personnel Management Con-
        ference in Harrogate, 20 October 1983; Comm-
        ission of the European Communities v United
        Kingdom of Great Britain and Northern Ireland
        (1982) ICR 578, IRLR 333, Christopher McCrudd-
        en, 'Industrial Law Journal'; NCCL Rights for
        Women Newsletter, especially the September
        1983 issue; Guardian, 28 March 1983, 15 Novem-
        ber 1982; Financial Times, 9 March 1982
(35)   On job evaluation see Tess Gill and Larry
        Whitty, Women's Rights in the Workplace
        (Penguin, 1983) p. 115-135; Scorer and Sedley,
        Amending the Equality Laws; Ann Phillips and
        Barbara Taylor, 'Sex and Skill: Notes Towards
        a Feminist Economics'' Feminist Review 6 (1980)
        pp. 79-88
(36)   Price v Civil Service Commission (1978) ICR
        127, IRLR 3; (1977) IRLR 291; Jenkins v Kings-
        gate (1981) ICR 592; Ojutiku and Oburoni v
        Manpower Services Commission (1982) IRLR 418;
        (1981) IRLR 156

(37)   Turley v Allders Department Stores Ltd (1980)
         ICR 66, IRLR 4
(38)   For discussion of alternative notions of sex-
         ist bias and law, see Elizabeth Kingdom 'Sex-
         ist Bias and Law' Politics and Power 3 (Lon-
         don: Routledge and Kegan Paul, 1981) pp. 97-
         114
(39)   There is an extensive literature on women and
         trade unions. See, for example, Anna Coote
         and Peter Kellner, Hear This, Brother, Women
         Workers and Union Power (New Statesman, 1980);
         Judith Hunt 'A Woman's Place is in Her Union'
         in Jackie West, (ed.) Work, Women and the
         Labour Market (London: Routledge and Kegan
         Paul, 1982) pp. 154-71; Jenny Beale, Getting
         It Together: Women as Trade Unionists (London:
         Pluto Press, 1982) Valerie Ellis, 'The Role
         of Trade Unions in the Promotion of Equal
         Opportunities' (EOC and SSRC, 1981); Coote
         and Campbell, Sweet Freedom, pp. 143-170. On
         women's position between house and work, see
         for example, Marilyn Porter, 'Standing on the
         Edge: Working Class Housewives and the World
         of Work' in West, (ed.) Work, Women and the
         Labour Market, pp. 117-134 and Anna Pollert,
         Girls, Wives and Factory Lives (London: Mac-
         Millan, 1981)
(40)   On legal provision for equal opportunities in
         the United States, see Sadie Robarts, Positive
         Action for Women: The Next Step (NCCL Rights
         for Women Unit, 1981); United States Commiss-
         ion on Civil Rights, Affirmative Action in the
         1980s: Dismantling the Process of Discrimin-
         ation (US Government Printing Office, 1982)

Chapter Five

PREGNANCY AND EMPLOYMENT LAW

Judith Mayhew

> "Quite frankly" said the Secretary of State for
> Social Services "I don't think mothers have the
> same right to work as fathers. If the Good Lord
> had intended us to have equal rights to go out to
> work, he wouldn't have created men and women.
> These are biological facts, young children do
> depend upon their mothers." (1)

This assertion indicates the problems of a government faced with high unemployment and a desire to
reduce spending on social services at a time when 40%
of the labour force were women and more than half of
the women between the ages of 16 and 59 were at work.
Married women now comprise one quarter of the total
labour force and outnumber single women by 2 to 1.
During the 1970s the number of women entering
the work force increased and the law encouraged and
reflected this trend with the enactment of the Equal
Pay Act 1970, Sex Discrimination Act 1975 and the Employment Protection Act 1975. The latter statute gave
for the first time some legislative protection for
pregnant employees in conjunction with rights to maternity leave and pay.
Legal policies have always been used by the government to encourage women to work when the economy
needed them in the labour force. An illustration of
this is seen in the way in which taxation policy has
affected the working patterns of married women. Although the relevant provisions of the three statutes
have encouraged women to continue to enter the work
force the law is not the only determining factor. It
alone cannot provide the necessary social and economic
climate to encourage and help women to enter the labour force. Without adequate social services such as
nursery care and school meals many mothers are unable
to take up or continue in paid employment even though

they may wish or need to do so. Such provisions can
be made if women are needed by the economy as seen by
the facilities provided during World War Two.
It is interesting to note that in the Employment
Act 1980 the government began to reduce the maternity
rights and benefits which had been created by the
Employment Protection Act 1975. This is a reflection
of the current government attitude which is that wom-
en with dependent children should remain at home thus
freeing jobs for unemployed men and reducing the amount of money spent on social services such as nursery
care and school meals.

THE PROVISION MADE BY THE LAW FOR PREGNANT EMPLOYEES

Rights During Employment
S.60 of the Employment Protection (Consolidation) Act
1978 provides that an employee shall be treated as being unfairly dismissed if the reason for her dismissal
is that she is pregnant or any other reason connected
with her pregnancy. Two exceptions are made to this
principle. The first arises if at the date of the
termination of her employment she has become incapable
of doing her work because of her pregnancy. The second exception occurs if her continued employment
would breach a statutory duty or restriction. An
employee may not rely on S.60 unless she has been employed for one year which is increased to two years
if her employer employs fewer than twenty workers.
In addition to this protection from dismissal all
pregnant employees are now allowed paid time off, for
a reasonable period, during working hours to receive
ante-natal care. This new right was created at the
Committee stage of the Employment Bill 1980 and is now
contained in S.13 of the Employment Act 1980. This
reflects the growing concern over the high infant mortality rate in this country and the reluctance on the
part of women to attend ante-natal clinics.

Maternity Leave and Pay
The qualifications for maternity leave and pay are the
same. The employee must not be in an excluded class
(2) and must have had two years' continuous service up
to the beginning of the eleventh week before the expected week of her confinement. (3) This does not
mean that she has to be at work until then because she
may have been away on leave or ill. Notice should be
given of her pregnancy at least twenty-one days before
her absence begins.

She is entitled to six weeks' pay from her employer at 90% of her gross weekly pay minus the flat rate maternity allowance which is payable under the Social Security Act 1975. This is deducted whether or not the employee is entitled to it in whole or part and in Cullen v Creasey Hotels (Limbury) Ltd. (4) it was held that if an employee has more than one contract of employment, the allowance is deducted in the calculation of each statutory maternity payment.

The employer may claim a rebate from the State Maternity Fund to cover in full the gross amount of the maternity pay. This rebate does not cover any additional benefits which may have been paid under any other agreement. If the employer fails to pay, the employee may complain to an industrial tribunal within three months and it has the power to order the employer to make the payment. The Fund may be used to pay employees who have not been paid by their employers despite having taken all reasonable steps to recover the amount due.

Women who satisfy the National Insurance contribution conditions are entitled to claim the weekly maternity allowance (5) from the State for eighteen weeks. This time runs from the eleventh week before, to the sixth week after the expected week of confinement. A woman must stop work before she can claim it. The amount of the benefit is reviewed annually and is currently £22.50p per week.

In addition to the maternity pay and the maternity allowance, a maternity grant (6) of £25 is payable at the birth of a child. This is dependent on the mother's or husband's (not the co-habitee's) National Insurance contribution record.

The DHSS in a consultative document published in October 1980 indicated a wish to simplify the system and achieve a more equitable distribution of resources without actually increasing the amount of money involved. Three options were considered. These were, a single lump sum, or a DHSS grant and an allowance for working women paid by the employer or finally a grant and allowance paid by the DHSA. The reaction to this Green Paper was sufficiently hostile for the government to announce in January 1981 that no major amendments to the maternity benefits would be made.

The Right to Return to Work
An employee is given a right to return to work by S.45 Employment Protection (Consolidation) Act 1978 if her absence from work has been because of her pregnancy. She may return up to twenty-nine weeks after the birth

of her child. (7) The right is to return to the job
specified in the original contract of employment or a
similar one with the original employer or where appropriate his successor.

This right to return has been reduced by the
Employment Act 1980 in two important ways. The refusal to permit a woman to return to her old job or an
identical one will not be deemed an unfair dismissal
if the employer employs five or fewer employees and
he can show that it was not reasonably practicable to
permit her to return or to be offered a not less favourable alternative. Nor will it be unfair dismissal
if irrespective of the size of the firm, it is not
reasonably practicable to reinstate her in her original job (for a reason other than redundancy) and
suitable alternative employment is offered and she
either accepts or unreasonably refuses that offer. If
redundancy prevents an employee from exercising her
right to return then any suitable alternative position
should be offered to her on terms not less favourable
than would have applied to her had she returned to her
original job. If she is redundant and there is no
vacancy for her then she may claim a redundancy payment.

S.11 of the Employment Act 1980 has also restricted the qualifications for the right to return to work
by imposing three extra notice requirements. An employee must now give written notice three weeks before
she begins her maternity leave and three weeks before
she exercises her right to return. If the employer
requires it an employee must provide additional writt-
en notification of her intention to return to work not
earlier than forty-nine days from the beginning of her
expected date of confinement. Failure to comply within fourteen days or as soon as is reasonably practicable will lead to the loss of her right to return.

These substantive and procedural changes to the
right to return have reduced it and made it more difficult to exercise the remaining original rights granted in the Employment Act 1975. The government justified their alterations by arguing that the original
rights were a burden on employers, especially on small
businesses and could actually be a disincentive to
employ women. The notice requirements were necessary
to prevent women from stating that they would return
when they had no intention to do so. However this is
still possible because no penalty is attached to failure to return after giving the prescribed notices. It
was argued that the new requirements would lead to
greater certainty for employers in planning and organ-
ising their staffing.

Pregnancy and Employment Law

These assumptions about the inconvenience caused
to employers are not borne out by the various studies
which have been done.

In December 1980, the number of people in employment in the United Kingdom was 21,812,000 of whom
9,168,000 were women. It has been calculated
that each year 3.6% of working women stop work to
have a baby (ie 330,000). Since approximately
760,000 have babies each year, 43% of all women
who have babies were working when they became
pregnant. (8)

Upex and Morris conclude that "apart from the
purely financial benefits, the impact of maternity
rights on the lives of working women has been neglig-
ible. (9) On the basis of figures supplied by the
DHSS they calculated that of all the women who have
babies in a year 60,000 (7.9%) qualify for no benefit
at all; 310,000 (40.9%) qualify for only the maternity
grant; 270,000 (35.5%) may claim the grant and the
allowance; 40,000 (5.26%) the grant and maternity pay
whilst only 80,000 (10.53%) qualify for all three payments. This trend is also illustrated by an EOC survey which showed that up to April 1977 only 202,776
women had taken maternity pay, that is only 3.1% of
the total female working population. More recently
an Industrial Relations Review and Report subscriber
survey found that the take up rate for maternity pay
was 1.9% and maternity leave 0.3%. (10) The conclusion that may be drawn from these surveys is that few
women qualify for the rights and benefits and even
fewer choose to exercise the specific right to return.
     Two surveys (11) have indicated that very few
employers have experienced difficulty with the maternity provisions and that the possibility of such
problems arising had not affected the recruitment of
women workers. The problems created by holding jobs
open appear to have been exaggerated and the government's policy which has been to restrict the right to
return appears to be an over-reaction to a very small
problem.
     One of the major factors highlighted by the sur-
veys is the large number of women unable to bring
themselves within the qualifying group because of
their lack of continuous service. For this group the
specific maternity provisions give no rights. However
the more general provisions of the Sex Discrimination
Act 1975 could provide some protection for these women
if the courts choose to interpret it widely.
     This Act has the potential to be used in several

situations when a women has suffered discrimination
in employment because of pregnancy. It could prevent
dismissal on the grounds of pregnancy when the employee does not fall within the qualifying group protected
by the 1978 and 1980 Acts. It could prevent an employer denying benefits such as access to training
schemes, promotion, seniority rights and other fringe
benefits. Whether the courts are prepared to interpret the Sex Discrimination Act 1975 to cover such
situations is not clear.

The issue whether the Sex Discrimination Act 1975
could be used by women who failed to qualify under the
1978 and 1980 Acts arose in the case of Reaney v Kanda
Jean Products Ltd. (12) The Industrial Tribunal approached the case on the basis of direct rather than
indirect discrimination. The question it raised was
whether the employers, in dismissing Mrs. Reaney on
the grounds of her pregnancy, were treating her less
favourably than they would treat a man. They stated:

> It is impossible for a man to become pregnant
> (at all events in the present state of scientific
> knowledge!). His situation, therefore, cannot be
> compared with that of a woman. The concept of
> discrimination involves by definition an act or
> treatment which in the case of a woman is less
> favourable than that which is or may be accorded
> to a man. The applicant was not dismissed on the
> assumed facts because she was a woman. She was
> on the assumed facts dismissed because she was
> pregnant, and it is only an accident of nature
> which bestows the burden and happiness of preg-
> nancy on the female sex... We are therefore
> driven to the conclusion that the Sex Discrimin-
> ation Act gives no remedy to the applicant here,
> nor indeed does any other relevant legislation.

The Employment Appeal Tribunal also considered
the issue in Turley v Allders Department Stores Ltd.
(13) Mrs. Turley complained that she had been dismissed by the respondents because she was pregnant. As
she lacked the necessary continuous service to bring
her claim under the unfair dismissal provisions she
too brought her complaint under the Sex Discrimination
Act 1975. The majority of the Employment Appeal Tribunal held that the Industrial Tribunal had correctly
concluded that to dismiss a woman because she is pregnant is not within the definition of discrimination
against women in S.1 of the Act, and that if the appellant was dismissed on the grounds of pregnancy it
did not amount to unlawful discrimination.

They argued that S.1 required the court to look
at men and women and see that they are not treated unequally simply because they are men and women. In
order to see whether a woman has been treated less
favourably than a man, the sense of S.1(1) is that
like must be compared with like. In the case of a
pregnant woman, this cannot be done. When she is
pregnant a woman is no longer just a woman. She is a
woman, as the Authorised Version accurately put it,
with child, and there is no masculine equivalent.
The dissenting judgment of Ms Smith takes a
broader approach:

> The case under the direct discrimination pro-
> vision - S.1(1)(a) - is a simple one. Pregnancy
> is a medical condition. It is a condition which
> applies only to women. It is a condition which
> will lead to a request for time off from work for
> the confinement. A man is in similar circumstan-
> ces who is employed by the same employer and who
> in the course of the year will require time off
> for a hernia operation; to have his tonsils rem-
> oved; or for other medical reasons. The employer
> must not discriminate by applying different and
> less favourable criteria to the pregnant woman
> than to the man requiring time off.
>
> That is the 'like for like' comparison, not
> one between women who are pregnant and men who
> cannot become pregnant.

This Industrial Tribunal should have asked:

1.   Did Mrs. Turley's pregnancy incapacitate
      her in her job?
2.   Would the employer have treated a man in
      similar circumstances differently - that
      is, a man requiring time off for a medical
      condition who is not incapacitated in his
      job?

If the employer shows that the man would not be
treated more favourably, then the Sex Dsicrimination
Act would not give the woman protection. The answer
rests on the facts and the test falls squarely within
the terms of S.1(1)(a).
This argument does not conflict with the Employment Protection Act. The right not to be dismissed on
the grounds of pregnancy and the maternity rights
under the Employment Protection Act are, following a
period of continuous employment, automatic unless S.60
(a) or (b) apply. The Sex Discrimination Act would not

108

give an automatic right; it would give a much more
limited right, resting on a comparison with other employees, a right not to be singled out for dismissal
for pregnancy - a female condition - as distinct from
other medical conditions. (14)
    This broader interpretation is consistent with
the reasoning of the Employment Appeal Tribunal in
Peake v Automotive Products Ltd. (15) when they stated that "in deciding whether the circumstances of the
two cases are the same, or not materially different,
one must put out of the picture any circumstances
which necessarily follow from the fact that one is
comparing the case of a man and a woman." Also in
Schmidt v Austicks Bookshops Ltd. (16) the Employment
Appeal Tribunal when examining whether dress restrictions placed on female employees were discriminatory
stated that the preferable basis of the decision was
whether the male employees also had restrictions placed on their dress. In this case the restrictions
would not be the same but this approach would be more
sensible than one which examines point by point, garment by garment. When a characteristic is shared by
the two sexes then the gender equality principle may
be applied. When it is not shared then the comparison
can only be made by using the equivalent or similar
characteristics. In the case of pregnancy any male
medical condition which required absence from work
would form the basis for comparison.
    An alternative approach under the Sex Discrimin-
ation Act 1975 would be to argue that a pregnancy
classification imposed by an employer amounted to indirect discrimination. It would require the employer
to establish that a requirement or condition which
has a disproportionately adverse effect on women was
justifiable. It would be similar to the reasoning
of the Employment Appeal Tribunal in Price v Civil
Service Commission. (17) This was raised in the dissenting judgment in Turley (18)
    The case law indicates that the tendency to see
pregnancy in a class of its own and not to compare it
with other incapacitating conditions, results in many
women being unable to claim under the Sex Discrimination Act 1975 when they have been treated adversely
for reasons related to pregnancy.
    The maternity rights and benefits although res-
trictive in practice show that a specific law is able
to recognise and deal with biological differences.
These provisions are seen by the courts as merely one
aspect of the wider law of unfair dismissal and are
treated as such. However problems have arisen when
women have tried to use the more general laws, such as

the provisions of the <u>Sex Discrimination Act</u> 1975, to
prevent discrimination on the grounds of biological
difference. Analysis of the cases shows that the courts have not been consistent in their approach and have
tended to retreat into a restrictive interpretation
of the Act.

NOTES

(1)   Secretary of State for Social Services as
       reported in The <u>Guardian,</u> 16th November 1979,
       as a quotation from the BBC television
       programme'Man Alive'.
(2)   These are the wife of the employer S.146(1)
       EPCA 1978, share-fisherwoman S.144(2) EPCA
       1978, policewoman S.146(2) EPCA 1978; and
       those ordinarily working outside Great Brit-
       ain S.141(2) EPCA 1978
(3)   S.33(3)a EPCA 1978
(4)   [1980] ICR.236.
(5)   S.22 Social Security Act 1975
(6)   S.21 Social Security Act 1975
(7)   This may be extended to thirty-three weeks on
       production of a medical certificate.
(8)   Maternity Rights - Illusion or Reality
       Upex and Morris, Industrial Law Journal 218,
       220
(9)   Supra p. 221
(10)   "Maternity Leave - The IR-RR Survey Part 1.
       The Act's Provisions in Practice". Indust-
       rial Relations Review and Report (IR-RR)
       No. 217, February 1980
(11)   W.W. Daniels Maternity Rights: The Experience
       of Employers, PSI Broadsheet No. 596 August
       1981. R. Clifton and C. Tatton-Brown Impact
       of Employment Legislation on Small Firms
       DE Research Paper No. 6, 1979.
(12)   [1978] IRLR 427
(13)   [1980] IRLR 4
(14)   Supra p. 6
(15)   [1977] IRLR 105, 108
(16)   [1978] ICR 85.
(17)   [1978] ICR 21
(18)   Supra

REFERENCES

Employment Law, Happle & O'Higgins
Striking a Balance, Lewis & Simpson
Maternity Rights Provisions - A New Approach, Winch
     1981 JSWL 321

Pregnancy and Employment Law

Maternity Benefits: Their Present Role and Future
      Development, Dalley 1981 JSWL 329
Maternity Rights - Illusion of Reality, Upex and
      Morris 10 ILJ 218.
Sex Discrimination and Pregnancy: Anatomy Is Not Des-
      tiny, Pannick 3 OJLSI

Chapter Six

WOMEN, IMMIGRATION AND NATIONALITY

W.I.N.G. London

The aim of immigration control for the last 22 years
has been to restrict the entry of black people
particularly black men, to this country. Immigration
laws have been used as a rationalisation and as a
justification of prejudice against black people. (1)
Instead of seeing the racism of the majority population as the major problem, lawmakers have preferred to
see black people coming here, or those already settled
here, as creating a problem. Immigration control is
always discussed with implicitly racist assumptions.
The fact that the majority of the people coming to this country, often to stay, are white, are neither coun-
ted nor noticed, is ignored. The fact that all the
citizens of all the EEC countries (except Greeks, who
will get this freedom in 1988) have a right to come
here to seek work is not seen as any "threat" but the
few British families from Malawi, of Asian origin,
coming to the country whose citizenship they hold,
created major media hysteria.
     The myth that "strict immigration control is good
for race relations" has been the basic tenet of successive governments' immigration policies, and has reinforced the view that the "problem" is black people
and fuelled demands either for a massive curb to immigration or for repatriation. It is not widely known
that the only people who can qualify for entry under
the immigration laws are the wives and young children
of men already settled here, that more people from the
Caribbean left the UK than entered last year, and that
there has been a net outflow of people from this country every year since 1977 (1979 excepting).
     From within this mythology and in from within
immigration policy women have not been seen as people
in their own right but either as "dependants" of men
living here, or as agents of male settlement. Immigration laws have enshrined the right for men to bring

112

their wives here, always explained by reference to
the "social problems" that result from keeping families apart (black men perhaps having sexual relations
with white women) but those aspects of the regulations
that have been changed most frequently are those per-
mitting or forbidding women living here from being
joined by their husbands; this double standard will
be discussed in more detail below. A central guiding
assumption of lawmakers is that women have no rights
in this matter but should automatically live where
their husbands reside and where their husbands decide
(2) they are not specifically mentioned in the law. (3)
        Modern immigration control begins with the 1905
Aliens Act, passed specifically in order to stop Jews
from Eastern Europe coming to the UK. Aliens Orders
were passed each year after that, gradually extending
control so that they could be used to exclude more
Jews fleeing from Nazism in the 1930s. Commonwealth
and colonial immigration was not restricted until
1962, again in response to racist agitation, this time
about Caribbean and Asian people coming here. In the
post-war labour shortage, people from the British
colonies had been encouraged to come here to work and
recruiting drives had been organised in the Caribbean.
The entry of people had closely correlated with the
demand for labour until 1961, when there were strong
rumours of impending immigration control and more
people rushed here to beat the expected ban. After
1962, people coming here to work had to obtain employment vouchers, granted only when there was a specific
vacancy to fill or a worker possessed a skill in short
supply. In 1965, under a Labour government which had
opposed the 1962 Act, the criteria for the grant of a
voucher were made still more restrictive.
        In the later 1960s, racist fears concentrated on
East Africa, where the population of Asian origin,
brought over by the British to administer the colonies,
was being squeezed out by the independent countries'
Africanisation policies. As many of them had not been
permitted to take the citizenship of the new independent countries, they were still British and not subject to immigration control. The 1968 Commonwealth
Immigrants Act, rushed through Parliament in three
days by a Labour government, subjected them to immigration control and in breach of all international
law and obligations prevented them from travelling to
the country of their citizenship unless they had first
obtained a "special quota" voucher to settle here.
This "special quota" voucher scheme is entirely discretionary, liable to be changed by the Home Secretary
and outside the jurisdiction of the Sex Discrimination

113

Act. The scheme is explicitly sex discriminatory in
that vouchers are only issued to "heads of households", defined as men, or single widowed or divorced
women. A married woman cannot be treated as the head
of household unless her husband is disabled. This
Act created great hardship for British Asians, unable
to make a living in East Africa or to go to any other
country; the hardship continues for those who went
"temporarily" to India and where people now wait over
seven years in the queue for vouchers. A woman who
marries while waiting loses her claim to a voucher.

The law in force at present, the 1971 Immigration
Act, consolidated the race and sex discrimination already operating, but also freed many people from control altogether. It invented the concept of "patriality", deciding who "belonged" to the UK. Commonwealth
citizens with a parent born here thus have the same
rights as British citizens and are free of control
so were Commonwealth citizen women married to British
men. Commonwealth citizens with a grandparent born
here are free to come to live and work here. The Act
came into force on 1 January 1973, the date the UK
joined the EEC. Under EEC legislation, nationals of
all the member countries are free to travel to take
or seek work in other countries and their spouses and
other generously defined family members are entitled
to accompany or to join them. Clearly, the majority
of these people are white and this is part of a deliberate policy decision, to tie the UK in more closely
with the rich, white world and to break links with the
rest of the Commonwealth.

At the same time, the legal and bureaucratic restrictions on other people have increased. People may
be allowed to come here as wives and children of men
living here, as husbands of British citizen women under certain conditions, as work permit holders if they
are coming for a specific, highly skilled job with a
specific employer who has been unable to find a British or EEC worker to fill the position, or temporarily
as visitors or students, as provided in the Immigration Rules, amplifications of the provisions of the
law. Sex and race discrimination, in the law and the
Rules and the attitudes and procedures of those who
operate them, is all-pervasive.

The most blatant view of women as appendages (4)
of their husbands is shown in the fact that a Commonwealth woman marrying a British man became automatically patrial, no longer subject to immigration control, whereas there has never been any corresponding
right for the foreign husbands of British women. The
scandal of "virginity testing" exemplified the prejud-

ices of the Immigration Service (largely male); although this practice has been stopped it is still assumed that an Asian woman must be a virgin on marriage
and that if she is not, she must already be married
and be attempting to avoid going through the proper
immigration control procedures. To avoid any possibility of a woman entering the country as a fiancee
when she should be a wife at least one Indian woman
at Heathrow and many more at Delhi were compelled to
submit to an embarrassing and degrading physical examination, justified on racist grounds as necessary for
maintaining strict immigration control, being concerned with statistics rather than people.
    The government's outdated and prejudiced ideas
are shown in the way the rules are written and operated. Because women are seen as appendages of men,
their own rights are non-existent and their wishes of
no importance. Women are not seen as workers in their
own right and the experience of those who have come
here independently to work and to support their families from the Caribbean, the Philippines, Latin America
- is ignored. Lesbian relationships are not recognised, neither are non-nuclear families; human rights are
ignored as the aim of curbing black immigration is
pursued.

FAMILY UNITY

As governments do pay lip-service to the idea of family unification, the immigration rules provide for
entry for settlement of some members of the families
of those already settled in the UK. The rules have
become increasingly restrictive over the years, so
that even those few relatives allowed to enter must
obtain entry clearance abroad, the sponsoring relative
in the UK must be able to maintain and accommodate
them without relying on public funds and they must be
without other close relatives outside the UK to turn
to.
    Each of these requirements is designed to place
obstacles in the way of family unification of non-
white families and only to admit those who will be no
burden on state resources and for whom no-one in some
other country can be forced to take responsibility.
The first requirement, that of prior entry clearance,
has been used since 1969 to delay entry, particularly
of wives and children in the Indian subcontinent,
where the queue in Dhake was allowed to reach over
three years in the mid-1970s. This is a queue for first
interview, which rarely results in entry clearance

being granted; applications are often deferred for
further inquiries to be made or referred to the Home
Office here.
    The second main requirement is that the sponsors
are able to support and accommodate their relatives
without state help. EEC nationals and Commonwealth
citizens who have the right of abode or were settled
here before 1973, are exempt from this requirement.
Everyone else must show that there is enough money to
support the family members coming. This means that
the sponsor must either be in work or have a very large amount of savings. Unemployed people and those on
social security cannot be joined by other relatives
here. The accommodation available for relatives must
be owned or already occupied by the sponsor. There
is quite literally one rule for the rich and one for
the poor.
    Apart from these general requirements, there are
specific additional requirements for each category of
dependant, ie wives, children, parents and other relatives. These rules are based on the model of the conventional Western heterosexual nuclear family. This
is not an appropriate definition to judge who is
"family" in non-British cultures, where far more extended networks of responsibility and dependence frequently apply. In general, only "legitimate" relationships are recognised.
    Children must generally be under 18, unmarried
and both their parents must be settled in the UK to
qualify. If only one parent is in the UK, the child
will only be eligible if the parent has had the "sole
responsibility" for the child's upbringing, or there
are "serious and compelling family or other considerations making the child's exclusion "undesirable".
Sole responsibility is difficult to establish when
by definition the parent, often the mother, has been
working in the UK for some years to gain settlement
here and the children have been left in the care of
another relative or friend in the country of origin.
Parents are expected to be able to produce not only
evidence of regular financial remittances but exchan-
ges of letters indicating a strong emotional bond and
a parental interest in decisions affecting the child's
life. Obviously, not everyone keeps a comprehensive
collection of suitable letters to and from their children and their temporary guardians and one wonders
whether many British parents with children in boarding
schools could produce the sort of evidence often dem-
anded by entry clearance officers in Ghana or India.
    Current Home Office policy is normally to accept
that children under 12 seeking to join a single parent

in the UK should qualify as those whose "exclusion is undesirable", though evidence of support and accommodation and suitable arrangements for the care of the child have to be shown. This policy, stated only in unpublished letters rather than in the official rules shows how the exclusion of children is normally to be considered desirable.

Once children reach 18, they lose their eligibility to come, although special provision is made for unmarried and fully financially dependent daughters between 18 and 21, if they formed part of the family unit overseas and have no other close relatives in their own country to turn to. Daughters are thus seen as more dependent than sons and the assumption is that in the UK they will remain at home, or will marry and become dependent on their husbands, rather than seek work in their own right. It is almost impossible to bring adopted children here.

Parents and grandparents will only be admitted for settlement if the maintenance and accommodation requirements are fulfilled, if they are wholly or mainly dependent on the sponsor here and have no close relatives in their own country to turn to. They must also be 65 or over, although widowed (but not separated, or unmarried) mothers who are younger may be admitted - again, it is assumed that women will not seek to work in circumstances where men would. Other, more distant relatives like brothers, sisters, uncles and aunts may only be allowed to come if they are living alone in the most exceptional compassionate circumstances, including having a standard of living substantially below that of their country of origin. As they also have to be mainly financially dependent on the sponsor here, this is virtually impossible. The rule is also interpreted restrictively; a woman who had been subjected to serious and frequent violence from her husband in Sri Lanka and escaped to join her parents and eight siblings settled here was told that her circumstances were not "exceptional" enough and that she had "chosen" to become dependent on her family in the UK so did not qualify to stay.

Even where families can satisfy the strict requirements of the rules and have a respectable chain of legitimate marriages and births, it may be very difficult to prove this to the satisfaction of the immigration authorities. Not every country in the world has a St. Catherine's House where all births and marriages can be traced. Relationships may have been formed by customary ceremonies of which no records are kept. Even where appropriate documents are produced, immigration officials will frequently allege that they

are not genuine and that family members are not therefore "related as claimed".

In the notorious case of Anwar Ditta, a British
woman with three children born in Pakistan had to
fight for 5 years to establish that she and her husband were their parents. The Home Office only finally
gave in after a television company had spent thousands
of pounds on an exhaustive investigation, including
expensive and complicated blood tests, proving as
conclusively as is possible that the children were indeed related as claimed. Needless to say, not all
families have Anwar's tenacity and few have the financial backing to establish their family bonds in this
way.

The immigration rules and practice are to be contrasted with the rules governing EEC nationals, which
are controlled by EEC law. All EEC citizens (not including Greeks until 1988) have the right to come to
the UK to take or seek work or set up in business or
self-employment. The family members entitled to come
to settle in the UK with them are much more loosely
defined than under British immigration law. They
include the spouse of either sex, all children under
21, older children and any grandchildren who are dependent, and dependent parents, grandparents and great-
grandparents. EEC law does not discriminate on the
basis of sex and there are no requirements that eligible relatives have no-one to turn to in their own
country. Nor do EEC citizens have to prove that they
can maintain and accommodate their family without help
from the state. The emphasis of EEC law is on the
right of a family to live together where it chooses
rather than the British obsession of limiting entry.

This means that citizens of other EEC countries
have much more chance of being united with their families in the UK than do British women. For example,
an Italian woman living and working in London has a
right to be joined by her 19 year old son, her married
but dependent daughter aged 30 and her two illegitimate children, whatever their citizenship and however
many other family members remain in Italy. A British
woman is not entitled to bring any of these relatives
to live with her.

MARRIAGE AND ASSUMPTIONS

The immigration rules relating to the admission of
husbands and fiances of women living here show most
clearly how women have no independent rights in immigration law and practice. Women are seen in this con-

text entirely as agents for male settlement here, the
settlement of those black men who must be kept out of
the country at all costs, and a woman's right to live
where she chooses with the husband she chooses is unimportant. As other areas of the immigration rules
have become still more restrictive, marriage has become almost the only way in which young men may still
be able to come to this country and this has made governments regard all husbands and fiances with suspicion.

Before January 1969, the husband or wife of a
man or woman settled here would be allowed to stay
here with her/him. On 30 January 1969, the Home
Secretary, Mr James Callaghan, announced that this
"concession" was being withdrawn from husbands and
fiances from abroad, because the numbers of Commonwealth citizens admitted for marriage to women resident in the UK "have risen sharply in the last year or
so and are now on such a scale that it seems that
marriage is being used by many young men of working
age as a means of entering, working and settling in
this country." He was supported by his junior minister responsible for immigration, Mr Merlyn Rees, who
said that "this rests on the idea that immigrants
should live in the man's country, not the woman's."

This rule, which did not permit the husband of
any woman living here to come to join her, was operated
by the next Conservative government but there was opposition to its injustice and the hardship it caused.
When Labour was returned to power there was an initial
refusal to change the rules again, Mr Roy Jenkins being afraid this would result in "a substantial and new
wave of male immigration, particularly from the Indian
subcontinent." However, on 27 June 1974, new Rules
were announced, allowing the husbands and wives of
people settled here to settle with them. Mr Alex Lyon
the Home Office Minister warned against the dangers of
any evidence of small numbers of marriages of conven-
ience being used as a pretext for introducing discrimination into the rules again. Yet on 22 March 1977
they were amended to give all husbands (but not wives)
a one-year probationary period here before being granted settlement. This gave the Home Office the pre-·
text for added surveillance of immigrants' marriages
and for intrusive questioning of couples about their
marriage. Allegations about "abuse" of the "concess-
ions" were made but never substantiated; from 1977 to
1979 less than 3% of husbands were refused permission
to settle after their first year, which included men
whose genuine marriages had broken down.

The new Conservative manifesto in 1979 stated,

"We shall end the concession introduced by the Labour government in 1974 to husbands and male fiances" but this was never seriously entertained as a possibility. The Conservatives' first concrete proposals exempted women born in the UK from the ban; this was shortly extended to women UK citizens who had a parent born in the UK. Mr William Whitelaw stated "We cannot go further and extend the provision for all women who are citizens of the UK and Colonies; this would mean leaving the door open to further primary immigration because of the facility of registering minor children as citizens under our nationality law", thus making the racist intentions of the change still more explicit. New provisions, stipulating that the marriage should not be entered into primarily to obtain admission to the UK and that the partners to a proposed marriage had met, were introduced specifically to be used against people from the Indian subcontinent. In the debate on the rules, Mr Timothy Raison, the Minister responsible for immigration, stated,"...we know perfectly well that sex equality does not exist under our nationality and immigration laws... there is a general aim simply of reducing numbers." This frank statement shows no concern for the women and couples whose lives have been distorted or destroyed by the racist policies of successive British governments.

After the 1979 rules came into force, they were challenged and contested in many ways, both by individuals fighting for their own lives and through legal channels, by women affected complaining to the European Commission of Human Rights that their rights under Articles 8 and 12 (the right to respect for private and family life and the right to marry and found a family) and Article 2 (against sex and race discrimination) had been breached as well as Article 3 (which protects individuals against inhuman and degrading treatment). In a preliminary hearing in May 1982, the Commission decided that the first three cases were admissible, and others would be considered on the same principles; there was thus a prima facie case that the British government's rules were unlawful.

Because of this and other pressure, new rules came into force at the beginning of 1983, at the same time as the British Nationality Act 1981. The government may have hoped that these would let them off the hook in Europe, but the Commission has not accepted this and a hearing before the European Court is expected in autumn 1984.

The Immigration Rules in force at present state that a husband or fiance may be allowed to come to or to stay in the UK if his wife or fiancee is a British

120

citizen, if the couple have met, if they intend to
live together permanently as husband and wife, if the
marriage was not entered into primarily for the man's
settlement in the UK, if the man has not remained illegally in the UK before the marriage and no decision
has been made to deport him and, if he is a fiance,
there are adequate arrangements for his support and
accommodation here before the marriage. There are
thus wide areas in which the individual judgment or
prejudices of an immigration officer, or an entry
clearance officer at a British post abroad can be used
to keep a couple apart.

The judgment of immigration officials is partly
dictated to them in secret, unpublished Instructions
to Immigration Officers which are written by the Home
Office and distributed throughout the world. Although
the present Home Office Minister, Mr. David Wadding-
ton, has stated that he is waiting for guidance from
the immigration appeals authorities to know how exactly the clause about the "primary purpose" of settlement should be interpreted, a leaked copy of the instructions of September 1983 shows that when a man is
interviewed in the Indian subcontinent it is relevant
whether he has already found employment in the UK,
whether he has already applied to come here for any
other reason in the past, or whether he has ever been
refused entry at a port; hypothetical questions such
as,"if your family had asked you to marry a local
girl, would you have done so?" should also be asked,
in the hope that a man may say something that could
be interpreted to mean that the primary purpose of the
marriage was to gain settlement in the UK. Exactly
the same considerations are said to be used for husbands - the fact that a relationship has existed for
some time and the binding contract of marriage has
taken place is not supposed to make any difference.

The rules are still sex discriminatory; only a
British woman has any claim for her husband or fiance
to join her, whereas a man of any nationality who is
settled in the UK may bring his wife here and she also
is not subject to a year's probationary period. A
man who is a student here or on a work permit here may
have his wife with him for the same length of time as
he is permitted to stay; there is no corresponding
provision for women. A woman who has been here temporarily because of her husband's status has no right
to remain if he leaves or if the marriage breaks up,
if she has not been granted settlement and the dangers
that she may face from an estranged husband in another
country are not normally considered by the Home
Office.

Case 1. In practice, the operation of these rules can
lead to enormous suffering. Mrs C., one of the three
first complainants to the European Commission, married
her husband in 1980 in the Philippines but she has
never yet been able to live with him, apart from two
short holidays there; she cannot return there to live
because her nursing qualification is not recognised
there and her husband has been continually refused
entry here until her application for naturalisation
was finally granted in April 1984.

Case 2. Kalsoom and Rustam were married in early
1980, when Rustam was here as a visitor; Kalsoom and
her family had lived here since 1969. Rustam was refused permission to stay here with his wife; Kalsoom's
application for naturalisation, made even before she
met Rustam, was refused on the grounds that her husband was not settled here and therefore she might not
intend to continue living in the UK if her husband
were not permitted to remain. They have been fighting
ever since then for Rustam's right to stay with his
family (they now have two British-born babies) but the
Home Office is adamant in attempting to deport him.
Kalsoom has applied again for British citizenship and
it is no longer Home Office policy automatically to
refuse an application made by a person whose spouse is
not settled here - but the application is still discretionary and there can be no guarantee that it will
succeed, or if it did, that Rustam would then be permitted to remain.

Case 3. Margaret married in 1982; she had custody of
her seven year old son from her previous marriage,
which had ended because of her husband's violence towards her. She did not know that her second husband
had remained in the UK without permission and he had
never dared to tell her. After their marriage he
applied to the Home Office for permission to stay here
which was refused, because he had overstayed his original permission to remain. In spite of the dangers
that would face Margaret and her son in returning to
Ghana, where she is sure that her first husband would
kidnap their son, and the birth of a daughter from her
second marriage, the Home Office still wants to deport
Yaw and has offered to pay Margaret's and the children's fare if they accompany him.

These are just a few examples of the human suffering

that is caused every day by the application of the
Immigration Rules in order to cut down on the numbers
of men settling here without regard to the suffering
caused to them and their families and the basic injustice of the law.

INTERNAL CONTROLS

Since the 1971 Immigration Act there has been increasing emphasis on internal immigration controls. Some
of these are a formal part of the administration of
immigration; they include the requirement for a husband from abroad to apply to lift conditions on his
stay after living with his wife here for a year. The
arrangements for tracing illegal entrants and over-
stayers are also part of this system of internal controls.
      But the administration of internal immigration
controls is no longer confined to individuals with
specific immigration control functions such as officers of the Immigration Service and the police. These
controls are increasingly coming to be performed by
those who administer public services. Thus the instructions issued by the General Register Office to deputy registrars sets out that when either party to a
proposed marriage comes from abroad they must request
proof of nationality and identity. Passports are
regarded as the best proof. The instructions state
that where deputy registrars "have good reason to
believe that a marriage is being contracted solely for
the purpose of avoiding the statutory controls applying to aliens or Commonwealth citizens or solely for
the purpose of acquiring citizenship of the UK and
Colonies they should notify this office."
      Entitlement to public benefits may depend on imm-
igration status or "ordinary residence" and the latter
requirement is often interpreted in a sexist way. A
woman may be considered "ordinarily resident" where
her husband lives. Thus one Asian woman who had been
brought up in Britain and all of whose family is here
was charged for National Health Service treatment.
Her husband was working in India and she had spent the
previous 11 months there with him so she was told
that she was not considered "ordinarily resident" here.
      Benefit officers at local DHSS offices are in-
structed to examine passports of "persons who appear
to have come from abroad" and to refer to the Home
Office, via the DHSS, those who appear to be in breach
of immigration conditions. Women married to men whose
immigration status is irregular may not claim benefits

to which they are entitled, because their husband has
no right to benefit. Women often bear the responsibility for approaching statutory agencies for family
support. It is upon them that the increased burdens
of internal controls and status checks frequently
fall. Even women who are entitled to state support
may be frightened off by these measures.

THE 1981 CHANGES

With the changes introduced by the British Nationality
Act 1981, the position of women in UK nationality and
immigration law was worsened.
      Women now have the worst of both worlds. The
special rights given to women as the dependants of
men - the automatic right to citizenship and to live
in Britain previously given to wives of citizens and
which husbands did not share - have been taken away,
leaving women no better off than men. But (with one
exception) the British Nationality Act only abolished
discrimination that benefited women. Women have been
left with seriously disadvantaged status in the immigration laws and rules. The basis of that disadvantage, as of the extra rights which have now been abolished, is the presumption that women are the appendages of men.
      Nationality laws have an historic quality - they
define the nation and give a sense of identity to its
members. While Britain's immigration laws and rules
are changed from year to year, the last big development in nationality law prior to the 1981 Act had
been a generation before in 1948. The 1981 Act made
fundamental changes and will inevitably have a long-term
constitutional impact. This was duly employed by the
British government to deflect by sleight of hand the
criticism that Britain had for nearly 20 years been in
breach of international law by refusing to admit its
own citizens - hey presto, the labels have been changed, and yesterday's black citizen deprived of immigration rights is today no longer even called a citizen
(South Africa has a similar policy, creating "home-
lands" for those it does not want). Thus through the
1981 Act Britain's law-makers not only perpetuated
past discrimination but tried to legitimise it, by enshrining it in a law that simultaneously carries constitutional weight and respectability and is a classic
of indirect discrimination.
      Although the British Nationality Act 1981 does
not contain many provisions which expressly discriminate on grounds of race and sex, it is built on disc-

riminatory foundations. In the pre-1981 period racist and sexist criteria had been employed to restrict the acquisition of citizenship of the UK and Colonies, and immigration laws had used racist and sexist criteria to define those citizens of the UK and Colonies (CUKCs) who were free of immigration control. Those excluded possessed citizenship that was second class in nature, although not yet in name. The change of name had to wait for the 1981 Act, which limited the acquisition of the new British citizenship, resplendent with first class immigration status, to those persons who had both acquired citizenship under previous discriminatory nationality legislation and been kept free of immigration control by previous discriminatory immigration laws. To discover whether you became a British citizen on 1 January 1983 you have to refer to S.2 of the Immigration Act 1971, the high point of discrimination based on ancestral connections with Britain through the legitimate male line. So, by dint of importing from previous discriminatory laws the central formula for determining who is to be a British citizen, the 1981 Act dispenses with the obligation to spell out the racism and sexism that underlies its structure.

Having excluded millions of CUKCs from acquisition of British citizenship on commencement, the 1981 Act goes on to restrict the numbers who can acquire it in future. For the first time, children born in Britain are being excluded from the club of British citizenship. To be a citizen a child born in the UK after 1 January 1983 must have at least one parent who is a British citizen or who is settled in the UK at the time of its birth. A parent for this purpose includes all mothers, but a father only if married to the child's mother. So, for example, if a Nigerian citizen woman with a time limit on her stay becomes pregnant by a British citizen and has the child in Britain without being married to the father or becoming settled or a citizen herself her child will not be a British citizen; Nigerian law will determine whether the child is a Nigerian citizen; otherwise the child may well be stateless. Children now being born in Britain without British citizenship are subject to immigration control. Those who do get citizenship need far more documents to prove it - a birth certificate alone for 1983 or later is no longer enough.

The justification put forward by the government for restricting access to the new citizenship was the need to cut off sources of future immigration. When it came to justification for the removal of rights from women, the government produced the rhetoric of

125

sex equality. It must be conceded that the Act did eliminate the inequality that has prevented women from transmitting citizenship to children born abroad. Previously women had been the passive vehicle for the transmission of their husband's citizenship to legitimate children born outside Britain. Now such children, legitimate or not, obtain the mother's British citizenship. But otherwise "sex equality" was achieved in the British Nationality Act 1981 by reducing the rights of women. Women's absolute rights were taken away. Then women were permitted to share with men something that is not even a right: the opportunity to apply for naturalisation, which can always be refused. This is really a process of levelling down.

On 1 January 1983 women lost two important and absolute rights. Under previous law a woman had acquired these rights the moment she married a citizen, and whether or not she had ever been to the UK. The loss of entitlement to citizenship for any woman married to a CUKC, Citizen of the United Kingdom and Colonies, received much publicity, and is dealt with below.

Less publicised was the fact that whereas women Commonwealth citizens formerly obtained the absolute right of abode in Britain through having married a man possessing this right, marriages taking place after 1 January 1983 would no longer produce this effect. The British Nationality Act amended the 1971 Immigration Act to prevent further women becoming patrial (the old term for the right of abode) through marriage to a patrial. No longer will marriage free a woman from immigration control - the Home Office has gained the right to choose whether she will be allowed to come to or stay in Britain.

No woman who had acquired patriality through marriage prior to 1 Janaury 1983 lost it as a result of the 1981 Act. But many women who possessed the absolute right to citizenship prior to the 1 January 1983 lost it on that date when the 1981 Act came into force, and others have lost it since. This is because through either widowhood or divorce they are no longer married to their citizen husbands. Those women who have hung on to the absolute right because they have stayed married will lose it on 1 January 1988 if they have failed to apply for citizenship during the intervening five years. This ending of an absolute right for wives is similar in many ways to the British Nationality Act's phasing out over five years of the absolute rights to citizenship of Commonwealth citizens settled in Britain prior to 1973. These changes are an example of a major purpose of the British Nationality Act - the erosion of absolute rights for immigrants and

their children, and a corresponding increase in the
power of the state to decide who shall be allowed to
live in Britain.
    The changes to the right of a woman to obtain
citizenship through marriage to a citizen deserve
looking at in more detail. Prior to 1 January 1983
any woman who had at any time been married to a citiz-
en had the absolute right to become a CUKC. This
process was known as registration. The right included
widows and divorcees. The woman did not have to be
resident or settled in the UK. In fact, she might
never have set foot in Britain. Once registered as a
citizen in the UK the woman became patrial - entitled
to the right of abode in Britain.
    From 1 January 1983 the British Nationality Act
abolished this absolute right to citizenship. Wives
married before the new law's commencement date of
1 January 1983 can still exercise this right provided
they apply before 1 January 1983 and are still married
at the date of application. Widows and divorcees lost
existing rights to citizenship based on the marriage.
Instead they were allowed 5 years in which to apply
for registration as citizens at the discretion of the
Home Secretary (ie it can be refused). So for widows
and divorcees an absolute entitlement has become a
claim that can be refused with no reasons given. If
no longer attached to a male British citizen a woman
is denied the rights she possessed until widowed by
accident or illness or divorced perhaps because of his
misconduct. Thus are presumptions of dependence preserved, for a transitional period, but the emphasis is
now on deriving benefit from present rather than past
connections with husbands. Women who marry a British
citizen after 1 January 1983 no longer get any absolute right to citizenship by virtue of the marriage.
Instead, spouses of both sexes, provided they are still
married, are enabled to apply for naturalisation after
3 years'residence rather than the 5 years laid down
for standard naturalisation. For the first time husbands get a claim to citizenship based on marriage.
    How much have husbands really gained?. Admittedly
spouses can apply sooner and pay lower, although still
exorbitant, fees than ordinary naturalisation applicants (currently £55 rather than £160). But naturalisation has always been a discretionary process and can
be refused. And with naturalisation there is the
critical requirement that the applicant is settled in
the UK at the date of application. This rules out
husbands in particular, because Home Office rules and
practice make it so difficult for them to settle in
the UK. With the retention of the settlement hurdle

for husbands and the imposition of that requirement
for the first time on wives, husbands have gained very
little of significance, while wives have lost an absolute right. An important route to security in Britain for women has been closed off.

This brief summary of some of the most sex discriminatory aspects of the immigration and nationality
law has shown how women have only recently been affected by the changes in climate of opinion about the
roles of the sexes. In immigration law, the control
of entry of black people has been seen as the priority
and the rights of women have been negated and ignored
because of the overriding aim of excluding black men.
Women are not seen as individuals in their own right
even now but always in relation to men, always as dependants - as wives, as daughters and as sisters.

NOTES

(1)   Rose E.J.B. (1969) Colour and Citizenship
      Oxford Ch. 2 pp. 16-23
(2)   Patrilocal residence is not a reflection of
      patterns of residence in modern western culture
      See E. Chinoy (1967) Society p. 145
(3)   See A. Sachs and J. Hoff-Wilson Sexism and the
      Law 1978 Martin Robertson London
(4)   Women have been treated as a male appendage
      throughout the law for further discussion on
      this see K.O'Donovan "The Male Appendage" in
      S. Burman (ed.) Fit Work for Women 1979
      Croom Helm

FURTHER READING

Chapeltown Citizens Advice Bureau Tribunal Assistance
      Unit and Chapeltown Law Centre Immigrants and the
      Welfare State
Dummett, A. 1976 Citizenship and Nationality Runny-
      mede Trust
Dummett, A. 1976 "Citizenship and Nationality" Runny-
      mede Trust
Evans, J.M. 1984 Immigration Law (2nd ed.) Sweet and
      Maxwell
MacDonald I.A. (1972) "The New Immigration Law"
      Butterworths
Rees, T. 1982 "Immigration Policies in the UK" pp. 75-
      97 in C. Husband (ed.) "'Race' in Britain"
      Hutchinson University Library

Chapter Seven

GENDER 'JUSTICE'? DEFENDING DEFENDANTS AND MITIGATING
SENTENCE

Susan Edwards

This discussion paper looks forward to new dev-
elopments and initiatives within reasearch and theorising on women and crime focusing on two hitherto relatively neglected areas, defences to crime and mitigation. Whilst much of the emphasis up till now has
been on the lenient or severe treatment of women
throughout the criminal justice system it is time for
taking new directions and exploring new interfaces.
In addressing the question of defences to homicide the
historical male formulation of what constitutes a defence and the criticism that a woman's formulation of a
defence might be excluded are factors examined. In
discussing mitigation the issue is rather more with
the extent to which a particular pattern of gender
role, motherhood, should influence sentencing decisions, together with concern that what passes as good
mothering will inevitably be based on judicial conceptions of appropriate motherhood and gender role.
      Decisions made within the 'justice' process are
based on tacit understandings relating to background
expectancies of crimes, probable offenders and possible or likely locations. Such expectations function
to confirm or reject the possibility of what we see.
Such that, the belief that people designated mentally
ill must indeed be so and all antecedent behaviour is
an indicator of this isolated judgmental decision,
left 'K's' friends as Dorothy Smith observed in no
dispute over the madness of her actions in their ret-
rospective construction of her behaviour. (1) Again,
it was just such tacit understandings about drug use
and users which as Jock Young found led police in
Notting Hill, in their isolation, to become suspicious
of and subsequently apprehend the stereotypical long
haired and bizarrely dressed hippy youth, (2) and for
Swigert and Farrell (1977), the criminal stereotype in
cases of homicide emerges as the "normal primitive".

Gender 'Justice'? Defending Defendants and Mitigating
Sentence

Within the criminal justice process detection depends
largely on characterisations of likely suspects wherein the evidence for suspicion in the initial stages
and during the prosecutorial, is negotiated to fit the
stereotype (Phillips and De Fleur 1982). Defendants
arraigned on charges of shop theft are described in
guise and pose as 'shifty and furtive', an indicator
of original suspicion and an indice of probable guilt.
Instances such as these may cause little concern understood as important indicators in the detection of
crime. It is only when characterisations of likely
suspects or defendants lead to an unfair disadvantage
as in aspects of legal defence and mitigation that
there is cause for concern. Yet it is this ready
reliance on background expectancies of offenders and
victims which leads police to suspect rape complainants
of consent and victims of violence in the domestic
situation of provocation or complicity.
    Studies of women's experience of the criminal
justice process examining the impact of gender ascriptions meets with the problems already existent from
within the criminological forum as well as theoretical
difficulties within feminism itself. Within criminology indeed as the very use of the term suggests the
emphasis has been on the individual and on theories of
crime causation. The problem with this perspective is
succinctly expressed:

> The fact that an act is considered to be a crime
> focuses attention on the offender as the cause
> almost to the exclusion of other elements in the
> crime situation - the opportunities, the physical
> environment, the victim or, indeed, the law its-
> elf. The excessive emphasis in the past upon the
> offender has not paid off and if we are to
> deal realistically with crime, it is necessary to
> study less romantic and dramatic elements - to
> emphasise things and situations in relation to
> decisions. (3)

By contrast, what we might loosely describe as the
socio-legal approach which rather than exclusively
focusing on the problems of offenders, considers their
treatment in and experience of the criminal justice
process from an interactionist perspective owes much
to Jeffrey (1959), who suggested that the definition
of crime, be it legal or sociological, must be based
on a study of law and society rather than on the individual offender. (4)
    Whilst the positivist 'criminological' approach
with its often highly theoretical abstractions and the

Gender 'Justice'? Defending Defendants and Mitigating
Sentence

interactionist approach which examines how people
experience the criminal justice system have developed
alongside one another neither have addressed, even less
marginalised, the question of women offenders or their
experience in the criminal justice process. Hutter
and Williams cognisant of this omission write:

> While mainstream criminology has been concerned
> with the pathology of criminals, little until
> recently, has been available on the pathology of
> the penal institutions and agencies of control.
> as a result we know even less about the treat-
> ment of female criminals within the penal system
> and the effects of taken for granted assumptions
> about female criminality which inform the Home
> Office policy makers. (5)

The emphasis on criminal justice as a consequential
process has been inspired by the work of Wilkins
(1964), Sudnow (1965), Skolnick (1966), Box (1971),
Bottomley (1973), (1979), and Newman (1975).

> The decision-making, functional approach has the
> advantage of cutting through the provincialism
> that has characterised criminal justice planning
> and programming... Decisions made by the police,
> such as whether or not to invoke the criminal
> process, and if so, how and how vigorously   are
> not merely in-house concerns. What the police
> do, or do not do, has a pervasive effect across
> the system, as do decisions made in other agenc-
> ies and offices. This whole approach demonstrat-
> es that the criminal justice system is a system
> not because of bureaucratic structure, for the
> agencies of crime control are relatively indep-
> endent, but rather because of the functional
> relationships among the enforcement efforts of
> the police, the prosecutory decisions of states'
> attorneys, the adjudicatory and sentencing funct-
> ions of trial judges, and the post conviction
> treatment of offenders in correctional agencies.
> (6)

   To the extent that the sentencing of criminal
defendants has become the concern of the more recent
research relating to women and crime, analyses have
too often concentrated on the disparities in sentencing patterns of men and women rather than on a more
detailed examination of the conditions, imperatives,
and mechanisms which give rise to this difference.
This has led to identification of an apparent lenient

treatment of women defendants as against men and to
the theorising for this apparent leniency. (See Pollak, 1950, Smith 1962, Giallombardo 1966, McClean and
Wood 1969, Devlin 1970, Simon 1975, Anderson 1976,
Chesney Lind 1977). In response to this there has
been a corresponding rejection of this claim arguing
on the contrary that women receive more severe treatment, sentencing and punishment by the courts and in
the criminal justice system. (Walker 1965, Foley and
Rasche 1976, Armstrong 1977, Hancock 1980, Klein and
Kress 1981). Hancock (1980) concludes that women are
not treated more leniently, on the contrary, 'Females
are more likely than males to be presented to court
on protection applications for juvenile 'status' offences, but are more likely than males, whose delinquency is defined predominantly in legalistic terms, to
receive a supervisory disposition.' (p.11).
Whilst studies have focused on leniency/severity,
issues in the sentencing, possibly because this stage
of the criminal justice system is more readily visible,
recently there has been an increasing focus on specific pre-trial investigatory and trial stages. The central guiding imperative in these studies has been with
a discovery of the particular factors which act on,
thereby influencing, the interpretation of rules and
procedures in respect of discretionary decisions influencing the recording of crime in respect of arrest,
bail, representation, plea and mitigation. In the
work of Radelet (1980), Smith and Visher (1981 : 169),
Visher (1983), the focus of the research has been on
pre-trial arrest decisions, in which Visher's research
in particular indicated that a lenient or harsh treatment by law enforcement agencies at any stage of the
process depended on the degree to which behaviour was
in accordance or at variance with the female role concluding:

> Chivalrous treatment at the stage of arrest dep-
> ends upon a larger set of gender expectations
> that exist between men and women in encounters
> with police officers, those female suspects who
> violate typical middle-class standards of tradit-
> ional female characteristics and behaviour (ie
> white, older and submissive) are not afforded any
> chivalrous treatment in deciding arrest decis-
> ions. pp. 22-23

Swigert and Farrell (1977 : 17), explained: the proc-
essual consequences:

> Stereotypes not only shape public attitudes and

behaviour towards deviants, but guide the very
choice of individuals who are to be so defined
and processed.

In the work of Swigert and Farrell (1977) and Nagel
(1981)are provided some important insights on the factors contributing to the exercise of discretion in bail
decisions. Similarly, Simon and Charma (1978), Bern-
stein, Cardascia and Ross (1979), found that the decision to prosecute was also effected by factors relating to gender congruency.
The process of mitigation in particular frequently
reflects gender role considerations such that the work
ethic is considered central to the male defendant's
gender role and thus the fact that the defendant is
employed or has a job to go to is invoked in mitigation of sentence. Women, on the other hand, are more
likely to be processed as 'sick', as mentally ill in
a non-clinical sense. Reports are more frequently
requested on social background, standards of maternal
care and the ability to cope with the domestic situation, and it is this domiciliary ability which is so
frequently put forward in mitigation of a sentence and
considered in appeal hearings. Eaton (1983), explores
the role of the family in both male and female mitigation, rather then the specific relation of men and
women in their respective roles in relation to family
responsibility, arguing that mitigating circumstances
reflect the defendant's relationship with or to the
social world. Should this relationship follow an accepted pattern it will be used to show that the defendant it not really criminal since the social identity
in question is basically conformist, criminal activity
presented as a temporary aberration.
Farrington and Morris's (1983) research revealed
that while sex per se is not of direct significance
in sentencing, magistrates gave weight to different
factors in the sentencing of males and females. The
major predictor in sentencing women was current problems, previous convictions, involvement of other offenders, number of theft offences, mental status, family
background. Pat Carlen (1983) in her work on women's
imprisonment makes the point that appropriate gender
role, wifehood and domesticity are factors likely to
affect sentencing decisions. As one magistrate expressed it, 'Other things being equal, the appropriate
sentence should indicate the appropriate measure of
social disfavour. Then you add on and take off marks
for particular social circumstances - a few marks for
having children, a few marks off if you haven't any.'
(p. 66) Though as Carlen observed, sheriffs tended to

Gender 'Justice'? Defending Defendants and Mitigating
Sentence

hold the view, 'If she is a good mother, we do not
want to take her away. If she is not a good mother,
it does not really matter.' (p. 67) Whilst studies
of women in prison tend to confirm that conformity to
gender role and patterns of domesticity is still required, such compliance is often regarded as a sign of
improvement and adjustment resulting in points for
remission (see Rowett and Vaughan 1981).

On this point researchers are unanimous, that
differences in treatment arise in relation to the
character of the crime, and the degree to which the defendant's behaviour is at variance with the female role
(Phillips and De Fleur (1982). Nagel (1981 : 144),
pointed out that it is not being female per se that
may result in a particular judicial outcome, but concluded that 'Females whose offence is more consistent
with sex role expectations seem to experience less
harsh outcomes than females whose offence is less
traditional.' As Phillips and De Fleur (1982 : 435),
write, 'if a woman is believed to have deviated from
femaleness in general (ie, she has in some fashion
stepped outside gender role expectancies, or she may
be attributed masculine characteristics presumably
necessary for criminality), she may be more likely to
be believed capable of criminal activity and deserving
a harsh treatment.'

Recently then, it can be observed that analyses
of women's treatment within the criminal justice system
have moved right away from the over-simplistic theorisation of leniency and severity in sentencing decisions to examine the conditions and the arrangement by
which women come to receive a harsher or more lenient
consideration, a special consideration as infanticide,
or indeed no consideration at all. At each successive
stage, this attempt to structurally situate the conditions which give rise to the various socio-legal response diverts attention away from amorphous theorising
about men or women per se, concentrating instead more
closely and more critically at:

    i)   the crime that has been committed and its
           congruousness with notions of typical female
           criminality,
    ii)   the degree to which the criminal law itself
           invites the defendant to neutralise her
           normative attachment to it,
    iii) the motives rendered and the motives avail-
           able for excusing or justifying the behav-
           iour in question in relation to the crime
           committed and,
    iv)   the degree to which she conforms to or dev-

134

iates from appropriate gender roles in everyday
life.

It is these considerations taken together which affect
the outcome of the case in question influencing the
overall assessment of criminal responsibility, culpability in the determination of guilt and the final
assessment of punishment. Thus sympathetic or lenient
treatment only takes place within a framework of what
judges see as normal and responsible. (Pattullo 1983 :
9)

TYPICAL CRIMES: TYPICAL WOMEN

It has already been suggested that whether as suspects, defendants or offenders, women are dealt with
in part in accordance with the degree to which their
behaviour deviates from what is expected of them in
their appropriate gender role. Pearson, (1976) and
Worrall, (1981), in their study of women in magistrates' courts explain that the fact that women are regarded as 'out of place' in the criminal justice system affects the way in which they negotiate the various escape routes. 'This fundamental incongruity may
be seen to advantage women, but it serves in fact, to
define the parameters of negotiation in a restrictive
fashion and causes breaches of those parameters to be
severely penalised',(Worrall 1981). (8) Thus women
find themselves 'on trial' in more ways than one, since imputations of mens rea, culpability, and responsibility may like mitigation and sentencing be influenced by the degree to which the defendant is a good
wife, mother and homemaker: honest, decent and moral
and above all feminine. From the decision to grant
bail, to prosecute, to charge and ultimately to sentence, the degree to which the defendant's gender behaviour is considered appropriate is an influential
factor. Thus the kind of justice received depends
very much on notions of what is 'normal' and 'abnormal' female behaviour and what is the typical 'normal'
and 'abnormal' female offender. Given the way in
which characterisations work one can envisage that in
the typical crimes of shoplifting, petty fraud, DHSS
fraud and forgery and where the defendant conforms to
the appropriate domestic stereotype of good wife and
good mother, then the criminal justice system tends
to treat her sympathetically and leniently especially
if she is seen to commit crime in order to provide for
the family. Where the defendant engages in a typical
crime and is not conforming to the generally accept-

able stereotypes of mother and domestic homemaker, the prostitute is a good example of this instance, then there is the tendency for the courts to emphasise re-socialisation often in the form of probation super-vision. Often in this instance, prostitutes who are also mothers work the streets in order to provide for the family. In this instance, her sexually unconvent-ional lifestyle is not excused and indeed the courts' response may be of two kinds; either to resocialise or in fact to treat her severely. Pattullo (1983 : 9) cites the case of one young mother who felt she had no option to return to shoplifting and prostitution to support her child, suffered the harshest punishment - she lost the custody of the child. Where the defend-ant commits an untypical crime and therefore does not conform to the image of typical female criminality the courts may treat her harshly. In cases of robbery, burglary and crimes of violence, especially violence outside the realms of a family or neighbour 'tiff' such as a violent assault in a pub, with a glass or knife, the defendant is treated harshly, regarded as a bad and wicked person. Where the defendant neither conforms to conventional crime nor conforms to convent-ional images of female domesticity and home centred-ness, then she is frequently regarded as dangerous, and if the crime is one of violence, particularly if against her own children, - a monster - in need of custody and treatment. Where women neglect their child-ren and are cruel to their offspring or take their lives, the law regards them as always 'sick' and to varying degrees as bad though this imputation is always dep-endent on the nature of the cruelty inflicted, whether it appears as a deliberate and wilful act - commission, or whether it appears as neglect, - ommission. In law acts of commission and omission may be defined as 'wilful neglect' as in Breeze, where the defendants did nothing wilful to the child - neither fed nor changed it and in consequence the child died of hypoth-ermia associated with malnutrition. (9)

    And so in cases where the mother is a good moth-er, where she keeps the family together, her criminal intent and responsibility becomes somewhat lessened in the eyes of the court and good mothering becomes a positive reason for treating her with leniency. Where the defendant has committed an untypical crime and where there is evidence of an untypical lifestyle, then this behaviour becomes seen in negative terms and goes to reaffirm the judgment that she is 'sick' and bad. Such that in the case of a woman who was convic-ted of cruelty to a child under sixteen and sentenced to two years' imprisonment, the fact that the defendant

was pursuing a degree course was taken as a further
manifestation of the kind of selfish woman she was.
The belief clearly held was that her wilful deviation
from home making and domesticity had in some way contributed to the crime. (Edwards 1984 : 177). Thus
broadly, women who have committed certain crimes yet
conform to the female stereotype, have more often than
not been treated sympathetically and with greater leniency. Victims and complainants who have appeared as
true victims conforming to appropriate female gender
and sexual roles have been similarly granted protection of the law.

Defences within the criminal law are too based
and predicated on versions of typical persons and
typical situations. In this case the defence to homicide is formulated on a model of the reasonable man,
in consequence such defences define women as sick, as
in infanticide predicated on puerperal pyschosis, or
else write them right out as in the defence of provocation.

In the precise context of the criminal law accounts for action rendered by defendants are not merely
as Henry (1976) asserts,'self defensive rationalisations', nor as Sykes and Matza (1957) originally proposed, 'techniques of neutralisation'. Instead the
structure of the criminal law paradoxically invites
the individual to neutralise his normative attachment
to it (1964 : 61). This invitation however, is not
held out at all. Indeed we frequently encounter a
discrepancy (10) between everyday versions of motiv-
ation for crime commission and the legal versions that
is the legal invitation available to the defendant.
Such as I have already indicated, persons may be convicted in law of 'wilful neglect' though their behaviour amounted to nothing deliberate or wilful, in the
everyday sense of the word. Similarly, in cases where
a mother has killed her newly born chld, evidence of
puerperal psychosis is necessary to sustain a charge
of infanticide, though the defendant's account of her
action may be more closely related to depression, economic circumstance, rather than to any physiological
prerequisites. In some instances the discrepancy
between everyday versions and legal invitations has
evolved along sex-gender lines. In the case of homicide for example, what passes as provocation is more
likely to take into account male characterisations of
response than the female response. That is not however, to set up a case for acknowledging any inherent
difference in response, merely to acknowledge that male
and female response are to varying degrees socially
tailored and unevenly represented in law. A

Gender 'Justice'? Defending Defendants and Mitigating
Sentence

comparative observation of male-female and female-male
homicide sheds light on this supposition since what
passes as provocation both in the legal and to a lesser degree in the everyday sense is formulated in conjunction with gender characterisations of typical responses of men and women, characterisations and expectations of what men and women in their appropriate
gender role might be expected to endure, characterisations of appropriate response and male versions of what
constitutes the legal parameters of provocations.
First, provocation as a legal defence is clear -
it is one of the legal defences to murder where there
is evidence of a sudden and temporary loss of self
control resulting in a reduction of a murder charge to
one of manslaughter (if accepted by the jury) the
effect of S.3 Homicide Act (1957).

> Where on a charge of murder there is evidence on
> which the jury can find that the person charged
> was provoked (whether by things done or by things
> said or by both together) to lose his self cont-
> rol, the question whether provocation was enough
> to make a reasonable man do as he did shall be
> left to be determined by the jury; and in deter-
> mining that question, the jury shall take into
> account everything both done and said according
> to the effect which, in their opinion, it would
> have on a reasonable man.

Provocation as a defence rests on what 'the reasonable
man' might consider constitutes provocation following
the Bedder rule (1954 38. Cr App R 133). This does
however, tend to exclude the exceptional as in excit-
ability, pugnacity, ill temper and drunkenness. The
jury must take into account:

1.   the events which have happened,
2.   the relevant characteristics of the defend-
     ant which may result in loss of self control.

Whilst provocation might well appear as a relatively clear legal category bound by rules and procedures, what precise forms of action, behaviour, manner-
isms, speech and situations, and relevant characteristics a jury may consider constitutes provocation, is
both arbitrary and ambiguous.
This matter will vary from individual to individual as it will from one jury to another. And the implicit rules which govern the adjudication of what
comes to pass or constitutes provocation have much to do
with background expectancies, understanding or situat-

ions, concepts of appropriate and inappropriate behaviour and what persons might be expected to tolerate. Thus decisions made concerning where and when retaliatory action is justifiable or excusatory are not immutable and given this human element may be informed by characterisations, prejudices and sophist sentiments.

On this issue alone, there is considerable discrepancy between women's everyday version of reality and the legal reality in homicide defences, since rules relating to homicide defence have emerged within the context of male orientated law, male judiciary and male criminology, in so far as Pattullo writes (1983 : 5), 'the fabric of the law and the assumptions of an overwhelmingly male legal profession affect the lives of women who come into contact with lawyers, defendants, victims and complainants'. Perhaps if these systems and beliefs were female dominated, or even equally power based, the question of cumulative provocation as a defence to murder under certain circumstances would not be untenable.

Along these lines, Lord Simon of Glaisdale:

> It is accepted that the phrase 'reasonable man' really means 'reasonable person', so as to extend to 'reasonable woman' (see, specifically, Holmes v DPP (1946) AC 588, 597). So although this has never yet been a subject of decision, a jury could arguably, consistently with Bedder and its precedent authorities, take the sex of the accused into account in assessing what might reasonably cause her to lose her self-control...take the insult 'whore' addressed respectively to a reasonable man and a reasonable woman. (R v Camplin 1978 AC 705)

Lord Morris of Borth-Y-Gest in discussing reasonable men asserted:

> If the accused is of a particular colour or particular ethnic origin and things are said which to him are grossly insulting, it would be utterly unreal if the jury had to consider whether the words would have provoked a man of different colour or ethnic origin.

and:

> if words of grevious insult were addressed to woman, words perhaps reflecting on her chastity or way of life, a consideration of the way in

which she reacted would have to take account of how other women being reasonable would or might in like circumstances have reacted. (11)

Given the essential component of a sudden and temporary loss of self control re-affirmed in <u>Ibrams</u> 74 CAR 154, immediately followed by the homicidal act, defendants who may wait before they retaliate have little ground for a defence of provocation. Provocation as a legal defence, is unlikely to be reflected by circumstances where a wife or cohabitee, although the victim of prolonged domestic violence and suffering, retaliates when the aggressor is asleep. 'Provocation may extend over a long period of time, providing it culminates in a sudden explosion.' (Smith and Hogan : 302). In 'cumulative provocation', its meaning is widely shared as involving a course of cruel or violent conduct by the deceased in the domestic setting, (Wasik 1982 : 29), where the victim of the torment or else someone acting on his/her behalf kills the tormentor. Reliance in this instance is placed on a course of conduct rather than one individual act immediately before the killing which reduces the crime committed to manslaughter. Although, the meaning and application of provocation still remains restrictive. The New Law Journal, reporting on the decision in Maw, stated that the admissibility of provocation as a defence, is very restrictive indeed. 'The fact is that their violent reaction to their situation cannot be explained at all in terms which even begin to do justice to them, on the basis of the wholly unrealistically restrictive view which the law takes of what is a permissible form of self-defence or excusable as a loss of self-control under provocation.' (NLJ 1980 : 1163) Therefore it can be supposed that the victims of 'cumulative provocation', are more likely to be women living with violent men, who when to quote the judge in Greig, 'the worm turns', may be denied protection or equal justice by the law and may be more likely to be convicted of murder rather than culpable homicide (manslaughter).

Consider these following cases of female-male spousal homicide, and patricide. Jones (1980), notes that in the US, Francine Hughes,   violent and bullying husband retaliated pouring gasoline around the bed where he slept; she was charged with first degree murder. (12) In Scotland in 1979, June Greig was sentenced to six years' imprisonment after being found guilty of the culpable homicide of her husband. The husband was a heavy drinker and there was a history of violence though on the fatal night in

140

question, the husband had not been violent, but Mrs
Grieg was afraid that he would become so. So she
stabbed him in the chest as he lay asleep. The judge
in dismissing her appeal against sentence maintained
that there were other remedies open to her. (HM Advocate v Greig, May 1979) (13) The impotency of these
'other remedies' is discussed in the contribution on
male violence. Mary Bernard (The Times 18th June 1982)
a Wolverhampton prostitute was not prepared any longer
to accept the brutal intimidation of a bullying and
violent husband who had forced her into prostitution.
She retaliated by pouring paraffin over him. She was
convicted of manslaughter and placed on probation for
three years. As the Criminal Law Revision Committee
para 84 states:

> ...the defence applies only where the defendant's
> act is caused by provocation and is committed
> suddenly upon the provoking event, not to cases
> where the defendants' violent reaction has been
> delayed; but the jury should continue to take
> into consideration previous provocation before
> the one which produced the fatal reaction.

In England, Celia Ripley, mother of two, shot and killed her husband after suffering years of violence and
abuse. She was convicted of manslaughter on the
ground that she had been provoked and at the time was
suffering from diminished responsibility. Celia Ripley
had already in effect served a six month sentence
whilst in custody awaiting trial, (The Guardian,
November 1 1983).
     It can also be seen that in cases of patricide
insufficient consideration is given to the motives of
the daughter(s) for their action. In 1976 Noreen
Winchester received a 7 year prison sentence for the
murder of her father. When at her appeal later the
circumstances of her actions were revealed - she had
been the victim of sexual abuse for years! Community
Care 19.5.78 The Maws sisters were imprisoned for three
years for manslaughter, on provocation after killing a
violent and drunken father,who had over a period of years
abused both the daughters and mother. In passing sentence
Mr Justice Smith said'...you deliberately and unlawfully
stabbed and killed your father...I bear in mind your
suffering, but the least sentences I can impose are
three years in prison for each of you'. (The Times,
18th November 1980). At the Court of Appeal, Annette
Maws' sentence was upheld but Charlenes' was reduced
from three years to six months. Lord Justice Lawton
at the Court of Appeal said:

Gender 'Justice'? Defending Defendants and Mitigating
Sentence

> What should be the attitude of the law to those
> who unlawfully and with violence kill someone who
> has treated them badly? Can the law tolerate
> this kind of behaviour when there are ample rem-
> edies. (Times 4th December 1980)

This important issue of defences to homicide
where defendants have been the victims of violent husbands who have physically and sexually assaulted them
has been the subject of international research (Fiora -
Gormally (1978)), Schneider (1980), Rasko (1981),
Scutt (1981), Bacon and Lansdowne (1982) and Rani
(1983). The work of Bacon and Lansdowne in particular, although limited in its sample size provides some
very valuable insights into this question which has so
often gone eclipsed.
In a study of 16 homicide cases where wives or
female cohabitees had killed their husbands, or lovers they examined the courts' perception and handling
of the cases. Finding that very rarely was the husband's or male cohabitee's violence and oppression
highlighted. 'Similarly, the difficulties they faced
in leaving the marriage were hardly ever explored
in a thorough or convincing way, that was sufficient
to overcome a jury's and judge's preconception that a
woman can leave a violent relationship if she wants to
and so cannot be said to be driven to homicide.'
(p 71) The authors maintained that in denying the
defendant's perception of the event in preference for
the legal version, resulted in the presentation of the
defendant's action as cold blooded and premeditated,
and not the act of woman forced to fight back in self
defence or provoked beyond endurance by a husband's
violence. In 6 of the 16 cases, the husband was
sleeping at the time and in most cases, there had been
some delay since the time of his last abuse or threat.
The authors inspired by the defendant's 'definition of
the situation' concluded that this 'apparent' delay-
ed response was the action of 'a woman too terrified
to fight back during an assault and physically incapable of doing so except with a weapon, and even then
only when her husband was incapacitated.' (p 71) In
14 out of the 16 cases, the women who had killed husbands or boyfriends had been assaulted in the past by
the deceased, and in some cases violence had been repeated extending up to 20 years. The authors describe
in some detail the dreadful and degrading way in
which these women offenders were abused and violated
by their husbands such that given this harbinger homicide became a means of self preservation. 13 out of
the 16 women interviewed stated that they killed their

142

Gender 'Justice'? Defending Defendants and Mitigating
Sentence

husbands in order to protect themselves from physical
harm. Yet when their cases came to court, although
the fear of further violence was presented as a motive, it was not presented as amounting to a defence
in law. The view taken by one of the judges, echoes
the views held by the trial judges in Greig and Maw:

> Given your domestic troubles, which as I find,
> were present but are not to be accepted in their
> entirety, the law itself is not without remedy
> and was not without remedy to you. There are
> friends: there are relations: there are community
> and Church and other avenues of advice: there
> are policemen, there are Chamber Magistrates:
> there are solicitors: there are means of protect-
> ion in the community. (p 84)

Bacon and Lansdowne draw attention to some of the
legal rules which by limiting the admissibility of
evidence may work against the female defendant. The
rules of evidence, specifically the hearsay rule require that only direct evidence of facts can be given,
any witness in court can only give evidence of what
he or she actually saw and not details of what the
woman said happened relating to her version of how
she sustained the wounds. As the authors point out,
'The law prescribes that judge and jury shall look
only at certain issues.' (p 87) Thus the Crown must
prove a death and establish whether the accused had
the intent, mens rea, to kill or to inflict grevious
bodily harm or reckless indifference as to whether she
did either - and whether she has a legal defence. The
authors argue that given the violence of the husbands
in 13 out of 16 cases, this was the direct and immediate reason why the homicide had occurred, 'one might
have envisaged that the defences would emphasise the
conduct of the victim and that self defence and provocation would have been argued frequently in the
cases.
Self defence was argued in one of the cases, and
raised on appeal in another. Provocation was argued
at the trial in four cases and raised by the trial
judge in another. 'In summary, of the 13 substantive
defences raised in these 16 cases, self defence was
argued twice: provocation 5 times and defences of
mental impairment 6 times'. (p89) Concluding that the
criminal law does not allow for a construction within
its legal categorisation of self-preservation, the
use of diminished responsibility in 6 cases tends to
suggest that these women were essentially 'abnormal'.
The limitations lie largely within the development of

legal defence:

> For example, the technical legal defence of self
> defence developed historically in the context of
> assaults between strangers, where the person
> attacked was assumed to be the physical equal of
> the attacker, and both able and willing to fight
> back in the course of the attack. (p 90)

And again in examining the gender basis of defences:

> This bias towards male reactions and single ass-
> aults means that the defence is quite inapprop-
> riate to situations such as a continuing relat-
> ionship where one party, the woman, is in an un-
> equal physical and economic position, and so is
> forced to remain in a marriage where she is re-
> peatedly battered.

Secondly, it seems reasonable to argue that what passes as provocation in the everyday sense and for the
purposes of mitigation, reveals a gender bias. What
amounted to provocation as a legal defence and influenced mitigation of sentence in the case of Wright
where the defendant had killed his wife with a hammer
as she lay in bed one morning, was the fact that he
had to put up with his wife's 'Saturday night and
Sunday morning activities' with boyfriends. This amounted to provocation, (The Times 14th October 1975).
In another case that of Asher (The Times 4th June
1981), the defendant was found guilty of manslaughter
and given a 6 months suspended sentence. Both the
legal defence and mitigatory circumstances reflected
the view that he was the victim of extreme provocation in the infidelities of a promiscuous wife. (14)
From Blackstone onwards, it has been a far graver
offence for the wife to kill the husband, than the
husband to kill the wife. In the case of wife-husband
homicide, it is akin to killing the king. In husband-
wife homicide, it is on the contrary permissible if
certain conditions prevail. Family civil and criminal
law has upheld the 'chastisement' of wives, whilst
some criminal codes explicitly state that if a man
kills his wife in the act of adultery, it will not be
unlawful (Scutt 1981). Again Blackstone states in
this context that such a case 'is of the lowest degree
of (manslaughter); and therfore... the court directed
the burning in the hand to be gently inflicted, because there could not be a greater provocation'. (Leading case Manning 1671 t. Raym 212). And although
words of adultery alone have not been sufficient in

Holmes v DPP 1946 AC 588), words alone have indeed in
other cases been taken to constitute provocation. (15)
Thus provocation may depend upon a subjective evaluation of the male response, the female response is therefore completely eclipsed.

TYPICAL MITIGATING CONSIDERATIONS IN SENTENCING

The criminal law not only invites defendants to neutralise their normative attachment to it via legal
defences, but also via a consideration of mitigating
circumstances, and everyday conceptions of motives
allows for a wide range of motive justificatory and
excusatory in accounting for action. In addition
courts pay much attention to the presence or absence
of conformity in other areas of the defendant's lifestyle, such that occupation and domestic role respectively become the key indicators of male and female
appropriateness.
        In a study of accounts rendered by female shop-
lifters and female prostitutes, motives for criminal
infraction varied according to whether the law was
considered correct in criminalising their behaviour.
Women who were charged with loitering for the purposes
of prostitution, predominantly accepted responsibility
for their behaviour offering only a justification for
their action in financial terms, in working for and
supporting the family. Women arraigned on charges of
shoplifting although typical and petty crimes tended
to deny full responsiblity. (Table 1) in fact 42% of
sample (33 persons) excused their behaviour appealing
to involuntaristic motives in the form of accident,
impulse, temptation, inebriation, whilst only 37% (29
persons) accepted full responsiblity, stating that
their action had been voluntaristic providing justificatory rationales predominantly in the form of financial imperatives. These financial imperatives accounting for 28% (22 persons), of the overall sample and for
76% within the voluntaristic category. Where responsibility was accepted and financial reasons were rendered in attribution, women could be seen acting in
supporting and working for their family, where women
stole groceries from supermarkets in order to feed
their family and stole cash in order to pay for elect-
ricity. In these cases, (22 in all) 50% were given
probation orders, 27% (6) conditionally discharged, 5%
deferred sentence and only 18% were fined, though
since three of these women were in receipt of supplementary benefit. This was not a realistic choice of
disposal one might think. Because the crime was typ-

145

ical and because of the woman's centrality within the
family, motive for action was in part due to family
and financial responsibility, the court treated women
leniently reflecting the view that theft of groceries
was indeed justified and could not be for gain. Most
accounts fell however, into the involuntaristic category, which tends to support the idea that the criminal law paradoxically invites the defendant to neutralise her normative attachment, since within the law,
accident, mistake, irresistible impulse, are well
understood as partial excuses. Women talked of irresistible impulse and then later rationalisations of
conduct were grafted on such that the conflation of
involuntarism followed by voluntaristic secondary motives, frequently characterised accounts.

> She finds it difficult to explain her recent
> behaviour and can only say that she acted on
> impulse (primary motivatory account) at a time
> of financial worry (secondary motivatory account)
> (Edwards 1984 : 157, my emphasis).

Women who were convicted of loitering for the
purposes of prostitution on the contrary, were not
concerned to neutralise their normative attachment to
the law, instead outrightly rejecting the normative
rule.   This led to the predominance of accounts,
wherein responsibility for action was fully acknowledged. (Table 2) In 62.5% (25 cases) voluntarism was
given in explanation whilst only 20% denied responsibility significantly, within this 5% included threats,
mistake, impulse from other men, 5% irresistible impulse, but the sick category was never invoked. 50%
of the total sample and 80% within this sub category
actually said that prostitution was a way of earning
a living. A significantly higher proportion engaged
in prostitution with the very deliberate and conscious
intent of providing for the family. The apologia was
not observable in their accounts, since like the political criminal, the prostitute is at variance with
the coteries of law making. In the voluntaristic
category, 44% of the defendants were predominantly
dealt with by means of a probation order, 8% received
community service orders, 8% were fined and 12% were
conditionally discharged. Where no explanation was
given, the defendants were dealt with as follows: 29%
were given probation orders, 14% were conditionally
discharged, 43% received suspended prison sentences
and 14% imprisonment. In both cases of shoptheft and
prostitution, female defendants primarily saw crimes
in terms of actually going towards preservation of

appropriate gender role in providing for family needs. Social inquiries and court verbalisations in mitigation took these factors into account, but financial difficulties in consideration of the appropriatness of financial disposal did not act to deter magistrates. They were only slightly deterred from imposing a fine where the defendant had sole responsibility for the family. Whilst the family needs were taken into account, acting apparently upon sentencing leniency, financial sentences doubly inflicted hardship on women whose poverty had initially set them on a course of theft and prostitution.

JUDICIAL MITIGATORY CONSIDERATIONS IN APPEALS AGAINST SENTENCE AND/OR CONVICTION

Thomas (1979 : 212), argues that family considerations have a mitigating effect on sentence particularly in the case of an offender who is a mother of young children and indeed some appeal hearings bear this out. In Charles, the defendant was convicted of unlawful wounding of another. The court suspended her sentence of 9 months, partly because 'she is the mother of a number of small children.' Further research is required to look at differences in sentencing between women who are mothers and women who are childless, to see to what extent sentencing varies with sex or gender role.
      Gender role appropriateness, obligations, and duties have influenced appeal decisions and provided the judicial justificatory rationale for varying sentence (see 1972 CLR 447; Thomas 1979: 213). In Arnold, the appellant received a 3 year sentence for bankruptcy offences. The court said that there was absolutely nothing wrong with such a sentence, but in view of the uncertain future of the appellant's children, from whose father the appellant had been divorced some years earlier, the court reduced the sentence to 18 months as 'some contribution towards keeping the family together as a unit'. (Thomas 1979 : 213). Similarly, in Parkinson the Court of Appeal declared that although sentences totalling 9 months for a young woman uttering forged banknotes were properly imposed, the sentences were reduced because of the effect on her two young children (Thomas 1979 : 212). In Owen (1972 CLR 324), the defendant stabbed her husband in his chest following a quarrel. She was sentenced to four years' imprisonment. The Court of Appeal took into special consideration that the appellant had five children: 'having regard to the interests of the children, and the birth of her latest child, the court

147

thought that the public interest would be adequately
served if, as an act of mercy, the sentence was varied
to 30 months'. But such considerations may not have
such a mitigating impact in offences of a rather more
serious and therefore untypical female crime. In
Ayoub for example, the sentence of 6 years was upheld
on a West African woman for fraudulently importing a
large amount of cannabis, though the appellant had 6
children (Thomas 1979 : 212). Family considerations
may weigh even more heavily when the appellant is a
single parent. In Fels the appellant, a single parent, had received five years for importing cannabis.
This was later on appeal reduced to 3 because her 5
year old son was suffering greatly in her absence.

In a study of 71 appeals against sentence and/or
conviction, heard at Manchester Crown Court 1981, the
reasons for allowing, varying or dismissing the appeal
(see Tables 3 and 4) were recorded. Though the majority of appeals were tendered on some legal technical-
ity, a significant number of cases were allowed on
matters strictly extraneous.

In 42 cases the appeal was allowed or varied (a
total of 60%). In only 29 of those cases the reasons
for allowing or varying the appeal were recorded and
therefore produced data that could be analysed. A
question of some considerable interest was whether
appeals were allowed solely on the basis of the judiciary's conception of the ability of the appellant to
fulfil gender role and family commitment and whether
gender role was more likely to be influential in cases
where the original sentence imposed was one of imprisonment. In 8 of these 29 cases (28%) the decision of
the court was based on gender role considerations relating to women's centrality in the family context. In
the remaining 72%, wholly technical matters decided.
What this really suggests is that where extraneous
considerations influence appeal decisions, they are
almost always related to women's responsibility appropriateness, the role within the family. In these 8
cases where gender was invoked, a sentence of imprisonment had originally been imposed.

However, it is also to be noted that we do not
know in cases where the appeal was refused (40%),
what proportion of applicants were good or bad mothers
as defined by the court and what was their crime. For
these results to be in any way conclusive we would
expect family considerations to have less or no effect
where appellants are considered bad mothers.

Therefore it was not motherhood per se which had
an influence on allowing the appeals against sentence,
but the question of whether the appellant was a good

mother. Evidence of bad mothering or evidence of
children already in care would not have the same effect as evidence of a strong family unit and a good
mother whose removal would have a poor effect, although the fact of a good mothering may not have weighed
so heavily in cases where the appellant was a single
parent. These speculative conclusions require further
testing and verification. The reasons listed for the
appeals against sentence were of this nature:

> To lock up the appellant would be destructive
> to the mother-child relationship. .....defendant
> said to be a good mother and lose custody of her
> children.

Always of central concern however was the extent
to which perceptions of a good mother in the eyes of the
court were based on a middle class version of the appropriate mother and appropriate wife. Most women
who had good relationships with their children may not
be seen to conform to this deserving of remission
stereotype, these 'other' good mothers might be single,
not in a permanent relationship, perhaps without an
appropriate accommodation, perhaps with a different
sexual life and therefore not considered eligible or
suitable mothers. If women are to be considered for
variations of sentence in appeal cases it may appear
that one important factor in the success of the appeal
will be their ability to conform to very conventional
and middle class role models, which whilst not only
perpetuating a model of motherhood, femininity, and the
centrality of the family may unfairly discriminate in
favour of those able to conform.
This discussion paper has brought together a number of important dimensions within recent investigat-
ions of gender and criminal justice. In rejecting an
implacable relationship between women and criminal
justice, the paper has instanced some precise locations within the legal process where particular images
of gender are invoked consciously or not, in negotiation of charge defence mitigation and later sentencing,
and appeal. The preoccupation has nevertheless been
with two recently emergent foci in the study of gender
and criminal justice; that of mitigation in crime generally and defence to homicide in particular. By
introducing the notion that legal defences to homicide
disproportionately accommodate everyday versions of
defences between the sexes, the proposition questions
the extent to which sex role characterisations of
response and criminal characterisations of typical
homicide criminality have had some influence in the

Table 1. The Function of Motive in Conduct: Shoplifting

Voluntarism

	No	%
(1) Financial	22	28.0
(2) Attention seeking	3	4.0
(3) Opportunism	2	2.5
Accept responsibility	2	2.5
		37.0

Intermediate

	No	%
(4) Mistake	5	6.0
(5) Unresponsible Illegitimate	5	6.0
Accounting		12.0

Involuntarism

	No	%
(6) Temptation/Compulsion	9	11.5
(7) No explanation Can't remember sorry	15	19.0
(8) Drugs alcohol	4	5.0
(9) Physiological episodes	2	2.5
Emotional	3	4.0
		42.0

	No	%
Non recordable Not guilty pleas not known	6	8.0
TOTAL	78	100

Table 2. The Function of Motive in Conduct: Prostitution

	Voluntarism		Intermediate			Involuntarism		
	No	%		No	%		No	%
Not a crime way of life	4	10	No explanation	7	17.5	Temptation	2	5
Financial	20	50				Alcohol/Drugs	4	10
Appeal to higher loyalties	1	2.5				Threats from men	2	5
TOTAL	25	62.5		7	17.5		8	20
						GRAND TOTAL	40	100

Table 3. Appeals: According to Offence and Outcome (Manchester Crown Court, 1981)

	Appeal against conviction allowed	Appeal against conviction sentence varied	Abandoned	Dismissed	Remitted to Magistrates	Total
Violence	1	-	-	1	-	2
Sexual Offences:						
Prostitution	-	1	-	-	-	1
Burglary	1	2	-	-	-	3
Robbery	-	-	-	-	-	-
Theft and handling	12	9	7	11	2	41
Fraud and forgery	-	5	-	-	-	5
Criminal damage	-	-	-	-	-	-
Other	8	3	2	6	-	19
	22	20	9	18	2	71

Gender 'Justice'? Defending Defendants and Mitigating
Sentence

Table 4. Reasons for Allowing or Varying Appeal

	Allowed	Varied
Not enough evidence to convict	9	–
Too severe/wrong in law	1	4
Not opposed by respondent	3	1
Court concern for family	3	5
Previously not represented	1	–
Time-lag between offence and prosecution	–	1
Recent good character	–	1
TOTAL	17	12

formulation of legal defences, both in the context of
the objective formulation and in its subjective interpretation. A consideration of mitigating circumstances in their relation to both the crime and the defendant provides an insight into the way in which criminality is constituted in conjunction with a consideration of ability to fulfil appropriate role models,
though on another level often extraneous to the offence
committed.

REFERENCES

(1)   Smith, D. (1978) 'K is Mentally Ill: The Anatomy
        of a Factual Account', Sociology, XII, pp.
        23-57.

(2)   Young, J. (1971) 'The Role of the Police as
        Amplifiers of Deviancy' p. 27-61 in S. Cohen
        Images of Deviance, Penguin

(3)   Wilkins, L. (1974) 'Directions for Correct-
        ions' Proceedings of American Philosophical
        Society Vol. 118 p.235-247 Reprinted in RM
        Carter and LT Wilkins (ed.) Probation,
        Parole and Community Corrections New York
        Wiley, p. 57 1976

(4)   Jeffrey, C.R. (1959) 'Historical Development
        of Criminology' Journal of Criminal Law Crim-
        inology and Police Sci. Vol. 50: 3-19

(5)   Hutter, B.A. Controlling Women London: Croom
        Helm p. 14/15 Williams, G. (eds.) 1981

(6)   Newman, D. cited in Bottomley, A.K. (1979)
        Criminology in Focus, London: Martin Robert-
        son p. 102

(7)   Farrington, D.P. and Morris, A.M. (1983)
        'Sex, Sentencing and Reconviction'. Brit
        Journal Criminology Vol. 23 No. 3 p.229/248

(8)   Worrall, A. (1981) 'Out of Place: Female
        Offenders in Court', Probation Journal 28
        p. 90/93

(9)   The Times, July 7th 1981 cited in Edwards
        (1984: 97)

(10)   Taylor-Buckner, H. (1978) 'Transformations of
        Reality in the Legal Process' in T Luckmann
        (ed.) Phenomenology and Sociology, - Harmond-
        sworth pp. 311-323

(11)   Elliot, D.W. and Wood, J.C. (1982) A Casebook
        of Criminal Law, Sweet and Maxwell London
        Ch. 9

(12)   Jones, A. (1980) Women Who Kill, Holt Rine-
        hart and Winston p. 281

(13)   Extracts of Greig Case in C.H. Gane and C.N.
        Stoddart - Casebook on Scottish Criminal Law

(1980) Green and Sons, Edinburgh p. 364
See also: The Times 22nd November 1979
The Times 19th November 1980 M. Wasik 1982
p. 29, 33, 36 Cumulative Provocation and
Domestic Killing Crim. Law Rev. pp. 29-37

(14)   Radford, J. (1982) 'Marriage Licence or
Licence to Kill: Womanslaughter in the
Criminal Law' Feminist Review 11 p. 88, 96

(15)   Smith, J.C. and Hogan, B. Criminal Law,
Butterworth 1983 5th (ed.) p. 301 nb 19,
1965 (ed.) 208 nb 17

BIBLIOGRAPHY

Adler, F. (1975) Sisters in Crime, New York: McGraw-Hill

Anderson, E.A. (1976) 'The "Chivalrous" Treatment of The Female Offender in the Arms of the Criminal Justice System. A Review of the Literature' Social Problems 23, 3: 349-57

Armstrong, G. (1977) 'Females Under the Law - "Protected" but Unequal', Crime and Delinquency 23, 2: 109-120

Bacon, W. and Landsdowne, R. (1982) 'Women Who Kill Husbands: The Battered Wife on Trial' in C O'-Donnell and J Craney Family Violence in Australia pp. 67-93 Melbourne

Bottomley, A.K. (1973) Decisions in the Penal Process, London: Martin Robertson.

Box, S. (1971) Deviance, Reality and Society, London: Holt, Rinehart and Winston

Carlen, P. (1983) Women's Imprisonment, London: Routledge and Kegan Paul

Chesney-Lind, M. (1977) 'Judicial Paternalism and the Female Status Offender', Crime and Delinquency 23, 121-130

Devlin, K.M. (1970) Sentencing Offenders in Magistrates' Courts, London: Sweet and Maxwell

Eaton, M. (1983) 'Mitigating Circumstances: Familiar Rhetoric' International Jnl of the Sociology of Law 11, 385-400

Edwards, S.S.M. (1984) Women on Trial, Manchester: Manchester University Press

Fiora-Gormally, N. (1978) 'Battered Wives Who Kill' Law and Human Behaviour, Vol. 2 No. 2

Foley, L., and Rasche, C. (1976) 'A Longitudinal Study of Sentencing Patterns of Female Offenders'. Paper presented at the American Society of Criminology, Tucson, Arizona.

Giallombardo, R. (1966) Society of Women: A Study of

Bibliography

    Women's Prisons, New York: John Wiley
Hancock, L. (1980) 'The Myth that Females are Treated
    More Leniently than Males in the Juvenile Justice
    System' Aust. and N.Z. Jnl of Soc, Vol. 16 p+3,
    p. 4-13
Heidensohn, F. (1981) 'Women and the Penal System' in
    A Morris and L Gelthorpe (eds.) Women and Crime,
    129/139 Cropwood Conference No. 13 Cambridge
Henry, S. (1976) 'Fencing with Accounts: The Language
    of Moral Bridging', British Journal of Law and
    Society 3 91/100
Klein, D. and Kress, J. (1981) 'Any Woman's Blues: A
    Critical Overview of Women. Crime and the Crim-
    inal Justice System' in T. Platt and P Takagi
    (eds.) Crime and Social Justice, London: Mac-
    millan, 153/183
Matza, D. (1964) Delinquency and Drift, Berkeley:
    University of California Press
McClean J.D. and Wood, J.C. (1969) Criminal Justice
    and the Treatment of Offenders, London: Sweet
    and Maxwell
Nagel, I. (1981) 'Sex Differences in the Processing of
    Criminal Defendants' in A. Morris and L. Gelsth-
    orpe (eds.) Women and Crime, Cropwood Round Table
    No. 13, University of Cambridge Institute of
    Criminology, p. 104/124
Norland, S. and Shover, N. (1977) 'Gender Roles and
    Female Criminality: Some Critical Comments',
    Criminology 15(1) 87-104
Pattullo, P. (1983) Judging Women, NCCL London
Pearson, R. (1976) Women Defendants in Magistrates'
    Courts, British Jnl of Law and Society V III
    pp. 265-73
Phillips, D.M. and Defleur L.B. (1982) 'Gender Ascrip-
    tion in the Stereotyping of Deviants', Criminol-
    ogy Vol. 20 No. 3/4 431/48
Pollak, O. (1950) The Criminality of Women, Philadel-
    phia: University of Pennsylvania Press
Radalet, M. (1980) 'The Effect of Female Social Pos-
    ition on Geographic Variations in the Sex Ratio
    of Arrests' Bulletin of the American Academy of
    Psychiatry and Law Vol. 8 465/476
Rafter, N.H. and Natalizia, E.M. (1981) 'Marxist Fem-
    inism: Implications for Criminal Justice', Crime
    and Delinquency Vol. 27, 81/91
Rani, M.B. (1983) 'Homicides by Females' Indian Jnl
    of Crim 11/1, 8-17
Rasko, G. (1981) 'Crimes Against Life, Committed by
    Women in Hungary' in F. Adler (ed.) The Incidence
    of Female Criminality in the Contemporary World
Rowett, C. and Vaughan P.J. (1981) 'Women and Broad-

moor Treatment and Control in a Special Hospital' in B. Hutter and G. Williams (eds.) <u>Controlling Women</u>, London: Croom Helm pp. 131-153

Schneider, E.M. (1980) 'Equal Rights to Trial for Women: Sex Bias in the Law of Self-Defense' <u>Har. Civ. Rights Civ. Liberties Law Rev.</u> 15/3: 623-47

Scutt, J. (1981) 'Sexism in the Criminal Law' in S.M. Mukherjee and J. Scutt <u>Women and Crime</u> George Allen: Australia pp. 1-21

Simon, R.J. (1975) <u>Women and Crime,</u> Lexington, Massachusetts: DC Heath and Company

Simon, R.J. and Sharma, N. 'Women and Crime: Does the American Experience Generalise' in F. Adler and R.J. Simon (eds.) <u>The Criminality of Deviant Women</u> - Boston Mass, pp. 391-400

Skolnick, J. (1966) <u>Justice on Trial</u>, John Wiley and Sons

Smith, A.D. (1962) <u>Women in Prison</u>, London: Stevens

Smith, D.A. and Visher, C. (1981) 'Street Level Justice: Situational Determinations of Police Arrest Decisions' <u>Social Problems</u> Vol. 29: 167: 77

Smith, J.C., and Hogan, B. (1983) <u>Criminal Law</u>, Butterworth, London

Sudnow, D. (1965) 'Normal Crimes: Sociological Features of Penal Code in a Public Defender Office', <u>Social Problems</u> 12, p. 255/276

Swigert, V. and Farrell, R. (1977) 'Normal Homicides and the Law', <u>American Sociological Review</u> 42, 1, pp. 16-32

Sykes, G. and Matza, S. (1957) 'Techniques of Neutralisation: A Theory of Delinquency', <u>American Sociological Review</u> 20 pp. 664-70

Thomas, D.A. (1979) <u>Principles of Sentencing</u>, London: Heinemann

Visher, C.A. (1983) 'Gender, Police Arrest Decisions and Notions of Chivalry', <u>Criminology</u> 21, p. 5-27

Walker, N. (1965) <u>Crime and Punishment in Britain</u>, Edinburgh: University of Edinburgh Press

Wilkins, L. (1964) <u>Social Deviance</u> London: Tavistock

Wasik, M. (1982) 'Cumulative Provocation and Domestic Killing,' <u>Crim Law Rev</u> pp. 29-37

Chapter Eight

A PLEA FOR PMT IN THE CRIMINAL LAW

Linda Luckhaus

In November 1981, two women walked 'free' from
English criminal courts and caused a storm of protest.
Sandie Smith (alias Craddock) and Christine English
had blamed premenstrual tension (PMT) for their violent criminal offences and the courts had apparently
accepted their 'excuse'. In the ensuing debate, played out initially through correspondence columns and
feature articles of the national news media, the fear
was expressed that PMT had been established legally as
a woman's all-purpose excuse. (1)
    The basis of this fear became apparent through
the objections raised, some more explicit than others.
Implicit was the idea that spurious claims would be
made by manipulative female criminals and that they
would 'get off' due to the difficulty of sifting the genuine from the non-genuine claims. Better articulated,
and more hotly disputed, was the doubt as to whether
PMT existed at all and even if it did whether it had
any relevance to explaining and justifying crime. (2)
    New life was injected into the debate in April
1982 when the Court of Appeal delivered its judgment
affirming the trial court's decision in Sandie Smith's
case. (3) More recently, clear and considered feminist contributions to the debate have appeared (4) un-
equivocally in one instance (5) dissenting from the
view that PMT should be capable of excusing· a female
offender in any way at all.
    One purpose of this paper is to raise doubts ab-
out such an unequivocal stance. The other is to expl-
ore, from a strictly legal perspective, the preliminary issue of whether PMT is or can be an excuse in the
criminal law and if so what form it does and can take.
To prepare the ground first of all, however, a brief
outline of the Sandie Smith and Christine English case
histories is given followed by an attempt to penetrate
the misty realms of the medical notion of PMT in order

159

A Plea for PMT in the Criminal Law

to describe its content.

THE CASE HISTORIES: SANDIE SMITH AND CHRISTINE ENGLISH

Sandie Smith, according to reports, (6) had a long
history of psychiatric disturbance, attempted suicide,
uncontrollable violent behaviour, and crime. Seen by
psychiatrists on 23 occasions, she was said to have an
untreatable unstable personality but no mental disorder. She had 45 convictions, mainly for violent offences. In 1980 she stabbed a barmaid to death during a
fight at work. She was charged with murder but while
on remand before trial and on the initiative of her
father, the apparent coincidence of her violent out-
bursts with her menses and premenstrual state was
investigated.
    A retrospective diagnosis of PMT was made, link-
ing all past offences with the timing of menstruation.
Medical evidence was offered in support of her plea of
not guilty to murder but guilty to manslaughter due to
diminished responsibility, a plea accepted by the
prosecution. Sentence was deferred for three months
to assess the efficacy of hormone replacement therapy.
On the reported success of the progesterone hormone
injections, the trial judge placed Sandie Smith on
probation for three years subject to her continuing to
receive the steroid hormone treatment. Some months
later she was before the court again, charged with
threatening to kill a police officer and with possessing an offensive weapon. It was this incident which
was given such extensive publicity in November 1981.
Evidence at the trial maintained that she had a grudge
against the police officer because he had allegedly
insulted her some years earlier. Threats to kill him
had been made in (disguised) writing, by telephone,
and through her appearance at the police station where
she had been discovered in possession of a knife. PMT
was again diagnosed! Her 'bizarre' behaviour was
explained by deliberate reductions in the massive,
painful, dosage of progesterone administered through
injections. Once the original large doses were rest-
ored, the 'hidden animal' in her was quelled and she
reverted to her normal 'benign' state. (7)
    On this occasion, Smith pleaded not guilty, att-
empting to deny criminal liability altogether, her
defence counsel arguing (inter alia) that the defence
of automatism was open to her. The trial judge refused to let this defence go before the jury who convicted her of the charges laid. She was again placed on
probation for three years subject to receiving proges-

160

terone treatment. She appealed against the judge's
ruling of no defence and in April 1982 the Court of
Appeal delivered its judgment upholding the trial
judge's decision, noting the excitement the case had
caused and welcoming the 'merciful' treatment of Smith
by the trial court. (8)
    Lenient non-custodial sentencing was also the
fate of Christine English. News of her case broke the
day after Sandie Smith had been released on probation
a second time. English had no previous convictions.
She had killed her lover, during a quarrel over another woman, by driving her car at him, pinning him
against a post. After the event, she could remember
clearly what happened, claiming that something had
snapped inside when he made a V-sign at her. She began menstruating soon after. This coincidence was
seized on by her solicitor. He had been alerted to
the possible relationship between menstruation and
crime through media coverage of the topic some months
earlier. (9)
    Medical and psychiatric opinion was sought and
English was diagnosed as suffering from PMT on the
basis of PMT diagnostic pointers: following pregnancy
she had suffered post-natal depression; she had been
sterilised; and at the time of the incident she had
gone some hours without eating. Failure to eat in PMT
sufferers, it is said, could produce hypoglycaemia, in
turn producing aggressive uncontrollable behaviour.
(10) Although she was charged with murder, her plea
of guilty to manslaughter due to diminished responsibility was accepted, supported as it was by medical
evidence. Treated exceptionally sympathetically, she
was banned from driving for a year and given a one-
year conditional discharge. Unlike Smith, she was not
even required to undergo treatment but like Smith one
year earlier she had evaded the stigma of a murder
conviction.
    Both women were freed in the sense they received
non-custodial sentences. Neither were freed in the
sense they were acquitted altogether. The misconceiv-
ed idea that both had somehow got off 'scot-free' was
subtly conveyed in news reports at the time. One can
only speculate as to what extent if any this fuelled
the public indignation, even outrage, expressed at the
manner in which these two women were disposed of
through the criminal process. (11)

PREMENSTRUAL TENSION: THE MEDICAL CONCEPT

What is premenstrual tension? Posing the question has

its problems not least because the medical profession
is deeply divided on the issue. More fundamentally,
posing the question could be taken to imply validity
of the notion itself. Laws (12) has made a strong
case for saying that PMT is not 'real' at all but an
ideological construct, a set of categories constructed
by the medical profession. These are imposed upon and
accepted by women who then experience the lived reality of continuous cyclical change through them, in
distorted fashion. Importantly, Laws does not deny
the lived reality of cyclic change to which PMT refers
but questions and ultimately rejects the kinds of
self-expression being offered through the medical categories. (13) The position adopted here is to treat
PMT as a medical construct, 'real' to the extent it is
recognised by some within the medical establishement,
but with limited validity, if any, beyond these confines.

The medical history of PMT dates back to the
early 1930s when Frank first attempted a systematic
description of it, linking its occurrence with the
female sex hormones. Its discovery coincided with the
first significant advances in medical research towards
isolating the female ovarian hormones, particularly
oestrogen and progesterone. Frank described the condition as 'indescribable tension', 'irritability', and
'a desire to find relief by foolish and ill-considered
actions'. (14) The first two existence and symptom-
seeking studies seem to be of two main types. One set
has sought to establish the existence of the condition
by linking the timing of deviant and criminal behaviour
by women with menstruation and the premenstrual phase.
Such studies (15) tend to subvert, if not ignore, the
subjective element (whether women complain of ill-
effects). They have been used as 'scientific' evidence for the proposition that PMT causes crime, in
particular by Sandie Smith's defence counsel at the
time of her trial. (16)

The second set has taken women complainants as
the focal point and concentrated on elucidating the
ill-effects reported as regularly concurring during
the crucial period of menstrual cycle. The combined
effect of both types of studies has been to produce
a bewildering array of some 150 symptoms. Not surprisingly, given this range of symptoms, estimates of
incidence vary enormously, from 20% to 95%. (17) For
the most part studies intended to establish the existence of PMT, its symptomatology, or its incidence are
no more than exercises in definition. The one factor
common to all studies, providing the one definitional
element. is periodicity.

Katharina Dalton, who is acclaimed for having put PMT
on the medical map a generation ago (18) and who was
expert witness for the defence in both the Smith and
English cases, defines the condition simply as:

> The presence of <u>monthly recurrent</u> symptoms in
> the premenstruum or early menstruation with a
> <u>complete absence</u> of symptoms after menstruat-
> ion. (19)

Dalton recognises that this is probably the only disease (sic) not dependent on type of symptom for definition or diagnosis. (20) She estimates the incidence to be 40% although only one in ten menstruating
women are said to suffer PMT severely enough to warrant treatment. (21) Because she is committed to her
yet unproven hypothesis that PMT is caused by a deficiency of the steroid hormone, progesterone, her
favoured treatment is progesterone replacement therapy. This costly treatment is however reserved for
those who are alcoholic, suicidal or violent, (like
Sandie Smith), undergoing marital stress or at risk of
being hospitalised. In other cases symptomatic treatment is advocated, including self help, diurectics,
anti-depressants, bromociptine and pyridoxine (Vitamin
B6). Spironolactone is not recommended. (22)
    There are no biochemical tests which can estab-
lish the existence of what Dalton calls a disease,
therefore diagnosis must be by way of observation and
scrutiny of the woman's medical history in search of
diagnostic pointers. Dalton is emphatic that particularly for medicolegal purposes diagnosis must be
based on establishing the regularly recurrent nature
of symptoms over at least three cycles. She believes
the onset of PMT occurs at times of hormonal upheaval
such as pregnancy, taking and coming off the contraceptive
pill, and sterilisation. Such events in a woman's
medical history (as in English's) can provide pointers
in support of a diagnosis based on observation.
Another diagnostic pointer, according to Dalton, is
the failure of a woman in her premenstrual phase to
take food for some period of time. This allegedly
gives rise to a hypoglycaemic episode, the precise
significance of which we shall return to in a moment.
    Dalton and others who advocate the hormonal theo-
ry of PMT have their critics even within the medical
profession. Clare, who notes that the great majority
of women notice some degree of physical, psychological
and behaviour change during the premenstrual phase, is
careful to avoid the term disease and would want to
confine the condition at least to those who suffer

A Plea for PMT in the Criminal Law

symptoms severely enough to seek medical intervention.
(23) D'Orban has gone on record as saying that PMT
'is a common syndrome and the psychological manifest-
ations are transient and rarely severe enough to be
regarded as an illness'. Moreover 'the aetiology of
PMT is as yet uncertain'. (24)
       This lack of evidence in support of the proges-
terone deficiency theory is not for want of trying.
A spate of studies conducted largely throughout the
1970s has failed to produce conclusive evidence confirming the hypothesis. There even seems to be doubt
whether biochemical assays can successfully measure
progesterone levels. In addition the only double
blind controlled experiment conducted to test the
efficacy of progesterone treatment over placebos failed to show that one was significantly better than the
other. (25) Trials on the other treatments, spironolactone, pyridoxine, monoamic oxidase inhibitors, diur-
etics and oral contraceptives have proved equally in-
conclusive and unconvincing. In more anecdotal vein,
medical experts here and abroad have publicly stated
their doubts about the theory and the treatment: even
if progesterone works, which it does not always do,
(26) it is not certain why, (27) the implication being
that controlling symptoms does not always mean curing
them.
       The uneasy regard which many within the medical
establishment now appear to have for PMT as a hormonal
disease and as an ostensible cause of female crime is
of particular relevance here. Though the expert medical opinion of Katharina Dalton at the trials of
Smith and English appears to have prompted little dis-
agreement, the body of critical opinion now forming
suggests she would not have such an easy ride, so to
speak, in the future, should another attempt be made
to use PMT as a legal excuse. The prosecution may
well marshal opposing expert evidence on the question
of diagnosis, on the relevance of PMT if any to the
offence, on the very idea of PMT itself. The legal
analysis in the following section, aimed at discovering to what extent PMT is or can be a legal excuse,
must therefore be read with these medical reservations
and the possibility of challenge in mind. First,
however, it is necessary to outline some of the symptoms of PMT.
       Clare suggests a three-fold classification of the
most common symptoms: physical symptoms, psychological
symptoms and behavioural changes. The latter include
a loss of efficiency, clumsiness and proneness to
accidents. Psychological symptoms embrace tension,
irritability, depression, tiredness, sleep disturbance,

mood swings (presumably not happy ones!), forgetful-
ness and feelings of loneliness. Dalton would agree
with this description of psychological symptoms, though the terms may differ, for example, she cites leth-
argy and amnesia. Physical symptoms included by Clare
range from painful breasts, headache, backache, skin
eruptions and stomach cramps to subjective feelings of
swelling and bloatedness which may or may not be accompanied by weight gain, the mechanism for the latter
being thought to be intra-cellular water retention.
    Though perhaps extremely painful for the woman
sufferer, these physical symptoms are of little medico-
legal relevance. Dalton would extend the range however so that they do become relevant. She classes as
neurological symptoms: migraine, epilepsy, and syncope
(fainting). Hypoglycaemia, a deficiency of blood
sugar, due partly it seems in PMT sufferers because
they tend to fast during the premenstruum (28) is
pinpointed as the mechanism responsible for these more
severe symptoms. She also suggests that panics, naus-
ea, exhaustion and aggression can be produced by
(premenstrual) hypoglycaemic episodes. This elevation
of hypoglycaemia onto the premenstrual stage was of
critical importance in the English case, although its
relevance to PMT has been criticised since.(29) Elsewhere it has been suggested that hypoglycaemia can
rarely occur in circumstances other than in diabetes.
(30) An expert witness for the Crown may well feel
inclined to challenge medical evidence of this nature.
    Before leaving this discussion of PMT, a counter
to the weight of medical discourse on the subject is
perhaps desirable, not least as a reminder that PMT
does indeed refer to lived experiences. The following
is a personal account of PMT published by a feminist
magazine:

    I usually get PMT around ovulation time. It gen-
    erally starts with two days of crashing depress-
    ion - then for the next two weeks I walk around
    feeling as if I've got a ball of cotton wool in-
    side my brain which cuts me off from the rest of
    the world. I tend to feel unreal, out of cont-
    rol of my actions and feelings and often paraly-
    sed. What other people do and say becomes par-
    anoidly significant, as if everyone was deliber-
    ately trying to get at me. Feelings such as
    anger and frustration get confused with guilt
    because of the uncertainty of knowing whether
    they are the result of PMT or real and justif-
    iable. (31)

A Plea for PMT in the Criminal Law

PMT AND THE CRIMINAL LAW

The criminal law is concerned with human activity prohibited because perceived to be harmful or dangerous
in some way. PMT provides a possible explanation for
such activity. Through the cases of Smith and English
it has achieved a status of 'credible cause' within
the criminal law. However, to assess its full potential from the defendant's point of view, we have first
to locate the role of causes in relation to decisions
made about an accused at various stages in the criminal process. Causes or explanations of behaviour could
be relevant at a number of stages: the decision to
prosecute; the decision as to criminal liability at
the trial; the decision on sentencing; and the decision whether to release from custody. It is proposed
to concentrate here on the trial and sentencing stages. Further, and because causes are not conceptualised as such within legal discourse but are regarded
as 'excuses', it is proposed to adopt a theoretical
framework which gives prominence to 'excuses', in particular three types of them. Following Wasik, (32)
the three categories of legal excuses are: excusing
conditions, partial excuses and mitigating causes.
Excusing conditions operate to relieve a defendant of
criminal liability entirely. Excuses or defences such
as insanity, automatism, duress or self-defence are
relevant here, though insanity can be distinguished
from the rest in terms of disposal. The special verdict of not guilty by reason of insanity is a double
edged sword. It absolves of liability but 'punishes'
through mandatory committal of a defendant to a special or psychiatric hospital there to be detained at
the Home Secretary's pleasure. (33) Absolution via
this route, with its indefinite detention, is not a
path taken by many (34) and will not be pursued here.
A PMT sufferer would be ill advised to take such a
course although, as we shall see, it may be one thrust
upon her.
     There is a clear distinction between excusing
conditions and the third category, mitigating excuses.
These are a class of mitigating factors which operate
at the sentencing stage, influencing the exercise of
discretion as to type and length of disposal, but which
do not negate criminal liability. Partial excuses sit
uneasily between mitigating excuses and excusing conditions. They do not relieve of criminal liability
although they can drastically affect sentencing discretion and have the important characteristic effect of
changing the category of offence with which the defendant is ultimately convicted. The two leading par-

166

tial excuses are provocation and diminished responsibility: they transform a charge of murder to a conviction for manslaughter if successfully pleaded. The
fixed life sentence for murder may then be avoided,
the sentencing for manslaughter being at the total
discretion of the judge. The special rule relating
to infanticide may be mentioned here. This rule en-
ables a mother who has killed her child to avoid a
conviction for murder and mandatory life imprisonment.
The statutory provision (35) requires the child to have
been less than 12 months and the cause of the killing
to have been the effect of giving birth and lactation.
Disposal, again, is entirely at the sentencer's discretion, and criminal liability is imposed but not for
murder.

CRIMINAL LIABILITY, CULPABILITY AND CAUSES

Before examining whether PMT can found an excuse in
any of these categories, some theoretical presupposit-
ions are laid bare. Criminal liability is used here
in a procedural sense and is to be distinguished from
the normative concepts of culpability and responsibility. The term implies a judicial process whereby a
person is found to be or held guilty according to
whether certain criteria are satisfied. Neither
'criminal liability' nor the criteria are abstract
reified notions which somehow attach to the individual
defendant and are there to be discovered through the
magic of the criminal process. On the contrary, it is
assumed that the criteria of criminal liability are
socially constructed mainly through the legislative
and judicial systems and are normative products reflecting different moral, philosophical, ethical, and
political values often competing with each other, and
subject to constant flux and change. In short the
criteria are not fixed, neither is their normative
content. The configurations of values which may be
embodied in one or more sets of criteria are complex
and many. It is these configurations which constitute
the multi-dimensional normative concepts of culpability and responsibility. Concepts of culpability are
relevant to the trial and sentencing stages: criminal
liability only to the former.
    Whether and to what degree causes and excuses
should affect criminal liability are normative questions. At present excuses have a restrictive and
peripheral role to play. Tight boundaries have been
drawn around the types of explanations considered
acceptable. Although moves are afoot to loosen the

bonds, cultural and economic factors such as
'prolonged social deprivation' still appear to be
well out of bounds. (36)   O'Donovan has shown
how the Criminal Law Revision Committee (1980)
has sought to enable the perceived 'real' envir-
onmental causes of child killing to be given
effect through the retention of the above now
discredited medical explanation for these events.
(37) Excuses and causes are also peripheral to criminal liability because they tend to operate by
way of afterthought.   The two principal criteria
of criminal liability, the two main determinants,
pushing excuses to the side lines are the two
legal theoretical constructs of mens rea and actus
reus.   These, and their place in traditional legal
analysis will now be considered.

TRADITIONAL LEGAL ANALYSIS

Mens rea (loosely but not helpfully translated as
guilty mind) relates to the mental elements of
intention, knowledge and recklessness.   To establish criminal liability it must be shown by the
prosecution that the defendant intended an act and
or its consequences or that she was reckless as
to the possibility of specified harm occurring
(the latter now including the objective test). (38)
The actus reus relates to the act which must be
voluntary and to any other external elements specified by the offence.   For example certain offences may require an act or conduct to take place
in (known) circumstances and have (intended) consequences.   The permutations of the various mental
and external elements constituting specific statutory and common law offences are considerable.
Rather than to resort to excuses or defences to
negate criminal liability, a PMT sufferer could
use her condition to show that in terms of traditional analysis an essential element of the
offence has not been proved.   In short she could
claim that the prosecution has failed to establish
that her act was voluntary or that she had the requisite mens rea, be it intention, knowledge or recklessness.
    Is she likely to succeed?   To do so evidence must
be adduced as to her state of mind at the time of the
event.   This could be provided by her own recollect-
ions. Expert medical opinion could be produced as
to her likely state of mind at the time.   Inferences could also be drawn from her conduct and other
circumstances. If she felt 'unreal' or 'paralysed' as

in the earlier personal account of PMT and her evidence was credible, it is questionable whether the
prosecution would be able to make out intention as to
the consequences of her actions as required in the
most serious crimes, for example, wounding with intent. (39)
     Even where it need not be shown that she meant
to bring about the consequences, it is possible that
her evidence will be sufficient to show that she did
not intend her actions, she did not know what she was
doing, or she did not appreciate the risks she was
running. The behavioural changes of clumsiness and
proneness to accidents noted by Clare could be relevant here. If she succeeds then the requisite mens rea
for the less serious offences such as unlawful wounding (40) would not have been made out either. Alter-
natively, should the prosecution establish the latter
intent but not the former (specific) intent, she may
be held criminally liable for the lesser included
offence (even if not specifically charged). Such a
compromise would not be unlike that reached via excuses in the partial excuse category.

Excusing Conditions
Conviction for the lesser offence may in any event be
in the defendant's best interests. Indeed, she may
be advised to ensure her evidence as to state of mind
is sufficient to establish the mens rea required by
the lesser offence or more simply to plead guilty to
the lesser charge. Otherwise, the Damoclean sword of
the special verdict and mandatory committal which
appears whenever a defendant puts her state of mind in
issue may come crashing down.
     Put in positive terms, if the evidence at a trial
goes to prove insanity, the issue is raised even though the defendant does not want it raised. In this
very restricted sense insanity is a 'crime' as well as
a defence, a duality justified by the social harm doctrine. (41) Insanity will be found where because of
a defect in the reasoning processes caused by a 'disease of the mind' the defendant did not know what she
was doing, she did not realise it was wrong. (42)
     The case of Clarke (43) is a nice illustration
of how the tables can be turned on the defendant in
this way. A woman charged with theft denied liability, claiming she had not intended to take the goods
but had done so in a fit of absent-mindedness. She
had been ill, suffering from diabetes, anxiety, and
depression. Medical evidence was called in support.
The trial judge ruled that on evidence the defence
was one of not guilty by reason of insanity, whereupon

the woman changed her plea to guilty and was convicted. The Court of Appeal quashed the conviction, not
because the judge had raised the insanity issue but
because he had misapplied the McNaghten Rules: they
do not apply to those who retain the power of reasoning but in moments of confusion fail to use it, only
to those who are deprived of it.

A similar cloud hangs over the excusing condition
or defence of automatism. Automatism is a legal concept defined in <u>Bratty</u> (44) 'as connoting the state
of a person who, though capable of action is not conscious of what he is doing...It means unconscious in-
voluntary action and it is a defence because the mind
does not go with what is being done'. Leaving the
issue of insanity aside for the moment, could a PMT
sufferer succeed under this category?

Sandie Smith tried when charged with threatening
to kill and failed. In evidence she did not deny
knowing what she was doing but she claimed she did not
mean it. Katharina Dalton, giving expert evidence,
did not suggest that Smith was not fully aware of what
she was doing when making the threats. On the contrary, inferences from her conduct - pasting letters
onto a paper rather than writing in her own hand, intelligent enquiries of the police officer's where-
abouts - suggested she knew exactly what she was doing.

Upholding the trial judge's ruling that Smith had
failed to lay an evidential basis for the defence, the
Court of Appeal concluded that far from being unconscious, or unaware of what she was doing, Smith knew
what she was doing and intended to do it 'but was led
into doing it because the dark side of her nature
appeared as a result of her being unable to control the
impulse which she would not have allowed to dominate he
normally, due to the lack of...progesterone'. (45)

Thus the defence failed for lack of sufficient
evidence of impaired consciousness. Since it is still
feasible for a PMT sufferer to be able to adduce such
evidence, the defence of automatism cannot be ruled out
for her. Smith's case could be distinguished on the
facts. Premenstrual hypoglycaemia, if it exists,
could be of relevance here.

Hypoglycaemia can induce an aggressive outburst,
as claimed in the English case, and it can also impair
consciousness, inducing a coma-like state. Hypoglycaemia (in diabetics) has come before the courts several times and clearly been held to be capable of producing a state of automatism. (46) Even if we get this far
however, that the PMT sufferer had the requisite impaired consciousness induced by non-disputed evidence
as to hypoglycaemia, the rule relating to self-induced

automatism may bar a successful defence, acquittal
and freedom.

For where the offence charged is one of 'basic'
intent such as unlawful wounding, the prosecution
could argue that the defendant had induced her incapacity by failing to take food and that on the authority of Bailey (47) this precludes the defence of
automatism unless she can show she was not reckless
(subjectively aware) as to the risk she was running
by failing to take food at such a time. Such considerations would not apply, however, where the more serious 'specific' intent offence of wounding with intent
is concerned. Here the defence of automatism may well
succeed if supported by (accepted) medical evidence as
to a hypoclycaemic episode giving rise to impaired
consciousness.

Medical evidence is necessary to support a defence of automatism. If it is adduced to show that for
some reason other than hypoglycaemia the defendant
lacked awareness at the time of the event, caution
must reign for again the Damoclean sword of the special verdict looms large. Under the McNaghten Rules,
insanity is proved if the defect of reason is caused
by a 'disease of the mind'. What constitutes 'disease
of the mind' is a legal issue not a medical one. The
medical profession rarely use the term (except to
humour the judiciary), (48) preferring such concepts
as psychosis and mental illness.

Hypoglycaemia, resulting from a diabetic's failure to match insulin intake with food, has been held
not to be a disease of the mind. Epilepsy has. The
essence of the distinction appears to be that the former is extrinsically caused, while the latter is due
to an inherent condition. In the absence of premenstrual hypoglycaemia, then, a PMT sufferer attempting
to establish a defence of (non-insane) automatism on
the basis that her impaired consciousness was a consequence of her PMT hormonal disorder, may well be
held to have a 'disease of the mind', her state of
mind being due to inherent causes. Her defence of non-
insane automatism will become unwittingly a defence of
insane automatism.

The lack of clarity in the law regarding the defences of automatism and insanity has been criticised
(50) and may well be subject to further change (or
confusion) in the near future. As to confusion, one
wonders what the outcome would be should a PMT sufferer seek to establish that her state of mind was caused
by an epileptic seizure in turn the product of a (premenstrual) hypoglycaemic episode, a scenario envisaged
by Dalton in her PMT symptomatology. And how would

A Plea for PMT in the Criminal Law

Sandie Smith's situation (assuming impaired consciousness) be accommodated within the framework? She had
an hormonal disorder (inherent condition) giving rise
to an (assumed) impaired consciousness because at the
time of the offence she had failed to receive progesterone treatment (extrinsic cause) which may or may
not have been self-induced! Before leaving this
category of excusing condition, mention must be made
of the 'novel' defence run by Sandie Smith's counsel
as an alternative to her defence of automatism. He
appears to have argued for a new general defence of
'irresistible impulse' stemming from her medical condition which when specified as PMT appears to have
been characterised as a special defence open to PMT
sufferers alone, either or both to be left to the jury
with the direction that it is for them to decide whether she the defendant is to be held criminally responsible. The Court of Appeal threw out these arguments by invoking the social harm doctrine (meaning
the public must be protected). Smith had (previously)
stabbed a barmaid to death. If acquitted and discharged: 'There would be no control over her by society
through the courts and she would continue to be a
danger to all around her.' (51)
    In sum, one can conclude that attempts by a PMT
sufferer to avoid criminal liability and secure acquittal and freedom by invoking a defence of automatism
or by denying in terms of traditional legal analysis
that the essential elements of the offence have not
been made out, will probably not succeed. Given the
risks she will run of a special verdict being returned, she may be advised to not even try.

Partial Excuses
Criminal liability is not avoided by successful stag-
ing of a defence in the partial excuse category. A
dangerous or harmful defendant will not thereby be
acquitted and discharged into the community. Perhaps
this accounts for the very liberal interpretation by
the courts of the excuse in this category relevant to
PMT sufferers: the defence of diminished responsibility.
    Section 2 of the Homicide Act 1957 requires the
defence to establish that the defendant accused of
murder was suffering at the time of the offence from
such abnormality of mind (whether arising from a condition of arrested or retarded development of mind or
any inherent causes or induced by disease or by injury) as substantially impaired her mental responsibility for the killing. Medical experts must attest to
the abnormality of mind and its aetiology. In Byrne

172

(52) 'abnormality of mind' was contrasted with the requirement in the insanity defence of a 'defect of reason'. It was described as a state of mind so different from that of ordinary human beings that a responsible person would term it abnormal. It was further said to include lack of 'ability to exercise will power to control physical acts in accordance with ...rational thought'. The latter element arguably opens the door to a defence of irresistible impulse, so firmly shut by the Court of Appeal in Sandie Smith's case.

On a strict approach, the medical testimony on mental disorder should be such as to meet the legal criteria relating to 'abnormality of mind' and should specify causes of a non-environmental nature. In practice, the medical profession are willing to stretch thin evidence to enable a defence to succeed. 'Abnormality of mind' for example is found in a reactive depression which moreover does not have inherent causes but is a response to extreme adversity. Morbid jealousy is classified as psychosis. The courts appear mostly to turn a blind eye to these discrepancies and accept the medical evidence. (53)

Could a PMT sufferer establish 'abnormality of mind'? On a lax interpretation, certainly; even on a strict interpretation, given the scope afforded by the loss of control element, a PMT sufferer (always dependent on the facts of the case) could probably meet the requirements of this limb of defence. As to the second limb, specifying cause of abnormality, Dalton is on record as classifying PMT as a disease; while D'Orban would prefer to regard its hormonal base as inherent causes. (54) The third limb requires the defence to show that the abnormality of mind 'substantially impaired her mental (meaning moral) (55) responsibility'. Although medical evidence can be and is given on this point it has been held to be a question ultimately for the jury. (56) In effect the jury is asked to decide, given the abnormality of mind, whether so little blame can be attached to her actions that she should not be held responsible and criminally liable for murder.

Both Sandie Smith and Christine English succeeded in establishing this defence. Acknowledging the former, a legal commentator suggests that PMT does not sit easily in a defence of this kind. (57) A rejoinder is that much may depend on the facts of the case, the quality and credibility of the medical evidence, and the normative framework within which this evidence is interpreted and applied. Williams would put all the emphasis on the normative dimension. His view is

that the defence of diminished responsibility "is
interpreted in accordance with the morality of the
case rather than as an application of psychiatric concepts." (58) The success of defendants in 'mercy
killing' and 'spousal jealousy' cases bears him out in
this respect.
    In practice and in the absence of a blaze of pub-
licity, a PMT sufferer is likely to succeed in her
plea of guilty of manslaughter due to diminished responsibility, avoiding conviction for the more repreh-
ensible crime of murder and the automatic imposition
of a life prison sentence. Such confidence is supported by empirical evidence which suggests that the
vast majority of pleas of diminished responsibility
are successful. Moreover, most are accepted by the
prosecution, without the need for trial by jury. (59)

Mitigating Excuses

Mitigating excuses do not negate criminal liability,
nor do they downgrade the offence for which the defendant is ultimately convicted. Their sole function
is to justify leniency in sentencing, where the sentencer has discretion as to type and quantum of punishment. Some penalties are fixed by statute and cannot
be varied. Life imprisonment for murder is one, the
mandatory committal to and indefinite detention in a
psychiatric or special hospital following the special
verdict is another. In such cases excuses are irrelevant, though they may become relevant later when the
decision as to release, for example on parole, is
being made.
    Penalties for most offences, however, are not
fixed by law, though they are usually subject to a
maximum. The maximum for manslaughter is 'life'; the
maximum for threatening to kill, for which Sandie
Smith was convicted, is ten years' imprisonment. A
wide range of factors are considered by sentencers
when deciding on disposal. (60) Some, such as recognised penal objectives - general deterrence, the need
to incapacitate the offender where there is risk of
future danger - can 'aggravate' the sentence, others
mitigate. Mitigating excuses are those prescribing
leniency on the grounds of lack of moral blameworth-
iness.
    In the sentencing process, all these factors go
into the melting pot. Certain items are then extract-
ed and given priority according to the circumstances
of the case and the sentencer's value judgments. If
the sentencer is inclined to regard an offender who
'could help herself (or himself)' sympathetically,

because of illness, stress, spousal provocation or
other reasons, there is no reason why PMT should not
be accepted as a similar excuse going towards mitigation. (61)   In the absence of aggravating factors
which could neutralise the effect of such an excuse,
lenient disposal should follow.   Leniency can take the
form of a short prison sentence or even a non-custodial sentence, the latter even where an offence of some
gravity has been committed.   Christine English, having
avoided the automatic life sentence for murder through
successfully pleading diminished responsibility, was
then disposed of by way of conditional discharge.
Such leniency is not restricted to PMT sufferers nor
women generally.   Men who have killed their wives (and
children) and have run a successful diminished responsibility defence have received like leniency. (62)
     Where a plea in mitigation based on PMT falls on
sympathetic ears, the sentencer may nonetheless take
a different approach to disposal, the 'individualised'
one. (63)   Here 'punishment' is conceptualised as
'treatment' to be applied according to the perceived
needs of the individual offender, which are invariably
regarded as psychiatric.   PMT in the process is sub-
sumed under the more general category of mental disorder.   Thus Sandie Smith received a three year psychiatric probation order (64)   because her mental condition was thought to require and be susceptible to
medical treatment and because she consented to undergo
such treatment.   Had her mental condition been more
serious, sufficient to warrant detention in hospital,
and a place in a (secure if necessary) psychiatric hospital could have been found for her, she would have been
made subject to a Hospital Order.(65)   So detained she
could be discharged at a later date by medical staff,
unless the court had also imposed a Restriction Order
in which case her release would be subject to the
consent of the Home Secretary. (66)   A Restriction Order could only be imposed if the court felt it necessary to protect the public from serious harm.   In extreme cases where the risk of dangerous re-offending is
high, and a secure hospital place could not be found,
the court could use the life sentence as an indefinite,
preventive, form of detention. (67)
     The humane, outwardly non-punitive, individualised
approach has several stings in its tail.   In order to
secure release on probation, the PMT sufferer like
Sandie Smith, must subject herself to what is in effect
compulsory treatment.   Because the principle of propor-
tionality (length and type of disposal should match the
gravity of the offence) tends to recede into the background when individual needs (and the risk of future

danger) are taken as the starting point, it is possible for an offender sentenced in this way to spend
more time in hospital or prison than would have been
the case had the non-individualised (tariff) approach
been adopted. In short, a PMT sufferer could be deprived of her liberty for a considerable period despite
the initial offence for which she was convicted having
been a minor one. Moreover, since individual treatment is accorded on the basis of extensive medical and
other reports which take time to prepare, time spent
on remand for this purpose may be longer than the custodial sentence warranted by the offence. (68)
    Disadvantages of another kind accrue to those
regarded mentally disordered or ill and subjected to
the individualised treatment approach. It has been
argued that they suffer the indignity of being treated mad not bad, or perhaps even both. This is particularly pertinent where women are concerned reinforcing
seemingly entrenched views about their natural contrariness and emotional instability linked nicely, where PMT is concerned, to views of inherently weak female physiology. To this point we will return. Arguably, however, the individualised approach is not all
minuses. There are some plusses especially from the
woman offender's point of view. An obvious point
neutralising the 'compulsory' nature of treatment specified as a condition of being released on probation
is that the woman may undergo the treatment in any
event. This was almost certainly the case with Sandie
Smith. A woman may do so because however risky the
treatment might be (and large doses of progesterone
with unknown long term effects must fall into this
category) no other immediate means are available to
relieve the physical and psychological pain she is ex-
periencing. If so, treatment is understandable if not
welcome and she surely might as well receive it outside prison as in. She can always cease medication
under a probation order, though she is likely to be
returned to the court for being in breach of the order.
    If as a matter of principle she refuses to con-
sent to treatment under a probation order, she may be
sent to prison where she will have the dubious satisfaction of receiving treatment 'voluntarily'. In any
event, the prison authorities for administrative reasons as well as humane ones might persuade her to take
medication or therapy, if she did not seek it voluntarily. Of course, if she is prepared to take the
treatment solely to avoid detention in custody, the
issues are somewhat different. But one wonders how
often this would be the case and in any event such a
decision is ultimately for her to take and for her to

be allowed to take it. To suggest otherwise would firstly be somewhat authoritarian and secondly would be extremely dismissive of the harshness and deprivation that incarceration in prison entails.

CONCLUSION

One purpose of this paper has been to examine the scope of PMT as an excuse in the criminal law. We have shown that for the woman defendant it has potential as a partial or mitigating excuse but less so as an excusing condition. In addition, from the woman defendant's point of view, it can be extremely beneficial, avoiding the stigma of murder and warding off not only inevitable life imprisonment but possibly, too, a custodial sentence of any kind. In short, it can be extremely useful in serving the immediate, short term, interests of a particular female offender. But what of her long term interests, and the interests of women in general? A critical approach towards the use of PMT in the criminal law from this perspective stresses two main points.

The first point, already alluded to, is that the PMT phenomenon represents yet another example of the tendency to 'medicalise' female deviance, to treat conforming behaviour as healthy, to treat non-conforming behaviour as sick, ill, or mad. This process has been patently at work in the construction of the idea of PMT itself. We saw earlier that women's deviant behaviour has been the starting point for many studies set up to establish the existence of PMT. Moreover, in one recent study of female offenders where a significant number committed their offence in the premenstruum but few complained of PMT, the authors of the study still concluded that progesterone treatment might be beneficial not for the few but for the significant many. They assumed a treatable condition existed, though their only ground for doing so, in most instances, was the criminal activity itself. (69) This tendency to equate deviancy with disease has been criticised (70) because it subjects women's behaviour to medical treatment and control, because it impugns the integrity of the female actor, stripping her action of cultural and political meaning and anaesthetising the social and economic origin and conditions in which that action takes place. It thereby reduces explanations of women's behaviour to 'pure' matters of biology.

The second argument against PMT and its legislation through the criminal law is related to the first

but envisages more devastating political effects for
women. Stripped bare of its (sometimes) sophisticated
paraphernalia, the medical construct of PMT is said to
be no more than a reassertion of age old beliefs about
the natural contrariness of women, about the inherent
pathological functioning of female biology, about, to
quote Katharina Dalton, women being 'at the mercy of
their raging hormones'. (71) The absence of defining
symptoms, the theoretical reliance on periodicity for
definition and diagnosis, the lack of supporting evidence for hormonal and other theories, and the conse-
quent electric therapeutic approach all bear witness
to this. In terms of specific political effects it is
argued that PMT by reinforcing a conception of women
as inherently intellectually, emotionally, and physically inferior to men gives substance to and legitimates views which can be used to discriminate against
them, especially in the employment field. In short it
can be turned round and used against women in their
claims for sexual equality.
  Are these fears of adverse political effects
justified? Edwards has pointed out how in the 19th
century women were systematically excluded from participation in public life as doctors, lawyers and
professionals because of their weak and inferior physiology. (72) It is feasible similar processes are at
work today though no doubt taking more subtle and
complex forms, making them doubly difficult to resist.
Resistance is nonetheless possible and, I would argue,
need not necessarily be constituted solely by outright
rejection of PMT in all spheres, including the legal.
What I would like to argue for here is a moratorium
on a PMT 'boycott' and limited space for a plea for
PMT in the criminal law.
  The reasons are two-fold: firstly because PMT
in its existing medical form may yet provide a life
line for female offenders who cannot avoid incarceration in prison by any other means; secondly, because
in rejecting PMT outright within or without the criminal law we may well run the risk of throwing the
proverbial baby out with the proverbial bathwater.
PMT, though constructed by the medical profession and
imposed upon women, does nonetheless refer to real
experiences. The danger in rejecting the PMT medical
construct is that this lived reality may get swept
back under the carpet from which it has only recently
been retrieved, there to be swamped in the layers of
shame, myth and taboo historically associated with it.
We need to challenge the medical notion of PMT while
continuing to acknowledge the lived reality of it. The
criminal courts may even provide one forum for doing so.

NOTES

My thanks go to Sue Edwards, editor, for her
encouragement and patience, and to Sue Atkins,
my colleague in the Law Faculty at the University of Southampton, for her tremendous help
in preparing early drafts of this paper.

(1)   See eg G.I.M. Swyer: letter to The Times,
        November 11 1981; M. Berlins and T. Smith:
        Should PMT be a Woman's All Purpose Excuse?:
        The Times November 12 1981
(2)   J. Nicholson and K. Barltrop: 'Do Women Go
        Mad Every Month?' New Society February 11
        1982
(3)   See eg D. Nicholson-Lord: 'Judges Reject
        Menstrual Tension Defence', The Times, April
        28 1982
(4)   H. Allen: 'At the Mercy of Her Hormones: Pre-
        Menstrual Tension and the Law', m/f No. 9
        1984: 20-43; S. Laws: 'The Sexual Politics
        of Premenstrual Tension', Women's Studies Int.
        Forum Vol. 6 No. 1 1983: 19-31
(5)   Allen, (1984) ibid.
(6)   D. Brahams: 'Premenstrual Syndrome: A Disease
        of the Mind?', The Lancet, November 28 1981;
        1238-40; Craddock (1981) CLY 476
(7)   The description used by the trial judge accor-
        ding to The Times report: November 4 1981
(8)   Smith: Court of Appeal Criminal Division:
        April 27 1982: Transcript No. 1/A/82; see also
        case note (1982) Crim. L.R. 531-2
(9)   The Times November 12 1981
(10)   See D. Brahams: The Lancet op. cit. No. 6 for
        details of the case
(11)   See eg Swyer: The Times op. cit. No. 1
(12)   Op. cit. No. 4
(13)   Ibid. Her prescription which is of relevance
        to the main argument of this paper is to dis-
        card the defensive attitude many women adopt
        on PMT, turn it round and challenge the med-
        ical profession and its categories and begin
        to construct less distorted forms of self-
        expression in relation to menstruation and the
        pattern of cyclic change.
(14)   E. Frank: 'The Hormonal Causes of Premenstrual
        Tension', 1931 Archives of Neurology and Psy-
        chiatry, 36: 1053-7
(15)   Eg K. Dalton: 'Menstruation and Accidents',
        British Medical Journal, 1960: 2: 1425-6;
        'Menstruation and Crime', BMJ, 1961: 1752;

'Menstruation and Examination', <u>The Lancet</u>,
1968: 2: 1386-8. A. Coppen and N. Kessel:
'Menstruation and Personality', <u>British Jour-</u>
<u>nal of Psychiatry</u>, (1963) 109; 711-21. C.M.
Tonks et al. 'Attempted Suicide and the Menstrual Cycle', <u>J. Psychosom Res</u> 1968: 11: 319-
23. R.H. Tuch: 'The Relationship Between a
Mother's Menstrual Status and her Response to
Illness in Her Child', <u>Psychosom Med</u>, 1975:
37(5): 388-94. J.H. Morton et al. 'A Clinical Study of Premenstrual Tension', <u>American</u>
<u>Journal of Obstetrics and Gynaecology</u> (1953)
65: 1182-119. J.R. Udry and N.M. Morris:
'Distribution of Coitus in the Menstrual
Cycle', <u>Nature</u>, 1968: 220: 593-6. P.T. D'Orban and J. Dalton: 'Violent Crime and the
Menstrual Cycle', <u>Psychological Medicine</u>,
1980: ;0: 353-359. See also M.B. Parlee:
'The Premenstrual Syndrome', <u>Psychological</u>
<u>Bulletin</u>, 1973 Vol. 80 No. 6 454-465 for a
review and trenchant criticism of these and
other studies conducted prior to 1973.
(16) He believes the evidence to be 'cast iron',
<u>The Times</u> April 28 1982
(17) See list of studies provided by A. Clare in
<u>Psychiatric Problems in Women: Part 3 The</u>
<u>Premenstrual Syndrome</u>, SK and F Publications
1982: 4
(18) C. Doyle: 'Mean Moody and Monthly', <u>Observer</u>
June 10 1983
(19) K. Dalton: 'Legal Implications of PMT',
<u>World Medicine</u>, April 17 1982: 93-4 Note
there is no symptom unique to PMT (called
premenstrual syndrome (PMS) in much medical
literature), nor is any one symptom common to
all sufferers.
(20) K. Dalton: <u>The Premenstrual Syndrome and Prog-</u>
<u>esterone Therapy</u>, 1977: 6
(21) Dalton: <u>World Medicine</u>, op. cit. No. 19
(22) Dalton: op. cit. No. 20: 96-100
(23) Even then there are problems of differential
self-diagnosis: see Clare op. cit. No. 17 and
<u>The Times</u> (letters) November 26 1981
(24) P.T.D'Orban: 'Premenstrual Syndrome: A Disease of the Mind?' <u>The Lancet</u>, December 19/26
1981: 1413
(25) G. Sampson: 'Premenstrual Syndrome: A Double-
Blind Controlled Trial of Progesterone and
Placebo', <u>British Journal of Psychiatry</u>,1979:
135: 209-15. See also review of studies in
this area in <u>The Lancet</u>, December 19/26 1981:

1394

(26)   Swyer, op. cit. No. 1
(27)   'I don't think progesterone works because
         there is progesterone deficiency,' said by
         Dr Ronald V Norris, head of the Premenstrual
         Syndrome Program in Reading. Mass., and rep-
         orted in the New York Times, July 22 1982
(28)   Because of premenstrual weight gain and ab-
         dominal bloatedness: Dalton: 1979 op. cit.
         No. 20: 28
(29)   Nicholson and Barltrop: op. cit. No. 2
(30)   Lynne Harne: published in Spare Rib March
         1982 with article on PMT by S. O'Sullivan.
(31)   M.E. Bennun and C. Gardner-Thorpe: 'McNaghten
         Rules Epilepsy-OK?', Modern Law Review 1984:
         Vol. 47: 92-8, 95
(32)   M. Wasik: 'Partial Excuses in the Criminal
         Law' MLR 1982 Vol. 45: 516-33. See also by
         the same author: 'Excuses at the Sentencing
         Stage', Crim. L. R. July 1983: 450-65
(33)   Criminal Procedure (Insanity) Act 1964 SS 1
         and 5
(34)   In 1981 the insanity defence was successfully
         raised in three cases
(35)   Infanticide Act 1938 S.1(1)
(36)   See G. Williams: 'The Theory of Excuses',
         Crim. L. R. 1982: 732-42, 741
(37)   K. O'Donovan: 'The Medicalisation of Infant-
         icide', Crim. L. R. 1984:259-64, 263
(38)   Caldwell (1982) AC 341
(39)   Offences Against the Person Act S.18
(40)   Ibid., S.20. It is assumed here as did the
         Court of Appeal in Bailey (1983) 1 W.L.R. 760
         that S.20 involves a subjective awareness of
         risk and not objective recklessness of the
         Caldwell (op. cit. No. 38) type
(41)   'It is (the judge's) duty to (raise the insan-
         ity issue) rather than allow a dangerous per-
         son to be at large,' per Lord Denning in
         Bratty v Attorney General for Northern Ireland
         (1963) A.C. 386
(42)   McNaghten's Case (1843) 10 Cl. and Fin. 200,
         8 E.R. 718 (known as the McNaghten Rules).
(43)   (1972) 1 All ER 219-21
(44)   Op. cit. No. 41
(45)   CAP Transcript op. cit. No. 8
(46)   Of the non-insane type: Quick (1973) QB 910;
         Bailey op. cit. No. 40
(47)   Op. cit. No. 40
(48)   G. Williams: Textbook of Criminal Law, 2nd
         (ed.) 644

(49)   Sullivan (1983) 3 W.L.R. 123
(50)   See eg C. Wells: 'Whither Insanity?' Crim
       L.R. December 1983 787-97
(51)   CAP Transcript op. cit. No. 8:10
(52)   (1960) 2 QB 396
(53)   See Williams: op. cit. No. 48 Ch on Diminished
       Responsibility 685-94
(54)   D'Orban: op. cit. No. 24
(55)   Williams: op. cit. No. 48: 686
(56)   Walton (1978) AC 788
(57)   Crim. L. R. (1982) 532
(58)   Williams: op. cit. No. 48: 693
(59)   S. Dell: 'Diminished Responsibility Reconsid-
       ered', Crim. L. R. (1982) 809-18.
(60)   D.A. Thomas: 'Principles of Sentencing', 1979:
       194-222
(61)   Dalton has cited quite a few instances known
       to her. See for example report of talk given
       to police surgeons in The Times June 20 1981.
       Five examples are given there including cases
       of a teenager harassing police with 999 calls,
       a student accused of arson, another accused of
       stabbing and 'an angry female throwing a brick
       through a window'.
(62)   Asher (1981) The Times June 9: man who stran-
       gled his wife in jealousy given suspended
       sentence; Guardian July 9 1983: man who stran-
       gled alleged mentally ill wife given condit-
       ional discharge.
(63)   Thomas: op. cit. No. 60: 17
(64)   Powers of Criminal Courts Act 1973 S.3
(65)   Mental Health Act 1983 S.37: she must be suff-
       ering from one of the four forms of mental
       disorder specified in the Act.
(66)   Mental Health Act 1983 S.41. It is now poss-
       ible where both a Hospital Order and a Restr-
       iction Order (but not mandatory committal) are
       in force for a patient to apply to a Mental
       Health Review Tribunal for release.
(67)   Thomas: op. cit. No. 60: 300
(68)   See S. Edwards: 'Premenstrual Tension', Justice
       of the Peace, August 7 1982; 476-8
(69)   D'Orban and Dalton: op. cit. No. 15
(70)   Eg by C. Smart: Women, Crime and Criminology:
       1976: 147 specifically in connection with the
       association between crime and mental illness
(71)   K. Dalton: The Menstrual Cycle, 1971
(72)   S. Edwards: Medico-Legal Conundrums - The Leg-
       al Organisation of Physiological Difference,
       British Sociological Association Conference
       Paper 1982

Chapter Nine

MALE VIOLENCE AGAINST WOMEN: EXCUSATORY AND
EXPLANATORY IDEOLOGIES IN LAW AND SOCIETY

Susan Edwards

This paper examines the subjection of women to
men, their victimisation and its legitimation by and
in the civil and criminal 'justice' system, which remains relatively immune to women's suffering in its
provision of impotent remedies. It explores too, the
interpretation of law by agents working in both the
civil and criminal 'justice' system, their use of discretion and their decision to invoke criminal or civil procedures. Male violence is explored and assessed in the context of the prevailing ideological backcloth coloured by a social fabric of attitudes regarding women's duties and obligations, men's rights and
privileges and the social pathology rationales so often
resorted to in explanation of male violence towards
women.
    The seriousness or triviality of violence against
wives or cohabitees was, as it is now,very often estimated and adduced according to whether 'she stays on'.
In attempting to understand why women stay with violent men or with men who resort to violence, there had
been a division clearly emergent between those who
contend that an adequate explanation can be found through the investigation of individual pathologies of
offenders (Faulk 1974, Brisson 1981, Fitch et al.
1983) and of victims (Snell et al. 1964, Gayford
1979, Tahourdin 1983), and those who conversely focus
on the socio-legal and structural imperatives which
define the parameters of forced dependency, (Hanmer
1977, Freeman 1979, Dobash and Dobash 1980, Griffiths
1980, 1981).
    Given that women have been historically dependent
on men, either fathers or husbands, for provision of
shelter, housing and the most basic of requirements,
the more recent suggestion that some women may be, as
Erin Pizzey explains 'prone to violence', is an erron-
eous interpretation masking the real structural ine-

qualities and imperatives, which can have nothing more
deleterious consequences for the endeavour to find
appropriate remedies for those so abused. This somewhat perverse theorisation gained significant ground
with the growing assimilation of psycho-analytical
ideas, an interpretation which in the earlier years
went largely unchallenged until in the mid sixties,
when with the emergence of the Women's Liberation
movement, the all too ready explanation of womens'
victimisation as the product of 'her' own personality
and pathology was confronted for the politically ex-
pedient orthodoxy it was. Instead, structural inequalities were accusingly identified and exposed for
the contributory role they played in such violence,
its normalisation and perpetuation. Male violence,
family violence and sexual violence were re-defined in
relation to the objective realities of women's subordination and powerlessness and male dominance and
power (Martin 1976). This redefinition was crucial
for the development of the remedies sought and the
ameliorative action taken (Hanmer 1977: Weir 1977,
1979, Freeman 1980, Jackson and Rushton 1982: 17)
    Structural inequalities in the distribution of
power in contemporary society have frequently been
masked, eclipsed or at the most, marginalised for a
preferred concern and focus on considerations and explanations of male violence toward women relating to
psycho-pathology. It has been frequently in this
enclave that both male 'offenders' and female 'victims' have been studied, despite the force of argument
identifying structural factors. As Straus (1977),
asserts: '...wife beating is not just a personal abnormality, but rather has its roots in the very structuring of society and the family; that is in the cultural norms and in the sexist organisation of society'. (1)
    In turning first to the evidence of the extent of
violence, from assaults to homicide, criminal statistics and research studies conclusively reveal a significant representation of violence against family
members and women within the family in particular.
Given this evidence, it is perhaps curious that so
little research has been conducted both into domestic
violence assault and domestic violence homicide, notwithstanding the work of Hanmer 1977, Weir 1977, Pahl 1982,
Dobash and Dobash 1980, Wassoff 1982 - on domestic
violence and - Wasik 1982, Pattullo 1983 - on domestic
violence homicide.
    What little research is available nevertheless
provides sufficient evidence of the victimisation of
women, which has as far as we can see, remained his-

torically consistent. As Dobash and Dobash (1980)
point out, 'In England and Wales for the years 1885-
1905, out of 487 murders committed by men, more than
a quarter of the victims, 124, were women murdered by
their husbands: another substantial proportion 115,
were mistresses or sweethearts of their assailants.'
(1980;15) Von Hentig in his analysis of 1931 data,
found that 62% of women victims of homicide, had been
killed by their husbands, whilst 14% of male homicide
victims had been killed by their wives. (2) Wolfgang
1958,(3) in his study of 588 victims of homicide,
found that 41% of female victims had been killed by
their husbands, whilst 11% of male victims had been
killed by their wives. (p. 212) There were too, significant differences between the sexes as to 'mode of
resentment' (method of commission of killing), and
place of incident. 45% of the wives were killed in
the bedrooms compared with 46% of the husbands, who
were killed in the kitchen. Men used a variety of
methods to kill and of the 45 wives killed, 17 were
shot, 15 beaten to death. McClintock, (1963) (4)
found that in approximately 27% of crimes known to the
police, the offender and victim were related by marriage. Gibson and Klein, (1969) (5) found that 63% of
all murdered women were married to the defendant whilst, Blom Cooper, (1964) (6) found that in 169 of 396
cases, the victim and suspect were intimately related.
    In criminology theory for example, significant
importance is placed on the subcultural theories in
the explanation of male violence. In the work of
Wolfgang and Ferracuti, (7) a subculture of male violence partly explains the shared willingness to express
disdain, disgruntlement, and other hostile feelings in
personal interaction by using physical force. Given
the general acceptance of this theorisation, it is
curious that such a view of male power within society
more widely, is not taken into some account when domestic violence assault and spousal homicide are analysed, since a culture of male power, domination and
physical force is endemic in the structure of society,
where women are physically and sexually abused. This
domination and codification of male force and violence
is explicated in an analysis of superstructures. [The
law in particular co difies, legitimates and sanctions
male dominance through the physical and sexual abuse
of women and it is to these two aspects of the ensh-
rinement of male power we now turn].

Male Violence Against Women: Excusatory and Explanatory
Ideologies in Law and Society

MEN'S RIGHTS - WOMEN'S DUTIES

First the chastisement of women that is their physical
abuse has been codified in the laws regulating marriage. Broadly speaking, marriage has provided the husband with a series of rights whilst depriving the wife
of the few she may have had before marriage. Marriage
provided the husband with precedent to chastise, to
confine, to demand consortium, whilst institutionalis-
ing his adultery. The interpretation of a husband's
rights has permitted extremes of behaviour in the
battery, imprisonment and rape of wives. Yet significantly, during the 19th century in particular, men
were extolled as the 'protectors' of women. Histor-
ians have written of the 'gentlemanly code of conduct'
and many argued that if men were the natural protectors of women, as Ruskin and others claimed, what need
had women of rights in their own name? It seemed no
problem to men that women had no <u>locus standi</u>. Blackstone (1775) asserted:

> We may observe,that even the disabilities which
> the wife lies under, are for the most part in-
> tended for her protection and benefit. (8)

Yet Sachs (1978) and others have contested that this
claim to male protectiveness was little more than a
myth, especially so with reference to working class
women:

> The fact that millions of women, both married
> and single, worked in paid employment outside the
> home, showed that there was no overwhelming biol-
> ogical or cultural aversion to women working for
> cash. There was nothing intrinsic to the female
> condition, no special frailty, that the male leg-
> islators and judges were bent on respecting. (9)

Thus the patriarchal claim to protect female sexuality
and femininity because women were, after all, passive
and weak, had little foundation in reality.
Moreover, far from supporting the view that men
protected women, J.S. Mill saw that women lay in their
complete power:

> The vilest malefactor has some wretched woman
> tied to him, against whom he can commit any atr-
> ocity except killing her, and if tolerably caut-
> ious, can do that without much danger of legal
> penalty. (10)

186

Male Violence Against Women: Excusatory and Explanatory
Idiologies in Law and Society

Such ideas as expressed by Mill the champion of wom-
en's rights, had already been expressed earlier by
J. Bentham, who urged that women were entitled to more
sympathy and protection.

> Under the present laws of marriage, Mill declar-
> ed, wives could potentially be forced to endure
> not merely the traditional forms of slavery, but
> the 'worst description' of bondage known to his-
> tory. Unlike most other slaves, a wife could be
> made subject to duty 'at all hours and all min-
> utes'. She could be denied even Uncle Tom's
> privilege of having 'his own life in his cabin'.
> She had no legal means, as existed in some slave
> codes, to compel the master to sell her. And
> worst of all, she could not refuse her master ev-
> en 'the worst familiarity' but must submit to
> 'the lowest degradation of a human being, that
> of being made the instrument of an animal funct-
> ion contrary to her inclinations'. (11)

Throughout the 19th century, philosophers, politicians and feminists exposed the indignities associated with marriage for the female sex, her total eclip-
se under rule of men who could do with her as his wish
or whim fancied. The reality of this protection was
further exposed by Matilda Blake:

> Their so-called protectors daily beat, torture
> and violently assault them, often with such
> violence that death results; while the male jud-
> ges, appointed by a government chosen by an ex-
> clusively male electorate, punish the offenders
> in a most inadequate manner, holding a woman's
> life at a lesser value than a purse containing
> a few shillings. (12)

The claim to male protectiveness and gentlemanly conduct with its accompanying chivalry, juxtaposed against the brutality, grossness and vulgarity of men's
'real' treatment of women appeared to be behavioural
conduct occupying the extremes of a continuum. On
one level, this was undoubtedly true, but it is more
accurately the case that brutality and chivalry in fact
stemmed from a common source - that of man's superiority and woman's inferiority. Chivalry became a
way of extolling female passivity and meekness as
qualities to be celebrated. But was the extolement of
passivity, meekness and subservience through the ideology of class etiquette and appropriate femininity
any different from enforcing subservience through a

187

Male Violence Against Women: Excusatory and Explanatory
Ideologies in Law and Society

demonstration of physical superiority in violent assault? As the anonymous writer of 'Outrages of Women'
noted:

> both the chivalrous act or rushing across a room
> to pick up a lady's handkerchief and the act of
> beating her to the ground though a very differ-
> ent thing, stemmed from man's superiority and
> perpetuated the weakness of woman. (13)

It was no accident that Engels wrote:

> The modern family contains in germ, not only
> slavery (servitus), but also serfdom. (p. 122)

but the result of a close analysis of the family and
denial of legal standing to women within that contractual relationship. Male power is further acknow-
leged by Engels:

> In order to make certain of the wife's fidelity
> and therefore of the paternity of the children,
> she is delivered over unconditionally into power
> of the husband; if he kills her, he is only ex-
> ercising his rights. (p. 122)

Given the lack of any legal standing, it is not surprising that his analysis of marriage at this time
was a reflection of the master and slave relationship,
his interpretation of the legal status denied to the
wife is clear:

> The legal irregularity of the two partners be-
> queathed to us from earlier social conditions
> is not the cause but the effect of the economic
> oppression of woman. (pp.136-7)

Within case law, as far as chastisement of wives
was concerned, the husband was always right. According to Fitzherbert, the only restraint imposed on a
husband's free rein to chastise a wife was that 'he
did so in a moderate manner'. In Bradley v Wife
(1663), the court upholding this right to chastise,
refused to bind the husband over unless it could be
proved that her life was in danger, 'because by law,
he had power of castigation'. (14) In Lawes' Resol-
utions of Women's Rights, (1632) we find that:

> A man may beat an outlaw, a traitor, a pagan,
> his villein or his wife because by the Law Comm-
> on, these persons can have no action. (15)

Male Violence Against Women: Excusatory and Explanatory
Ideologies in Law and Society

Frances Power Cobbe, some two hundred years later
pointed to the analogous classification of women alongside minors, idiots and criminals in so far as they
were denied legal standing. But as Whatley in The
Bride Bush (1617) pointed out, beating a wife was
only justified in circumstances of 'the utmost extrem-
ities of unwifelike carriage'. Such that the root of
all good carriage is withered should she stand upon
terms of equality. We can only conclude that appropriate wifelike carriage was then as indeed was true
for the 19th century and to a lesser extent today,
that of complete subservience and obedience, without
self-assertion or challenge to male power.
        Later, the legal authorisation became increasing-
ly clarified wherein the circumstances considered relevant to the 'sanction' of wife beating were enunciat-
ed. In the commentaries of Sir William Blackstone,
(1775) the husband is empowered to correct his wife,
wives being classified along with children:

        For as (husband) is to answer for 'misbehaviour',
        the law thought it reasonable to intrust him
        with this power of chastisement in the same mod-
        eration that a man is allowed to correct his app-
        rentices or children. (17)

This question of a husband's rights in relation to a
wife's duties, is a matter which has interfered with
the wife's right to protection as a person. It is
perhaps not altogether surprising then, that the earliest official context in which the 'tariff' and
'range' of sentences are known to have been proposed
was in a Home Office Inquiry into wife beating. (18)
And so it seemed that within the law, provision for
beating was institutionalised, normalised and accepted under the guise of chastisement. The 'rule of
thumb' is referred to and so it appears the 'normal'
wife beating involved the use of sticks no thicker
than a man's thumb. Jeaffreson in Brides and Bridals,
(1872) maintained that it was possible to thrash a
woman with a cudgel, but not to knock her down with an
iron bar. (19)
        Of course violence against wives frequently res-
ulted not in a divorce action or a charge of violence,
but in murder; yet very few husbands were brought to
justice in the real sense. Most faced charges of manslaughter where the penalties ranged from a fine to a
few months in prison, whilst wives who murdered husbands faced more serious penalties. Such disparity
again is found enshrined in law. Blackstone's Commentaries reflected this:

> ...we [must] recollect that if the feme kills
> her baron, it is regarded by the law as a much
> more atrocious crime; as she not only breaks
> through the restraints of humanity and conjugal
> affection, but throws off all subjection to the
> authority of her husband. And therefore the law
> denominated her crime a species of treason, and
> condemns her to the same punishment as if she
> had killed the king. (20)

Again in case law too we find the parameters of chastisement being established, and with the legal enshrin-
ement of the doctrine of provocation, the concept of
'victim precipitation' blossomed to its fullest flow-
er. Numerous defendants on charges of wife assault
and wife murder said in their defence that they were
provoked or aggravated. One such case was heard before the Warrington County Police Court in 1880, where
the defendant was charged with brutally assaulting
his wife whom he had repeatedly kicked in the head and
ribs whilst she lay barely conscious. The Illustrated
Police News, 20th May 1880, reported the defendant as
saying he was aggravated and was sentenced to 14 days'
hard labour.

Provocation was invariably invoked in cases of
wife murder. The report from the Illustrated Police
News, 8th August 1885, characterises the deceased wife
as addicted to drink and frequently misbehaving,
whilst the defendant was a sober hardworking man -
who on the fatal night in question had been provoked
to the point of frenzy, upon which he had an epileptic
seizure and killed her. The jury found the prisoner
guilty of manslaughter and sentenced him to 5 years.

The belief in the 'provoking woman' influenced
the administration of legislation, decisions in case
law and decisions in the coroner's court, for it was
here that the murder of a wife was frequently reduced
to manslaughter.

In reality, the extent of this 'provocation' extends very often to 'a bell not answered with the
required promptitude - a dinner somewhat late or badly
cooked - a pair of slippers not to be found when wanted - a book carried off - a set of papers disarranged
...' (21) Yet the same author of the above quotation
adds that:

> 'it cannot, we are afraid be concealed, that there
> are often provocations arising from the conduct
> or behaviour of the woman herself'. Adding to
> that 'Some women have an unfortunate way of what
> is called "nagging" and finally, 'What are called

unprovoked assaults, we suspect are the except-
tions to the rule.' (22)

Similarly, objectors to the various aggravated assault
Bills, objected on the ground that women were very
much to blame for violence perpetrated against them.
In opposition to the 1860 Bill, Mr Clive asserted:

> But though there were many cases in which delic-
> ate women came forward and claimed protection
> against brutal husbands, it must be remembered,
> on the other hand, that a mischievious and ill
> tempered woman could very easily impose on a
> magistrate, and by aggravating her husband until
> he struck her, might continue to bring him into
> a police court, rid herself of his society, and
> disgrace him by the punishment which this Bill
> proposed to inflict. (23)

Mr. Caly, warned Honourable Members of 'the violence
of an angry woman's tongue'. (24) Many allegations
were doubted, indeed the attitude of the police courts
to allegations of marital cruelty were clear during
the 19th century and this was viewed very much in the
same light as if the woman was 'suffering from nerves'.
    Of course, it is generally agreed that the common
law right of a husband to physically chastise his wife
was finally abolished in R v Jackson, 1890 1 AB:671.
But that is a somewhat naive and short-sighted interpretation as Meacher v Meacher 1946 [P] : 216 amply
demonstrates, since the judge first held that a man
was within his rights in assaulting his wife because
she refused to obey his order not to visit her relatives. (See Freeman 1980 : 239).
    Husbands have also been granted the right to sex-
ually abuse wives, although within the law this has
been referred to discreetly as a husband's right to
consortium. In marriage a wife was owned by a husband,
she had a monetary value as any other goods or services. Prior to the royal assent of the Matrimonial
Causes Act 1857 (S.59) a husband could bring an action
for damages against his wife's seducer, adulterer or
rapist, even if his wife previously deserted him.
Such civil actions were know as Crim Cons (criminal
conversation) and enabled the husband to issue a 'writ
of ravishment or trespass vi et armis de uxore rapta
et abducta', under which he could obtain damages
against any man who had taken his wife away (Bromley,
1976 : 123). Compensation for the loss of a wife's
services provided a form of monetary redress for a
husband's wounded honour, yet no such action or redress

was made available to the wife. In <u>Macfadzen v Oliv-
vant</u> (1805 East 6: 387), where a plea of trespass was
proposed, the defendant with 'force and arms' made an
assault upon G. the plaintiff's wife, and then and
there seduced her, whereby the plaintiff during all
the time aforesaid, lost and was deprived of comfort,
society and fellowship'. In summing up Lord Chief
Justice Ellenborough declared that since the body and
mind of the wife had been corrupted, the wife was
'less qualified to perform the duties of the marriage
state'.
    <u>Crim cons</u> were abolished under the 1857 Act, be-
ing replaced by a statutory claim for damages (S.33),
which provided the following: the wife's earnings
were seized by the husband; and the wife was subjected to physical punishment. In such claims, the 'value'
of a wife was assessed on two grounds: pecuniary
'value' was assessed according to her moral character
and, the second ground was the injury to a husband's
feelings. In <u>Lynch v Knight</u> (1861 ER 11), Lord Wen-
sleydale declared that the loss of a wife's consortium
(sexual congress and household duties appropriate to
the female role) 'is of material value, capable of being estimated in money', thus the 'reputation of chastity' of a wife would affect the amount awarded for
damages. The loss of the consortium of an immoral
wife, even though she may well have been good, kind
and gentle, was considered less than the loss of consortium of a moral wife, even though she may have been
aggressive, slovenly and cruel. In such actions, a
clear distinction emerged between the wife who encouraged or precipitated such infidelity and the wife who
was seduced, thereby creating two categories of immoral woman. In <u>Keyse v Keyse and Maxwell</u> (1886, XI,
PB), Sir James Hannen said to the jury, '...you are
not here to punish at all. Any observations directed
to that end are improperly addressed to you', explaining the principle of loss: 'If he did not seduce her
away from her husband that makes a very material difference in considering the damages to be given.' A
principle reiterated in <u>Butterworth v Butterworth</u>
(1920, 36 LTR). Judge McCardie declaring, 'If the wife
be of wanton disposition or disloyal instincts, it is
obvious that her general value to the husband is so
much the less.' Again in <u>Comyn v Comyn and Hump</u> (1860,
32 LJ) Mr. Justice Cresswell conjected; 'If a woman
surrenders herself very readily to a man, who takes no
pains to obtain her affections, or if you have reason
to suppose that she had made the first advances, you
are to estimate, as far as you can form an estimate in
money, the loss the husband has sustained.'

Similarly, Sir James Hannen declared in Darbishire v Darbishire (1890, 62 LTR), 'Now, remember, there
is a particular distinction between the value of different wives...if she has led a loose life before marriage, her value is not the same as that of a virtuous
woman...If a man's wife goes and walks the streets,
the husband is not entitled to come here and recover
damages against any man who goes and consorts with
that woman.' So much for the protection extended to
women in and by law. It appears from the consortium
action that they were owned as property - their worth
being estimated according to their chastity value.
The right to consortium of a wife extended beyond the
award of damages to a wounded husband in the event of
his wife's adultery. It codified the 'right to rape'.
In The History of the Pleas of the Crown first published in 1736, Hale asserted:

> But the husband cannot be guilty of a rape comm-
> itted by himself upon his lawful wife, for by
> their mutual matrimonial consent and contract the
> wife hath given up herself in this kind unto her
> husband, which she cannot retract. (26)

It is worth noting the remarks of the judge in Smith
v Kaye (1904) 20 Times L R disclosing the double
standard: 'Apparently the law takes the view that the
wife has no such right of control or claim to a husb-
and's services as is possessed by the husband with
regard to the wife.' He continued by saying that the
wife had made a contract that she could not retract.
The principle of the 'right to rape' was enshrined in
R v Clarence (1888, 22 QBD) which stands as a test of
the Hale doctrine. Mr. Justice Hawkins, the presiding
judge asserted:

> The sexual communion between them is by virtue of
> the irrevocable privilege conferred once and for
> all on the husband at the time of the marriage,
> and not at all by virtue of a consent given upon
> each act of communion, as is the case between un-
> married persons.

During the 19th and 20th centuries several actions for marital rape were brought by the wife. In
R v Jackson (1891) 1 QBD 1 671) where the husband enforced his conjugal rights, Halsbury held that a husband could be convicted of assault in this case, but
could not be convicted of enforcing his conjugal
rights. During the 20th century certain exceptions
to this rule have evolved. Consider, for instance

the case of R v Clarke (1949, 2 ALL ER) where Mr.
Justice Byrne decided that a husband could be found
guilty of raping his wife if a separation order had
been granted, since such an order would automatically
revoke her consent to intercourse. In R v Miller
(1954, 2 All ER), Mr. Justice Lynskey decided that a
husband could be found guilty of rape if he and his
wife had entered into a separation agreement containing a non-molestation clause. In this particular case
there was no separation order or agreement in force.
The judge held that the husband could not be guilty
since there was no evidence in law that the wife's
consent had been revoked. The principle in Clarke
was entended to R v O'Brien (1974, 3 ALL ER). The
judge declared that where a decree nisi brings the
marriage to an end, a husband could be found guilty of
rape. And, more recently, a husband can be guilty of
rape after his wife has obtained a non-molestation injunction. The real extent of this prodigious desire
to protect women can be summed up in the words of
Lord Dundedin in the normalisation of the exercise of
gentle violence:

> If the wife is adamant in her refusal the husband
> must choose between letting his wife's will prev-
> ail, thus wrecking the marriage, and acting with-
> out her consent. It would be intolerable if he
> were to be conditioned in his course of action by
> the threat of criminal proceedings. (27)

This 'iron law' right of men to women's bodies
is now being resisted, and criticised from within and
outside the law. The Working Paper on Sexual Offences
(1980) (Criminal Law Revision Committee) recommended
that rape in marriage should be an offence, but as a
safeguard prosecutions to be brought only by the DPP.
(28) Although in Scottish law the position adopted
in Duffy might be considered a significant move in the
right direction. Lord Robertson in HM Advocate v
Duffy asserted:

> I can see no logic in justifying such a law by
> making a differentiation between a man and woman
> who happen to have gone through a ceremony of
> marriage and ones who have not, and I do not un-
> derstand why the mere fact that the marriage bond
> has never been formally broken should make any
> difference...To some extent it might be a quest-
> ion of degree, but I do not think that it can be
> affirmed as a matter of principle that the law
> of Scotland today, is that a husband in no

194

circumstances can be guilty of the crime of rape
upon his wife. (New Law Journal, 13th Jan. 1984)

And more recently, the 15th Report of the Criminal Law
Revision Committee on Sexual Offences concluded:

We recommend that the offence of rape be extended
to enable a prosecution to be brought for rape
where a man has sexual intercourse with his wife
without her consent when the two are not cohabiting with each other. (para 2.85)

Although they remained divided over whether other instances of non-consensual intercourse in marriage
should be deemed as rape (p. 93-4).(29)
     There is no doubt that forced sexual intercourse
in marriage is a component of domestic violence assault. Mrs Z in giving evidence to the Select Committee on Violence in Marriage (5/8/75 p. 22) described
one incident at the hands of a brutal husband, where
she was stripped and with a wet towel, beaten severely
by her husband and his friends. The committee asked
whether she had ever been raped. She replied, 'No,
I had to give in to what they wanted because I was so
scared.' (p. 25).
     Any move in the direction of law reform in this
area, would be welcomed since many wives living with
husbands and estranged wives, many alone, are continually subjected to such violence without any protection from the court. In R v Caswell (Crim Law Rev
1984: 111), the estranged wife was attacked, kicked
in the face and ribs and forced to suck his penis
(which Crim Law Rev points out, was 'activity they had
performed consensually during cohabitation'). What we
are to make of this addendum is clear! Although a
divorce petition was issued, there was no court injunction, this being the case the wife's deemed consent upon marriage was not terminated and the husband
was immune to criminal liability for rape or indecent
assault.

WOMEN'S RIGHT TO SELF PRESERVATION

Women have however, won some limited protection within
civil law, from violent partners, husbands or cohabitees with the introdution of The Domestic Violence and
Matrimonial Proceedings Act (1976) and later, The
Domestic Proceedings and Magistrates Courts Act (1978).
The 1976 provision enabled women to seek some protection from violent husbands without the pre requisite of

divorce proceedings. The act provided that the injured party may make an application for an injunction
against the aggressor S.1 (i) empowering the courts
to exclude the man if necessary from the family home
S.2 (i)(c) . In addition, in cases of grave violence,
a power of arrest could be attached S.2 (i).

With regard to the procedures necessary for the
granting of an injunction, the aggrieved applies for
an injunction in the presence of the alleged male-
factor. This procedure may take some weeks, thus in
the meanwhile, the aggrieved and the accused may well
and indeed are likely to be cohabiting. In some cases, ex parte applications can be made and interim injunctions granted. This Act requires applicants to
seek redress through the County Court, which involves
a lengthy and timely procedure. The 1978 Act created
two remedies; first it enabled a speedier application
via the magistrates court, for in this case a 'protection order' to be made. (S.16) Second, it provided
a partial remedy to the problem in the provision of an
eviction order, which empowered the courts to evict
the aggressor from the matrimonial home, under an
exclusion order S.16(3)(c) (i) and (ii) .

In practice, of course the interpretation of the
letter of the law is left very much to the judge, and
the effectiveness of legislation depends too on the
ability of the police to arrest, their preparedness
to enforce injunctions, council authorities to rehouse
or provide emergency accommodation. The effectiveness
of remedies available depends on a close liaison between all levels of jurisdiction, social welfare law,
local authority housing policy, as well as civil and
criminal law. In so far as the gravity of injunctions
is concerned, most women suffering violence seek interim injunctions, many needing immediate protection
and not a promise of protection some weeks ahead. But
the power to make ex-parte injunctions is very restrictive indeed [Coote and Gill 1979: 12].

Following Ansah v Ansah (1977) 2 All ER: 638,
Ormrod LJ advised that this power be 'used with great
caution and only in circumstances in which it is really
necessary to act immediately'. The judge's discretion in such matters inter alia, granting an injunction, attaching a power of arrest excluding the aggressor from the home, is quick,general and unfettered.
If a power of arrest has not been attached, the women
would have had to return to the court and ask for a
committal. In cases where a man and woman cohabit
under the same roof but live in separate rooms, the
judge may decide that they are not living together as
man and wife, S.1 (2) 1976, and thus may not grant an

196

injunction. <u>Adeoso v Adeoso</u> (<u>Times</u>, July 22nd 1980).
Despite the obvious progress made by the decision in
<u>Davis v Johnson</u> (1978 1 All ER) 1132, the 1976 Act was
interpreted to include those who were cohabiting, the
response of the judiciary remains ambiguous. As Aled
Griffiths observes:

> One judge, is reputed to have said that applying
> for an injunction with powers of arrest was main-
> ly a ploy by solicitors to increase costs.

The interpretation of these statutes and the intention of parliament differs in some detail. Since
the 1976 Act applications for injunctions under S.1
have increased each year, still a very significant
proportion of applications are refused and of those
granted a small proportion have a power of arrest attached. Figures for 1978 reveal 6386 injunctions
granted, [1489 with a power of arrest, 4897 without
power of arrest] and 516 refused, the number of injunctions granted increased in 1979 to 6794, [5092 of
those without power of arrest, 1702 with power of arr-
est] whilst 439 were refused. In 1981 a total of 6399
injunctions were granted [4846 without power of arrest
and 1553 with] whilst 300 were refused. In 1981 6809 injunctions were granted [5035 <u>without</u> powers of arrest
and 1774 with] whilst 301 were refused. In 1982 figures
reveal a total of 7474 injunctions granted under section 1 [5598 without power of arrest, 1876 with] and
217 refused. (<u>Judicial Statistics</u> Cmnd. 7627, 7977,
8436, 8770, 9065 respectively). But, as G. Ritchie
(1979: 1079) observes, non-molestation injunctions do
not always achieve the peace, security and protection
required. Women's Aid Refuge in Cambridge said, 'Rather then inhibiting the man, obtaining the injunction
provokes him to subject the woman to further assaults.' (30) In the process of seeking an injunction
with or without a power of arrest, the advice and assistance of a solicitor is normally required. And at
this juncture, already there are various problems.
First, not all solicitors are committed to legal aid
work. Secondly, they do not always know the law in
this context. At the other end of the continuum, the
police do not always enforce the law or offer initial
protection to an aggrieved party. The Home Office
Circular No. 68 (8) 1977 states that the power of arrest is discretionary not mandatory, (31) therefore,
even given that a judge may attach a power of arrest,
it is by no means certain that the police will enforce
this   (Coote and Gill: 1979 : 16).
    A protection order or non-molestation order can

often only be safely ensured by excluding the violent
partner from the home. And here we encounter another
vague and ambiguous area of law, wide open to differing
interpretation. Applications for exclusion orders
are made under S.2 (i) (c) of the 1976 Act, and initially given for three months, although there are no
guidelines as to the exercise of discretion. There
may be a reluctance to exercise discretion to grant
exclusion orders. Stamp LJ reflected such reservatory
reluctance in <u>Cantliff v Jenkins</u> 1978 1, ALL ER 836:

> Much depends on the circumstances of each case,
> but I find it difficult to believe that it could
> ever be fair, save in most exceptional circum-
> stances, to keep a man out of his own flat or
> house for more than a few months.

Applications for exclusion orders may be refused, the
judge may adjourn the application to see what happens
as in <u>Spencer v Camacho</u> 1983, FLR 4, 11: 662. Griffiths 1981, 11: 28, found that judges often did not
approve of exclusion orders or think refuges were
suitable places for bringing up children. In order to
get adequate protection, the applicant may make countless and successive legal aid applications extending
over months and years. Yet in <u>Davis v Johnson</u> 1979
AC; 264, Lord Scarman said that the remedy of the Act
is to deal with an emergency, 'a species of first
aid'! It is disturbing that the legislative remedies
available to women who have been subjected to male
violence are anything but a species of first aid.
Moreover, following the decision in <u>Richards v Rich-
ards</u> (1983) 2 All ER 807 county courts may be even
more intransigent in their reluctance to grant ouster
injunctions. (For further discussion see <u>Legal Action</u>
March 1984 p. 25.)
    Violence against wives or cohabitees has been
seen apart from violence committed between strangers,
or violence on the street. When wives and girl-
friends are assaulted, then this violence involving
equally bruises, broken bones and broken spirits, is
a secret matter, cloaked in a respectable veil called
family privacy, supported by explanations or pathology.
The response of the aggressed, the aggressor and legal
and social agencies, is one of passive reluctance to
get involved, which thereby leads to a cycle of
'laissez faire', in the hope that by ignoring the
problem, it may well disappear.
    Within this 'laissez faire' covert policy, it has
been said that whilst the aggrieved may well have very
good self-preservatory motives for not reporting the

Male Violence Against Women: Excusatory and Explanatory
Ideologies in Law and Society

incident, the police do not have such justification
for not regarding 'domestics' as they are separately
called, as 'real' police work (Coleman and Bottomley
1976: Chatterton 1976: McCabe and Sutcliffe 1978).
    Consider for instance that statistics for hom-
icide in England and Wales have consistently revealed,
for the period between 1972 and 1982, that between 21%
and 29% of all victims have been acquainted as spouse,
cohabitant or former spouse or cohabitant, and lover
or former lover. Taking these two categories together, they formed 21% of all homicide in 1972, 27% in
1973, 26% in 1974, 28% in 1975, 29% in 1976, 27% in
1977, 27% in 1978, 29% in 1981 and 25% in 1982. (32)
A further breakdown of the homicide statistics for
1982 is as alarming as they are illuminating. Out of
a total of 576 cases recorded as homicides a total of
143 cases were between spouses, lovers or former lovers, cohabitants or former spouses or cohabitants.
Cases between spouses totalled 116 and are better analysed separately from lover or former lover, a category which incidentally yielded a total of 27 victims,
26 male perpetrators, 1 female, and 19 female and 8
male victims suggesting a high proportion in this category of homosexual homicide (30%). (33)   In the
spouse, cohabitant, former spouse, former cohabitant
category 104 victims were female and 12 victims male,
a ratio of 9 females to 1 male. Therefore out of a
total of 576 victims of homicide 104 were women murdered by spouses in the domestic setting, a total of
18%.   How women are represented as victims of male
violence in other categories of (2) Attempted murder,
(5) Wounding (8) Other wounding (9) Assault, is a very
'dark figure' indeed. In order to get some rough
estimate of the tip of the iceberg following the Select Committee on Violence in Marriage (House of Commons, 329- i) (9), it was recommended that police forces should keep statistics about incidents of domestic
violence (Table 2.5, Criminal Statistics, England and
Wales 1980, Cmnd 8376).
    In Table 2.5: serious offences of violence bet-
ween spouses recorded by police in categories (1-4)
including murder, manslaughter, attempted murder and
threats to murder; taking figures available for both
years, in 307 cases women spouses, cohabitees were
victims, whilst in 65 cases male spouses, cohabitees,
were victims. In category (10) including wounding
and other acts endangering life, women spouses, cohabitees numbered 320 compared with 206 husband victims.
In categories (8-9) including other wounding and serious assaults, women spouses cohabitees numbered
10,270, whilst male spouses, cohabitees as victims

numbered 775. (34) Compared with the ratio of male
violence to women for homicide here women are represented much less significantly as victims in violent
assaults, ratios for categories (1-4) female to male
5:1, category (10) female to male 3:2, categories
(8-9) female to male 4:1. This table was subsequently
dropped because it was decided that the figures were
of little value because of the large proportion of
incidents which may not have been reported to, or recorded by the police.

But these figures even given their unreliability
tell us something about domestic violence assault.
Two possible interpretations can be derived. First,
it may be adduced that women are becoming increasingly
involved in violent crime. Second it may also be
adduced that women 'victims' of violence within the
marital or cohabiting situation may have certain motives for silence making them less likely than male
counterparts to report their victimisation.

If we carefully examine the first interpretation
relating to the possibility that women are becoming
more violent looking at Criminal Statistics (1982)
Cmnd 9048 Table 5.1 the ratio of male to female crimes
of violence is 13:1 inconsistent with the much closer
ratios deduced from violence between spouses. It is
unlikely that the depicted increase in violence of
wives towards husbands or female to male cohabitees
reflects any 'real' increase. It is indeed far more
likely and consistent with our information on women's
predilection to report violence against them by spouses or cohabitees that women are especially reluctant
to report such incidents (Binney 1981), the closer
ratios observed reflecting a great hidden element of
violence towards women which goes unreported and
therefore unrecorded.

Yet statistics on male violence against women
other than criminal homicide perhaps contain the dar-
kest figure of all, since women for multivarious
reasons do not report crimes of violence perpetrated
against them by spouses or cohabitees. Hough and Mayhew in The British Crime Survey 1983 : 21 (35),
found that 10% of assault victims were women who had
been assaulted by their present or previous husband
or boyfriend. Even in crime victimisation surveys, it
is clear that such incidents will continue to remain
eclipsed for women fear to disclose such details of
assault to an interviewer, as the authors of the report observed, 'Their assailant may be in the same room
at the time of the interview.' (p. 21)

Not only is domestic violence under-reported, it
is also under-recorded (Wassoff 1982: 188). Chatterton

Male Violence Against Women: Excusatory and Explanatory
Ideologies in Law and Society

writes:

> One of the most extensively documented facts
> about police work is that the police under-enfor-
> ce certain laws and jealously protect the dis-
> cretion which that implies. (1976: 133, Oppen-
> lander 1982: 449)

Certainly following R v Metropolitan Police Commiss-
ioner Ex parte Blackburn (No. 3) 1973 QB 241, we
might turn the proposition on its head and argue that
in the case of domestic violence, the police 'are
possessed of a discretionary power not to prosecute',
(Scutt 1980: 725, see also Parnas 1967: 930). The
role of the police in domestic violence disputes has
been seen to be one of 'peacekeeping'. As Parnas
observes (1967: 919), the settlement function appears
central. This is based on the presumption that 'many
disturbance calls require the services of the beat
officer in settling quarrels and neighbourhood problems. These calls are often non-criminal in nature
that do not require arrest and in fact have no grounds
on which to base legal arrest'. (Training Bulletin,
quoted in Parnas 1967: 919, Parnas 1978: 188.)
      In Britain the role of the police has been sim-
ilarly one of 'peacekeeping'. In fact this role of
mediator or indeed one of non-intervention can be observed from evidence of the Metropolitan Police Department in its submission to the Parliamentary Committee on Marital Violence, 1975:

> Whereas it is a general principle of the police
> practice not to intervene in a situation which
> existed or had existed between husband and wife
> in the course of which the wife had suffered some
> personal attack, any assault upon a wife by her
> husband which amounted to physical injury of a
> serious nature is a criminal offence which it is
> the duty of the police to follow up and prosec-
> ute. (Dobash and Dobash 1980: 210, see also Dow
> 1976: 129.)

Given this non prosecution stance, there is a discrepancy between citizens' allegations and police response
according to recording procedure, classification, investigation and prosecution. (McCabe and Sutcliffe
1978: 58, Pahl 1982: 343,). Therefore as McCabe and
Sutcliffe observe, 'In peace keeping, in the maintenance of social order, in rejecting or accepting definitions of criminal activity made by the general public, police organisation is not at all bureaucratic

and their system of records, their paper work, bears
this out.' (1978: 37).

In these cases, official action was most likely
to be avoided 'cuffing' being a well recognised strategy for dealing or not dealing with incidents considered trivial or not police work. (McCabe and Sutcliffe 1978: 29, Loving 1980: 114, Chambers and Millar
1983: 26-34). Indeed there is evidence that police
may redefine or reclassify incidents in such a way
which avoids police action or even police record.
Parnas (1967: 927) notes, 'A call that is apparently
concerned with violence (eg. a neighbour is beating
his wife) is often classified by the dispatcher as a
domestic disturbance rather than as a battery.' Similar conclusions were drawn by McCabe and Sutcliffe
(1978: 5). In an effort then to avoid prosecution
police would then 'no crime' domestic violence incidents. Coleman and Bottomley found that regarding
domestics 'the essence of the police 'no crime' decision was that these inter-personal disputes were in
a real sense not the proper concern of the criminal
law or the police, but ought to be sorted out privat-
ely or in a different public arena, (1976: 353), (see
also Dobash and Dobash 1980: 207). Most researchers
conclude that police rarely make arrests when there
is a legal cause to do so and in the words of Nan
Oppenlander 1982, may be seen to be 'copping out'.
Their neutrality has been widely observed and criticised (Borkowsi et al. 1983: 192). The result is that
there is an alarmingly low number of prosecutions in
relation to the estimated number of reported domestic
violence. (Borkowski et al. 1983: 21) Police success
or effectiveness is rightly or wrongly so frequently
measured in terms of the preparedness to prosecute.
This is undoubtedly an oversimplification of the problem, and whilst the police may well underforce the
law, it is far from certain that a prosecution orientated policy would provide the remedy for domestic
violence.

Certainly disenchantment with the police force
extends beyond prosecution policies. In a study conducted by Binney et al. (1981: 15) of 59 women interviewed in 8% of cases the police did not come to the
scene of the violence, in 51% the police said it was
domestic dispute, so no practical help was given, in
17% the man was charged with assault or with breaking
an injunction, in 20% practical help was given and the
woman in question was referred to a refuge or the man
taken away for the night and the final 4% were classified as other. Of 42% (25 cases which involved life
threatening attacks, strangulation, drowning or resul-

ting in Hospitalisation) only 5 of the men had been
charged. The justificatory rationale for this non-
interventionist stance is explained in a variety of
ways. Prosecuting offenders in such cases is usually
perceived as a waste of police time as women are considered to withdraw their complaint. Yet counter indications have revealed that charges are not dropped
with any greater frequency in this as compared to any
other charge. Wassoff (1982: 194) reported 2 out of
59 cases where charges were dropped; whilst Dobash
and Dobash found that charges were dropped in 6% of
cases. In response to this particular criticism and
following the Select Committee recommendations which
proposed that chief constables should review their
policies with regard to domestic violence (para. 44),
Bedfordshire police responded by initiating a new
arrest policy. Husbands who had assaulted wives were
arrested, charged and taken to court. During the first 6 months commencing February 1976, 288 acts of
violence came to the attention of the police. In 184
cases (63.9%) the complainants did not wish to pursue
their complaints, in 104 cases, complaints were substantiated, arrests were made and proceedings initiat-
ed, in 18 of those cases, 17.3%, complainants with-
drew their complaints. Only 3 men were given immediate custodial sentences. (Freeman 1979: 190) This
new 'initiative' has been similarly implemented in
several American States, and new laws in 20 States
have greatly expanded police arrest powers. (In this
respect some proposals contained in the Police and
Criminal Evidence Bill, whilst giving police wider
powers to arrest, and to arrest in domestic violence
cases, it is feared that these powers will be abused).
As a result of initiatives in America, several States
have produced written guidelines on when and where
the power of arrest should be implemented in domestic
cases. There is a general agreement in recognising
only serious assault as indicative of police action.
The police Executive Forum Report 1979, recommends
arrest in:

i)   cases involving serious injury, use of a
      deadly weapon,
ii)   and/or violation of a restraining order.
      (Loving 1980: 13).

Similarly arrest is indicated in Chicago Police Department:

i)   where there is serious, intense conflict,
ii)   where there is use of weapons,

    iii)   where there has been previous injury or
             damage,
    iv)   where there has been a previous court app-
             earance or
    v)   a previous attempt to sever the relation-
             ship,
    vi)   where the call to the police is a second
             or subsequent call,
    vii)   where children or mentally deficient part-
             ies are involved.

In the Westchester County NY districts, similar standards apply. Arrest is tenable:

    i)   Where there is a gun or deadly weapon,
    ii)   where there is reasonable cause to believe
             that a felony has been committed,
    iii)   where there is maiming or serious injury
             ie. where there is a history of criminal
             activity where in the judgment of the pol-
             ice officer, arrest is necessary for the
             future protection of the victim.

With the result that the majority of domestic violence
disputes are accorded a low priority. These new initiatives, so called, result in the kind of lack of
action British police are criticised for - ie. not
going to initial, but subsequent calls, not responding unless there is serious violence or unless there
is some breach of civil law injunctions.

    This kind of under-enforcement has been very much
criticised from a civil liberties viewpoint and indeed
in Oaklands California in 1976, a group of battered
women brought a class action law suit against Oakland
Police Department, charging that wife battering calls
were given low priority. The Scott v Hart suit
(1976), the primary cause of which was based on the
Equal Protection Clause of the Fourteenth Amendment
and the Civil Rights Act of 1871, such that it was
argued that arrest avoidance policy was insidious
discrimination against women and is biased and arch-
aic. A settlement was reached and the police in justification of non-intervention asserted that 'They
acted to prevent aggravation of the dispute', and to
minimise danger of injury to officers; they believed
that women would not prosecute; they contended that
the batterer would 'lose face' if arrested at his
home; and that arrest would result in family break up
(Gee 1983: 559).

    Following on from this, an arrest policy has been
implemented in Minneapolis, where over a 16 month

period during 1981/82, police officers used three
different strategies to respond to 252 cases of 'moderate' domestic assault, defined as assault, which
did not cause life threatening injuries. The strategies were:

    i)   arrest,
    ii)   mediation,
    iii)   ordering a violent spouse to leave for 8
          hours.

Police response was assigned to them randomly. The
results of the study disclosed that of those men arrested, only 10% went on to repeat the offence. Of
those cases where mediation was the assigned strategy,
16% committed the offence again and of those ordered
to leave the house, 22% committed the offence again.
The Police Federation in conclusion: 'the findings of
the study suggest that arrest may be the most effective approach and separation the least effective'.
    But it is not only the impotency of criminal
prosecution and the ineffectiveness of civil law in
providing protection for women married or cohabiting,
with violent men, it is also the anaesthetised response
of other agents and agencies within the criminal justice process and within welfare provision, which result
in women's forced dependency on violent men which
makes 'staying on' a lesser of the evils awaiting.
    Perhaps one of the greatest problems faced is in
the provision of alternative, adequate and appropriate housing. I say this since if an abused wife
leaves the matrimonial home not wishing to return for
fear of further violence, if she finds herself in
accommodation not considered adequate for the need of
her children, she may in the event of the husband being competent to care for the children, lose custody.
This threat of loss of custody results in many women
staying with violent men. Women's access to housing
is limited and although The Housing (Homeless Persons)
Act 1977, recognises women victims of domestic violence as homeless, the intention of this Act is certainly not incorporated to the letter and indeed housing authorities differ in their interpretation of this
legislation by imposing their own private definition
of what they consider to be the "cop out" clause
'intentional' and 'unintentional' homelessness. In
theory then, section 1 (2)(b) reads:

    A person is homeless for the purpose of this Act
    if he has accommodation but -

b) It is probable that occupation of it will
   lead to violence from some other person residing in it or to threats of violence from
   some other person residing in it and likely
   to carry out the threats.

First of all, the housing authority to whom she had
made an application may not recognise her as genuinely
homeless and refuse any suggestion that they have an
obligation to house her. On the other hand, if she
is recognised as homeless, the genuineness of her
destitution will be tested in the coming months as she
is moved into and out of usually squalid bed and
breakfast accommodation into and out of dilapidated
temporary accommodation. Finally, if this nightmare
is survived into the first offer of permanent housing,
for no further offers are open to this second class
housing applicant. This can be called the 'destitution test'. Those whose spirit is broken by the insec-
urity of such provisions and who then return to violent husbands are not considered genuinely homeless.
Within all this, a mother is always faced with the
possibility that during these uncertain months, the
emergency accommodation might be considered inappropriate for her children, and the threat of losing custody is forever present.
     In Re W and W (Interim Custody) CA FLR 4: 11:
686, the mother who had left the matrimonial home and
was residing with her two children at a woman's refuge
sought:

i)   an interim custody order and
ii)   an exclusion order.

The judge found no case to exclude the father, granted
an interim custody order to the mother. The mother
refused to return to the matrimonial home and appealed
against the refusal to grant an exclusion order, the
father cross appealed seeking interim custody of the
children. At a resumed hearing the matter came before
a recorder, the mother applying for a continuation of
interim custody and a reapplication for an order to
exclude the husband from the family home. The recorder was of the view that the mother should return to
the family home and refused her application for an
exclusion order. At the appeal hearing it was decided
that in the interests of the children who otherwise
would be living in refuge accommodation which the
court considered most unsatisfactory, that interim
custody be given to the father with reasonable access
to the mother.

Male Violence Against Women: Excusatory and Explanatory
Ideologies in Law and Society

The decision reached in this case well illustrates a mother's invidious dilemma. Judges are reluctant
to exclude the man from his home and so if battered
wives or cohabitees are to avoid further abuse they
are forced to leave, finding herself dependent on refuge or similar emergency accommodation. The courts
take the view that these provisions are unsatisfactory
for children in the majority of cases and thus women
are forced to stay on with violent husbands or else
as in this case forfeit her children.

INDIVIDUALISING THE PROBLEM - PRIVATISING THE EVENT

Given this civil, criminal, housing and legal impotency together with the social fabric of structured
institutionalised inequality it is surprising that
welfare workers, doctors, psychiatrists and those
working in legal and everyday practice consider pathological explanations or relevance to understanding
this form of male violence. Indeed the Select Committees' deliberations, on violence in marriage were influenced by just this kind of dogma. Erin Pizzey in
giving evidence had this to say:

> In a democratic society, laws are made for reas-
> onable men... These men are outside the law, they
> have been imprinted with violence from childhood,
> so that violence is part of their normal behav-
> iour. All the legislating and punishments in the
> world will not change their methods of expressing
> their frustration. I believe that many of the
> children born into violence grow up to be aggress-
> ive psychopaths, and it is the wives of such men
> we see at Chiswick. I feel that the remedies lie
> in the hands of the medical profession, and not
> in the court of law, because the men act instinc-
> tively not rationally.

Indeed as Wilson (1983: 198) observes, recommendations were 'heavily weighed in the direction
of types of prevention and education that assumed the
root cause of domestic violence to be psychologised'.
This tendency to find individual solutions to social
problems has been the matter of considerable comment
in the work of Halmos, (1978), Cohen (1979). But it
was C Wright Mills (1943), who clearly pointed to the
role of <u>political expediency</u> in this personalisation.
The consequence is as Jackson and Rushton (1982: 17)
observe:

Male Violence Against Women: Excusatory and Explanatory Ideologies in Law and Society

...the problem is individualised, seen as something affecting only a minority, the maladjusted or socially deprived, whose lives bear no resemblance to those of normal women and their families. This emphasis successfully diverts attention away from the power structure of the family, to the subordination of women within it and the oppression they experience as wives and mothers. The problem is restructured in terms of the unusual social or psychological characteristics of those who suffer from or give way to the temptation of violence.

The genesis or origin of the contemporary formulation of women as masochistic, is derived largely from the writings of Freud and the neo-Freudians of the right, in the work of Rado and Deutsch, Deutsch being the key spokesperson of this view. In her early work The Psycho-analysis of the Sexual Function of Women (1925), she set out to explain the normal psychic life of women and their conflicts, of which the traits of femininity, narcissism, passivity and masochism were examined. But it was not until the publication of Female Masochism, that her ultimate treatise on the female sub-conscious desire for violence, was presented. Here in this seminal paper, we find that women indulge in fantasies of violence and rape, 'Girlish fantasies relating to rape often remain unconscious, but evince their content in dreams, sometimes in symptoms, and often accompany masturbating actions. In dreams, the rape is symbolic: the terrifying male persecutor with knife in hand, the burglar who breaks in at the window, the thief who steals a particularly valuable object, are the most typical and frequently recurring figures in the dreams of young girls.'(p.255) (37). Of those conscious masochistic fantasies Deutsch explains 'The conscious masochistic rape fantasies, however are indubitably erotic, since they are connected with masturbation, they are less genital in character than the symbolic dreams, and involve blows and humiliations, in fact, in rare cases, the genitals themselves are the target of the act of violence.'
The wish to be beaten, she considers a masochistic perversion in women who may see violence perpetrated against them as an expression of male love. Women, she explains are happy in their subordinate role and repress their erotic longings, 'The little stenographer who worships her boss, whoever he may be, and who bears with him in his worst moods, allegedly in order to keep her job, the sensitive woman who cannot leave her brutal husband because she loves him, despite

(actually because of) his brutality, and the active
and tolerated woman collaborator who devotes all her
intuitive gifts to her master's production, are all
happy in these roles and repress their erotic longings.' (38)
     The message from the writings of Helene Deutsch
is clear, women accordingly desire rape, violence,
mental humiliation and these desires are not a deviation from normal female development, but an expression
of normal femininity. Her work is essentially biologically determinist where the cultural complex is regarded as the effect of anatomical characterisations.
Masochism is perceived as the genesis of femininity.
     By contrast, the work of neo-Freudian Karen Hor-
ney takes issue with the very prise de position presented in Deutsch. Horney regards the development of
the psyche in relation to cultural meaning, her work
presents a direct confrontation with the biological
determinism of psycho-analysis. Masochism in and so
far as it exists is for Horney cultural, she rejects
Freud's premise that masochistic phenomena are more
frequent in women because masochism is inherent in the
very essence of femaleness. Instead she argues masochistic phenomena may be more prevalent in women
because of their social conditioning (p. 214). Moreover, in criticising the work of Deutsch and Rado,
she argues that there is no data to substantiate their
claims. She explains:

> In particular one must consider the fact that
> when some or all of the suggested elements are
> present in the culture complex, there may appear
> certain fixed ideologies concerning the 'nature'
> of women; such doctrines that woman is innately
> weak, emotional, enjoys dependence, is limited
> in capacities for independent work and autonomous
> thinking, one is tempted to include in this cat-
> egory the psycho-analytical belief that woman is
> masochistic by nature. It is fairly obvious that
> these ideologies function not only to reconcile
> women to their subordinate role by presenting it
> as an unalterable one but also to plant the bel-
> ief that it represents fulfilment they crave, or
> an ideal for which it is commendable and desir-
> able to strive. (39)

As Horney points out, 'it is hard to see how any woman
can escape becoming masochistic to some degree, from
the effects of the culture alone...' (40)
     The consequences of too ready acceptance of the
Freudian view of woman as essentially masochistic can

be seen in some of the remedies sought to the problem
of domestic violence. This assumption has also guided
some of the research in the field, some of which bears
witness to the pathologisation of the abuse of women
and rejection of cultural and social factors, which
enforce dependency. The work of psycho-analytical
schools in the definition of the essential female,
has had a profound impact on interpreting domestic
violence and its mythologies have persisted into the
present day. Storr (1968) cited in Miller (1975) individualises the problem invoking the nagging wife
myth. 'The nagging, aggressive women is often uncon-
sciously demanding that which she most fears. By
irritating a man, making unreasonable demands and
criticising, she is really trying to evoke a dominant
response by attacking him for his lack of virility.
Her aggression is fulfilling a double purpose, both
protecting her against male dominance and at the same
time demanding it.' This view significantly shifts
the focus of attention away from structural imperatives onto wives as the sole cause of their own victimisation. Faulk (1974: 181), Gayford (1975, 1979) share
his view and Snell et al.(1964) found that wives were
'aggressive efficient masculine and sexually frigid',
who were capable of provoking men by simply not being
the 'typical' wife. Gayford for example, in a study
of 100 women (who had said they were victims of violent assault) monitored them for family background,
country of origin, social class, family employment,
education, psychological history, drugs and alcohol
abuse and found that 46 had received some form of psychiatric consultation. He concluded that the role of
the wife as provocateur was an important one. Snell
(1964), points out that both the inadequate as well
as the intelligent woman can be provocative. Thus,
women who are seen to provoke violence for whatever
reasons are seen to step out of the traditionally accepted female role and confront male power.
    The final myth that women need or desire assault
and domination is supported in some psycho-analytical
writings. Recent chemical theories and their adoption
in understanding violence have suggested that men and
women have a chemical need for excitement through
violence. Erin Pizzey's theory presented in Prone to
Violence (1982) proposes that women get excitement and
stimulation from violence. This leads to an addiction to
violence in the excitement they crave; pain and danger
within this become conflated and confused with love
and addiction develops as a result of body chemistry.
Writing recently in New Society, (1981) she had this
to say: 'Violence prone is the only phrase I can find

Male Violence Against Women: Excusatory and Explanatory
Ideologies in Law and Society

that defines as accurately as possible, women who
experience gross physical and mental abuse, but who
choose despite other viable and attractive alternatives, to remain within the confines of their abuse
relationship.' Continuing in this view she typologises
two kinds of 'battered women':

   i)   the one who is genuinely the victim, who
         wishes to leave and seek the help and ass-
         istance of supporting agencies, and
   ii)   the other who seeks out a violent relation-
         ship or a series of violent relationships
         with no intention of leaving.

'She is powerfully addicted to amounts of violence in
their relationship and cannot help going back to it.
Having been reared on violence, she will only feel
alive and satisfied in a situation of danger, so she
often deliberately provokes a man to the point where
he will hit her.' Pizzey writes further, 'the grave
danger in these relationships is that since pleasure
is found through pain, the ultimate orgasm is death'.
(1981: 170) Women on the whole, act as the cortisone
type victim - that is eliciting a predominantly 'cortisone response' to a violent situation where the victim 'plays possum'. Men on the other hand, are predominantly 'adrenalin personalities', that is to say
they react to violent situations by actively taking
the role of the aggressor. Taking this distinction
further (p. 179), she points out that the adrenalin-
aggressive personality is prone to diseases that result from the body's operating in an adrenalin high
state of constant arousal. These ill founded views
have implications for the treatment of violent men and
women who 'stay on'. Pizzey advocates research and
treatment programmes along the lines of chemotherapy
taking us, full circle back to the notion that domestic violence is an individual problem and aberration,
locating the solution to the problem in changing the
chemical make up of individuals.
     Male violence towards women has always been with
us and always been permitted whether by turning a
blind eye, upholding male right, or because of the ineffectiveness of legislative remedies. Male violence
must by analysed within the arena of sexual politics
and removed from the protective arena of family privacy. Whilst some violent men are indeed sick, the
vast majority are not, considered by society and by
themselves as 'normal' men excercising their rights.
This prerogative of men to chastise women is endemic
in our cultural attitudes and in the arrangement of

power between the sexes as codified in law and custom.
Opportunities for male violence are increased through
women's total vulnerability in her economic dependency
on men for resources, for housing, for custody. Women
will remain totally unprotected from violent assault,
grevious bodily harm and murder so long as legal and
social welfare agencies prefer not to recognise their
obligations and duty to the protection of women instead of, as appears to be the case, favouring the
recognition of male power to abuse.

REFERENCES

(1)   Straus, Murray (1976) 'Sexual Inequality,
        Cultural Norms and Wife-Beating'in J.R. Chap-
        man and M.Gates (ed.) Women into Wives.
        Sage, Beverly Hills/London p. 59 pp.59-77
(2)   Von Hentig, H. (1948) The Criminal and His
        Victim, New Haven
(3)   Wolfgang, M.E. (1958) Patterns in Criminal
        Homicide, Philadelphia Univ. of Penns, Oxford
        Univ. Press.
(4)   McClintock, F.H. (1963) Crimes of Violence,
        London, Macmillan.
(5)   Gibson, E. and Klein, S. (1969) Murder [1957-
        1968], London HMSO Home Office Research
        Study No. 3
(6)   Blom Cooper and Morris, T. (1964) A Calendar
        of Murder, Michael Joseph, London
(7)   Wolfgang, M.E. and Ferracuti, F. (1967) Sub
        culture of Violence, Tavistock, London.
(8)   Blackstone, W. (1775) Commentaries on the
        Laws of England Book 1, p. 445 Oxford
(9)   Sachs, A. and Hoff-Wilson J. (1978) Sexism
        and the Law, Oxford, Martin Robertson. p. 59.
(10)   Mill, J.S. (1978) edition The Subjection of
        Women, p. 35 The MIT Press, Cambridge,
        London, England.
(11)   Mill, J.S. The Subjection of Women pp.36-37
(12)   Blake, Matilda (1892) 'Are Women Protected?'
        Westminster Review Vol 137, p. 44
(13)   Anonymous (1856) 'Outrages on Women', North
        British Review p. 133
(14)   Cleveland A.R. (1896) Women Under English
        Law, London Hurst and Blackett p. 222
(15)   Lawes Resolution of Women's Rights. 1632
(16)   Whatley, W. (1617) The Bride Bush or Wedd-
        ing Sermon 1975 reprint English Experience
        Series No. 769 W.J. Johnson
(17)   Blackstone, W. (1775) Commentaries on the
        Laws of England.

(18)   Sentences of Imprisonment - A Review of
         Maximum Penalties - Report of the Advisory
         Council on the Penal System. London HMSO.
         1978, p. 29
(19)   Jeaffreson, J.C. (1872) Brides and Bridals
         London.
(20)   Blackstone, W. quoted in Scutt J. 'Sexism
         in Criminal Law' p. 10 (1981) in Mukherjee
         S. and Scutt J. Women and Crime George Allen
         and Unwin, Sydney, London, Boston.
(21)   Anon. Outrages on Women, p. 237
(22)   Ibid., p. 239
(23)   Hansard, (1860) Vol. 158 c 524
(24)   Ibid., c 519
(25)   Pizzey, E. and Shapiro, J. (1983) Prone to
         Violence, London Hamlyn, p. 75
(26)   Hale, M. (1971) The History of the Pleas of
         The Crown (1736), reprint London Professional
         Books at 629
(27)   Smith, J.C. and Hogan, B. (1973) Criminal
         Law: Cases and Materials London Butterworth
         p. 325
(28)   Working Paper on Sexual Offences, Criminal
         Law Revision Committee (1980) London HMSO
         at para. 42
(29)   Sexual Offences 15th Report Criminal Law
         Revision Committee Part II S(ii), London
         HMSO p. 93-94
(30)   Ritchie, G. (1979) Non-Molestation Injunct-
         ions, New Law Journal, Nov 1st p. 1079.
(31)   Home Office Circular No. 68 1977, Domestic
         Violence and Matrimonial Proceedings Act
         1976.
(32)   Criminal Statistics 1982, England and Wales,
         Cmnd 9048, Table 4.4
(33)   Home Office Statistical Breakdown on Homicide
         for 1982
(34)   Criminal Statistics (1980) Cmnd 8376 Table
         2.5
(35)   The British Crime Survey: First Report, Home
         Office Research Study No. 76 HMSO, London.
(36)   Pizzey, E. Minutes of Evidence of the House
         of Commons Select Committee on Violence in
         Marriage 75-76 [H.C. 553: 2]
(37)   Deustch, H. The Psychology of Woman, London
         Grune and Stratton, p. 255
(38)   " p. 276.
(39)   Horney, K. (1967) Feminine Psychology, London
         WW Norton p. 214.
(40)   " p. 231.

BIBLIOGRAPHY

Binney, V.G., Harkell G. and Nixon, J. (1981) Leaving
    Violent Men Women's Aid Federation, England.
Borkowski, M., Murch, M. and Walker, V. (1983) Marital
    Violence Tavistock, London.
Brisson, N.J. (1981) Battering Husbands; a Survey of
    Abusive Men Victimology 6, No. 1-4, 338-344.
Bromley, P.M. (1976) Family Law, London Butterworth.
Cohen, S. (1979) The Punitive City   Notes on the
    Dispersal of Social Control   Contemporary Crises
    III pp. 339-63.
Coleman, C.A. and Bottomley, A.K. (1976) 'Police
    Conceptions of Crime and No Crime', Criminal Law
    Review 334
Dicks, H. (1967) Marital Tension, Routledge and Kegan
    Paul, London.
Dobash, R. and Dobash, R.E. (1980) Violence Against
    Wives, New York Free Press.
Dow, M. (1976) Police Involvement in M. Borland
    Violence in the Family   MUP pp. 129-135.
Faulk, M. (1974) 'Men Who Assault Their Wives', Med-
    icine, Sci, Law 14, 3: 180-183
Fitch, F.J. and Papantonio, A. (1983) Men who Batter;
    some pertinent questions   Characteristics   Jnl
    of Nervous and Mental Diseases 171/3 190-2
Freeman, M.D.A. (1979) Violence in the Home, Gower
Freeman, M.D.A. (1980) 'Violence Against Women: Does
    the Legal System Provide Solutions or Itself
    Constitute the Problem', Brit Jnl of Law and Soc-
    iety Vol. 7
Gayford, J.J. (1975) 'Wife Battering: A Preliminary
    Survey of 100 Cases', Brit Med Jnl 1: 194-7
Gayford, J.J. (1979) 'Aetiology of Wife Beating',
    Med. Sci. Law 19: 1 19-24.
Gee, P.W. (1983) Ensuring Police Protection for Batt-
    ered Women.   The Scott v Hart Suit Signs Vol. 8
    No. 3.

Bibliography

Griffiths, A. (1980) 'The Legacy and Present Adminis-
    tration of English Law. Some Problems for Batt-
    ered Women in Context'. Cambrian Law Review
    Vol. 11 p. 29-37.
Griffiths, A. (1981) Some Battered Women in Wales.
    An Interactionist View of Their Legal Problems.
    Family Law No. 11 pp. 25-29.
Halmos, P. (1978) The Personal and the Political London
    Hutchinson.
Hanmer, Jalna (1977) 'Community Action, Women's Aid
    and the Women's Liberation Movement', p. 91 in
    Marjorie Mayo (ed.) Women in Community, Routledge
    and Kegan Paul, London.
Jackson, Stevi and Rushton, Peter (1982) 'Victims
    and Villains: Images of Women in Accounts of
    Family Violence', Women Studies International
    Forum Vol. 5 No. 1 p. 17-28
Loving, N. (1982) FBI Law Enforcement Bulletin Spouse
    Abuse: The Need for New Law Enforcement Responses
    pp. 10-16.
Maidment, S. (1978) 'The Laws Response to Marital
    Violence: A Comparison Between England and USA'
    In Eekelaar J. and Katz S., Family Violence
    Butterworths, London.
Martin, David (1964) Delinquency and Drift, John
    Wiley and Sons
McCabe, S. and Sutcliffe, F. (1978) Defining Crime
    Research Study No. 9 Oxford Centre for Criminal
    Studies
Miller, Nick (1975) Battered Spouses, Studies in
    Social Administration No. 57 G. Bell.
Mills, C. Wright (1943) The Professional Ideology of
    Social Pathologists American Journal of Sociology
    XLIX, 2, pp, 165-80.
Oppenlander, N. (1982) Coping or Copping Out Crimin-
    ology Vol. 20 No. 3 and 4 pp. 449-65
Pahl, J. (1982) Police Response to Battered Women,
    Jnl of Social Welfare Law, pp. 337-43
Parnas, R.I. Police Response to Domestic Disturbance
    Winconsin Law Review Vol. 1967 914 960 fall.
Pattullo, Polly (1983) Judging Women, NCCL London
Pizzey, Erin (1981) 'Choosing a Violent Relation-
    ship' New Society 23rd April.
Pizzey, Erin and Shapiro, Jeff (1982) Prone to Viol-
    ence, Hamlyn London.
Scutt, J. (1980) Spouse Assault: Closing the Door on
    Criminal Acts. The Australian Law Journal Decem-
    ber 1980 pp. 720-31
Sherman, L.W. and Burk, R.A. Police Responses to Dom-
    estic Assaults: Preliminary Findings. A Police
    Foundation Working Paper

215

Bibliography

Snell, J., Rosenwald, R.J. and Robey, A. (1964) 'The
    Wife Beater's Wife' 11 Archives of General
    Psychiatry, pp. 107-112
Stark, E., Flitcraft, A. and Frazier, W. (1979)
    'Medicine and Patriarchal Wisdom: The Social
    Construction of a "Private" Event', International
    Journal of Health Services 9, No. 3 p. 466
Straus, M.A. (1977) 'Sexual Inequality, Cultural Norms
    and Wife Beating', in Women into Wives, J.R. Chap-
    man and M. Gates (ed.), Sage Public. p. 59
Tahourdin, B. (1983) 'Family Violence', Int. Jnl of
    Offender Therapy and Comparative Criminology
    Vol. 27 No. 1: 79-83
Wasik, M. (1982) Cumulative Provocation and Domestic
    Killing Criminal Law Review: 29-37
Wassoff, Fran (1982) 'Legal Protection from Wife
    Beating: The Legal Processing of Domestic Ass-
    aults' Int. Jnl of Soc of Law, Vol. 10: 187-204
Weir, Angela (1977) Battered Women: Some Perspectives
    and Problems, in Marjorie Mayo (ed.) Women in
    the Community, Routledge and Kegan Paul, London
Wilson, Elizabeth (1983) What Is To Be Done About
    Violence Against Women ?' Penguin

NOTES ON CONTRIBUTORS

Beverley Beech is the mother of two boys and has been actively involved with maternity care since 1974. She is Chairperson of the Association for Improvements in Maternity Services and an adviser to the National Perinatal Epidemiology Unit at Oxford, a founder member of the Maternity Defence Fund and DRUGWATCH, (a group that was set up to examine the activities of the Committee of Safety of Medicines in the drug industry and campaign for changes). She is co-author with Ros Claxton of the Health Rights Handbook for Maternity Care (1983).

Susan Edwards is currently Research Fellow at the Polytechnic of Central London, where she is engaged in a study of legal response to domestic violence. She has one daughter, and has contributed regularly to sociological, socio-legal and medical journals on women as victims and women in the law. Dr. Edwards is author of Female Sexuality and the Law, Martin Robertson (1981) and Women on Trial, Manchester University Press, (1984).

Peggy Kahn currently teaches politics and labour studies at the University of Michigan at Flint, USA. She was previously a research officer at the National Union of Mineworkers and an active member of various groups concerned with women and employment. Dr. Kahn is a co-author of Picketing: Industrial Disputes, Tactics and the Law, Routledge and Kegan Paul (1983) and has written elsewhere on employment law, trade unionism and the coalfields.

Linda Luckhaus LL.B., M.A., is now lecturer in law at

the University of Southampton, teaching Welfare, Family Property and Sociology of Law. She sees as central to research and to ching practice the development of a feminist perspective on law and the treatment of 'women's issues' within discreet areas of law. She has published an article on Social Security and the Equal Treatment Reforms in the Journal of Social and Welfare Law, November 1983.

Susan Maidment was senior lecturer in law at the University of Keele from 1976-1984. She is now a practising barrister. She has written extensively in the field of family law with special emphasis on children. She is author of Child Custody and Divorce: The Law in Social Context, Croom Helm (1984).

Judith Mayhew is both a barrister and solicitor of the Supreme Court of New Zealand. She has an LLM from the University of Otago and is currently lecturer in law at King's College, University of London. She has written several articles in the field of women and the law. She has recently been a visiting lecturer at the University of Malaysia.

Katherine O'Donovan teaches law at the University of Kent and contributes to the Women's Studies programme there. Born in Dublin and educated there, in France and the United States, she has taught law at universities in Belfast, Addis Ababa, Sussex and Kuala Lumpur. Her book on sexual divisions in law will be published by Weidenfeld and Nicolson in 1985.

The Women, Immigration and Nationality Group, grew from a conference on this subject held in October 1982, when over 200 women of many nationalities met to discuss how to end sex discrimination in immigration and nationality law. Groups of women have continued to meet since then, working on specific issues - the immigration rules about marriage, the problems of babies born here not British, researching into the experience of women under immigration and nationality law. The women involved in writing chapter 6 were Rosemary Davies, Louise London, Fiona MacTaggart and Sue Shutter.

INDEX